AN
ECONOMIST
GETS
LUNCH

ALSO BY TYLER COWEN

The Great Stagnation

The Age of the Infovore

Discover Your Inner Economist

TYLER COWEN

AN ECONOMIST GETS LUNCH

New Rules for
Everyday Foodies

DUTTON

DUTTON
Published by Penguin Group (USA) Inc.
375 Hudson Street, New York, New York 10014, U.S.A.
Penguin Group (Canada), 90 Eglinton Avenue East, Suite 700, Toronto, Ontario M4P 2Y3, Canada (a
division of Pearson Penguin Canada Inc.); Penguin Books Ltd, 80 Strand, London WC2R 0RL, En-
gland; Penguin Ireland, 25 St. Stephen's Green, Dublin 2, Ireland (a division of Penguin Books Ltd);
Penguin Group (Australia), 250 Camberwell Road, Camberwell, Victoria 3124, Australia (a division
of Pearson Australia Group Pty Ltd); Penguin Books India Pvt Ltd, 11 Community Centre, Panchsheel
Park, New Delhi–110 017, India; Penguin Group (NZ), 67 Apollo Drive, Rosedale, Auckland 0632,
New Zealand (a division of Pearson New Zealand Ltd); Penguin Books (South Africa) (Pty) Ltd, 24
Sturdee Avenue, Rosebank, Johannesburg 2196, South Africa

Penguin Books Ltd, Registered Offices: 80 Strand, London WC2R 0RL, England

Published by Dutton, a member of Penguin Group (USA) Inc.

First printing, April 2012
1   3   5   7   9   10   8   6   4   2

Copyright © 2012 by Tyler Cowen

Ⓩ REGISTERED TRADEMARK—MARCA REGISTRADA

LIBRARY OF CONGRESS CATALOGING-IN-PUBLICATION DATA
Cowen, Tyler.
An economist gets lunch : new rules for everyday foodies / Tyler Cowen.
p.   cm.
Includes bibliographical references and index.
ISBN 978-0-525-95266-4
1. Food habits—Economic aspects.   2. Food preferences—Economic aspects.
3. Food industry and trade.   I. Title.
GT2850.C69 2012
394.1'2—dc23   2011035174

Printed in the United States of America

*It is a hard matter to save a city in which
a fish sells for more than an ox.*

—Cato the Elder

Contents

1

On the Eve of
the Revolution

American food is in crisis, and rarely has more disruption loomed before us.

People are rebelling against current food-production methods involving long-distance shipping, fertilizers, and genetically modified organisms. Many people have returned to eating locally grown food from small farms, and there is a fear that our agricultural practices lead to mass-produced food products that are bad for our health and worsen climate change. But is this fear well founded? Is local food a good thing?

On the other side of the ledger, we are spending more and more on fancy restaurants. At a time when many economic sectors are struggling, the choices for fine meals are expanding in most American cities. But are we spending our money in the best way possible, or are we overlooking cheaper and possibly superior alternatives?

In a world with some pretty big problems, is it even appropriate to think of food in aesthetic terms as much as we do? The backlash drove a recently published article in the *Atlantic Monthly* to suggest that foodies are evil for aestheticizing the experience of eating. But what could be morally wrong with eating good, even beautiful food?

The food crisis is not confined to cultured readers of urbane magazines. As the fallout from our larger economic crisis continues, more than forty-four million Americans are receiving food stamps. High unemployment has persisted far longer than politicians expected. Starvation is no longer a major American problem, but obesity is—especially among lower earners. The prevalence of diabetes continues to rise.

The news isn't all bad. The American restaurant scene has been transformed over the last few decades since Calvin Trillin wrote (hilariously) about pretentious dining establishments, which he collectively referred to as "La Maison de la Casa Haus." Bolivian, Laotian, and North Korean dishes are staples of my dining out. I know how "Husband and Wife Lung Slices" taste (not bad). Where government regulations allow, food trucks are proving more popular than a lot of sit-down restaurants—and it's not just a desire to get away from those lung slices.

But most seriously, as our global population grows to nine billion and beyond and agricultural productivity slows, another Green Revolution propelled by agricultural innovations will become increasingly imperative. Food prices have been rising, contributing to political unrest in Egypt and Tunisia, and help on this front seems far away. Countries are stockpiling foodstuffs; and when prices spike, governments shut down food exports with the ostensible goal of feeding their populations. The global trade network isn't as robust as we have wanted to believe.

Since Upton Sinclair self-published *The Jungle*, his exposé of the meat packing industry in Chicago in 1906, Americans have been repeatedly alerted to disturbing realities of their food quality and economy. However, this is an especially critical moment.

When it comes to food, the whole world needs some big changes. These changes will happen only gradually, but this book is about how you can start eating better food now for your own good and for everyone else's. We need a special kind of revolution.

Let's start with a personal story about finding good food no matter how exotic or ordinary, about finding food that simply tastes good. Constructing a better eating experience and understanding where the quality of that experience comes from, is, strangely enough, the first and most important step toward feeding those nine billion people.

A Journey into the Unknown

I was on my way to Nicaragua. No one had seemed enthusiastic about Nicaraguan food and the guidebooks were not overflowing with praise. I decided I would figure things out on arrival. Let's be clear: Every meal really matters to me.

A bit of bread and cheese accompanied me on the flight to Managua. That was to hold me over, since my flight was not arriving until the late lunch hour of 1:30 P.M. It was cheddar cheese from Safeway, extra sharp, and three-day-old sourdough bread from Whole Foods. The point of the snack was to avoid showing up famished; getting too hungry leads to all sorts of problems, including eating before you have found the best available place. You could also think of it as a kind of reverential abstinence before a culinary adventure.

Anyway, I got off the plane and searched for a taxi. Inside the airport terminal I negotiated the price to León, a city about two hours north of the Managua airport. Outside I picked a relatively old taxi driver. An old driver is a good way to get personal safety, good local stories, information—and, well, a good way to find a place to eat, maybe the best way. The fare was set, but once we were under way I negotiated a separate price for the first step of my odyssey.

"I'd like to stop for something really special to eat, something very Nicaraguan. I'll offer you ten dollars for your time and I'll also invite you there for lunch." I probably didn't need to pay so much, but I was excited.

He accepted my offer and told me we would stop at a *quesillo* near León. A food cart? A bar? A brothel? I didn't know. He warned me that it was near the end of our trip. I was hungry but, thanks to the bread and cheese, could be patient. I reflected as the miles bumped by that *quesillo* probably refers to *queso*, the Spanish-language word for cheese.

We were about half an hour from León when I saw an official-looking road sign saying there are *quesillos* ahead. A few minutes later I saw about five on each side of the road. They were all open-air restaurants, and all had customers. The indications were positive.

The cabbie said he knew a special *quesillo* in the small town of La Paz, so we stopped there, in the second cluster of *quesillos*. I was told only one cooked dish is served and it was called . . . you'll never guess: a *quesillo*. The choice is between "without onions" and "complete." I ordered mine "complete," without asking what that meant.

It turns out that a *quesillo* is pretty simple. The dish is cool, liquid white cream, rolled in a thick warm tortilla with gooey cheese, with onions inside and a splash of vinegar. The tortilla and the cheese are made on the premises each day. The onions give it a sweetness and soft grit to the texture, while the vinegar adds its goodness. Simple. Awesome.

Total price for lunch: $12,
including the extra payment to the cabbie

We continued the drive to León together in his rather ramshackle vehicle, chatting about the colonial architecture and all the places to visit in Nicaragua. As we crossed the countryside, I marveled at the beautiful volcanoes and the lakes, but I also noticed the local agriculture. Immediately outside of León I saw a few small farms—*very* small farms—that raised and sold chickens. Duly noted.

Once we arrived, I quickly became fond of León. It's one of the most charming Latin American towns I've seen; a kind of magical dream that you think cannot exist outside a magic realism novel, except it does. Run-down enough to evoke the past, the buildings are still attractive and everyone seems to have deep roots in the place, with a town square that comes alive at dusk with families, teenagers courting and flirting, merchants selling balloons, and older people sitting on benches.

At first I thought I would try the town's best restaurant, but I wasn't encouraged by what I heard. Both my hotel and my guidebooks claim that the best place is a restaurant called El Mediterráneo, which, as the name indicates, serves Mediterranean food. It might be good, but is that what I flew down here for? Besides, I liked the atmosphere of the town square.

I walked around and I noted about five vendors selling the same thing: fried chicken with French fries—El Salvador style, as it was called. Five looked like a lot of vendors in this square. It was a sign of a healthy competitive market as any economist might tell you. I figured the chicken was from those local farms, so I ordered some from the freshest-looking stand. If it wasn't any good I could just leave it and go to El Mediterráneo. But it was delicious—as good as the fried chicken you get in those hot-spot Manhattan restaurants experimenting with the concept, for instance Jean-Georges's place on Perry Street, where I recently had inferior fried chicken for more than ten times the price.

Total cost: $2

The woman selling the chicken sprinkled some delicious crumbly, sweet-salty white cheese on top of it all, a Central American standard. I'm still entertaining the hypothesis that Nicaragua has the best fresh white cheese in the world, El Salvador included.

As of the time I ate the chicken (and cheese), I'd only been in the country for six or seven hours, but I'd begun formulating my hypothesis about how the food supply chain works: The wealthy people have servants cook for them, so a lot of the upper-end dining establishments are only so-so. There's not much of a formal dining culture, at least not in restaurants. There is an alternative and quite fantastic food world, manifest in fresh corn products, perfect white cheese in various forms, and baked goods, which I began to observe all over León. That food culture is where locals go for their favorite meals; I just had to find my way into it.

After six or seven hours in Nicaragua, I don't think my hypothesis deserves a formal academic paper. But I'm going to use it—until it's proven false.

Before going to bed, I bought a chocolate ice cream cone, knowing that Nicaragua is a major producer of cacao. Bull's-eye.

Another dollar on my running tab

Day 2

I was determined to avoid my hotel's breakfast buffet. Breakfast can be the best street-food meal of the day, though in hotels it is usually the worst. I headed over to the Mercado Central, which is also a food market. Not having a clue what to order, I walked into the food section of the market and saw everyone ordering the same thing: a mountain of yucca surrounded by fresh cabbage, rice and beans to the side, and on top of the yucca about five pieces of pork, fried in what appeared to be a red achiote sauce.

The yucca was soft, moist, and luscious, unlike the fried pieces of rock you often get in U.S. Latino restaurants. The pork was a little chewy but flavorful and the achiote sauce gave it a tanginess. I munched on the cabbage and worried slightly about getting sick.

Getting a drink was a little tougher. They offered me "juice of orange," but when it came it was essentially water with a bit of artificial orange flavoring in it. I repeatedly asked about the freshness and safety of the water but always got the same answer. The server confidently said it was *"agua corriente,"* namely "running water." I wasn't sure if that was good or bad news and didn't take the drink. I got a Coca-Cola—not my ideal breakfast beverage, but it was the cane sugar version rather than the standard U.S. corn-syrup one.

My "drinks," by the way, cost fifty cents—total—for two. How can this be? Well, they took my remaining Coca-Cola (most of it) and poured it into an empty plastic bag—for resale—then stuck the bag in a tray of ice. Yes, I was putting the bottle directly to my lips. My lean entrepreneur food vendors also took the rejected orange drink and did the same, thus indicating they eventually would receive more than my fifty cents.

Rule number 2,367B for food-and-drink safety: Don't drink anything that comes in a hand-tied plastic bag.

Total cost for breakfast: $3

On my way out of the food market I bought a baked good, halfway between a cookie and bread, with something slightly sweet on top. I'm not so good at figuring out the contents of baked goods, in part because I don't bake, but these items were justifiably popular with the residents of León. A lot of other people were buying them too. The price is included in the three-dollar sum above.

I had eaten three delicious meals and the expense had been minimal. But maybe the highlight of the trip was during another cab ride, when I offered the driver some extra money to take me to a tamale stand.

He had a hard time finding one, as most of the tamale sellers close by the afternoon, when the product is no longer fresh. After about ten minutes of driving around neighborhoods, we came across a woman transporting a basket of tamales on her head. We stopped and I bought a corn tamale from her, and also bought a tamale for the driver.

The two tamales cost 20 córdobas, or about one dollar. I had no bill smaller than 50 córdobas and the woman had no change. We were in the middle of a residential neighborhood with no one in sight and no store nearby. I insisted that she keep the change and that I was pleased to have my sweet corn tamale. She refused. I asked again. She refused again. So I had to wait ten minutes in the cab while she went off to find change for the bill. At least I had a home-cooked tamale to eat—and it was probably my best meal in Nicaragua.

I can't say I *proved* the hypothesis about the corn and the cream being the keys to the cuisine, but at the end of my four-day trip I had a lot of confirming evidence. Only one of my meals in town, this time seafood, was less than excellent and led to a new hypothesis. It needs further field testing, but here goes:

When donkey carts are common and women carry baskets on their heads, eat your fish right by the ocean or lake.

Another way of putting it is that if transportation is slow, and refrigeration is a recent innovation, fish and indeed any seafood you find as little as ten miles from the water won't taste so good.

Food Snobbery

As it stands, food writers, commentators, and foodies are misled by three doctrines, useless in Nicaragua, useless at home, and misleading almost everywhere else:

1. The best food is more expensive. (Assume time is money, and it follows that slow food is better.)

2. Our largest source of cheap food—large agribusiness—is irredeemably bad.

3. Consumers are not a trusted source of innovation; rather, they are to be constrained, nudged, taxed, and subjected to the will of others—chefs, food writers, cultural leaders, and, especially, political officeholders.

Taken together these views constitute our generation's food snobbery. These prejudices are apparent in gourmet food magazines such as *Bon Appétit* and the now defunct *Gourmet*, in anti-agribusiness documentaries such as *Food, Inc.* and *Super Size Me*, and in restrictions on food carts, street food, nonpasteurized cheeses, and the numerous government interventions that stand between us and better, cheaper food. Author Michael Pollan, who has made some valid arguments about food in the modern world, tells us to leave food on our plate in his most recent *Food Rules*. I say, find or make good food—and eat it.

For all the lofty rhetoric about "locavores" and "slow food," this food snobbery is pessimistic, paternalistic, and most of all it is anti-innovation. Neither the consumer nor the businessperson is trusted to innovate; there is a false nostalgia for primitive agriculture, based on limited transportation and the arduous conversion of raw materials into comestible commodities. Rarely is it admitted, much less emphasized, that cheap, quick food—including its embodiment through our sometimes obnoxious agribusiness corporations—is the single most important advance in human history. It is the foundation of modern civilization and the reason why most of us are alive. Before there was an Industrial Revolution, which eventually brought the conveniences of modern life, there was an Agricultural Revolution, which created a large enough social surplus to make further economic development possible. It enabled us to pull people off the farm and employ them as scientists, engineers, inventors, and entrepreneurs.

Earlier food worlds were no paradise. If we go back to the middle of the nineteenth century, American consumers were suspicious of the concepts of fresh fruit, vegetables, meat, and milk, unless it came from their farm or a neighbor's. In practice "extremely fresh" and "spoiled" were close concepts, as even today any amateur cheese or sausage maker will attest. Back then, people did not know where "fresh" food came from or how long it had been sitting exposed to the heat and elements. There was no expiration date on the package and perhaps no package. Foods alternated between periods of extreme glut and extreme scarcity, depending on the seasons and the locale. High transport costs kept most fresh foodstuffs from most parts of the world. Most foods were local but no one was especially proud of that fact. Costs of refining and processing were almost nonexistent—sugar being one notable exception—if only because there were so few ways of usefully transforming food for broader marketing and sale, given the technologies and the economic constraints of that time.

Many foods were preserved, often using centuries-old techniques. Vegetables were pickled in salt brine and vinegar, not always the most flavorful combination. Fruits were dried, using the sun if possible. Meats and fishes were salted and smoked or stuffed into tightly sealed jars. Food poisoning was common. Making and taking care of the food involved a lot of hard work. There were some fine meals, and a lot of people felt "close to the land"—too close—but overall this was not a culinary world to envy.

By the 1920s all this had changed, at least in the United States. Canals, railroads, and later trucks lowered transportation costs—including food transportation costs—to a fraction of their former level. In this new world, riches were made from foodstuffs that lasted long enough to bear transport. Entrepreneurs therefore invested in technologies of shipping, storage, and preservation—and so began the modern world of rich and plentiful food ingredients. Americans received far more access to food than was ever the case before in the history of the world. No longer was supply limited to the pickled, the preserved, and what was grown on the family farm. Relative to wages, food was suddenly much cheaper and supply was more reliable.

Some mediocre frozen and canned foods became possible too, but don't damn commercialization for that reason. The printing press brought us both good and bad novels, but was a cultural boon nonetheless.

Appreciating agribusiness doesn't mean you have to deny the problem of fertilizer runoff, endorse government subsidies to corn syrup, or dine at McDonald's. Modern, cheap agriculture can be thought of as a *platform* upon which subsequent food innovation will occur. The platform needs reform, but for the most part it has fed humankind very well. If we do not understand the useful components of this platform, we will fail in finding the best and cheapest meals, and furthermore we will endanger the platform itself. Were it to collapse, famines would become ordinary.

In the meantime, we need to learn how people—right now—are using the platform for better and more humane ends. The food in Nicaragua really *was* wonderful and it is a testament to the creative powers of the individual, even the very poor individual. The United States however does not and cannot organize its food network in the same ways. France and Japan are different yet. So to eat well, to be environmentally friendly, or to make the right food decisions about our laws or our diets, we need a comprehensive understanding of how food markets work. We need a better understanding of how to take all the information before us and turn it into something useful.

Why Every Meal Counts

Nicaragua is an unusual environment, but my experiences there illustrate the compelling messages I hope this book will make clear.

1. Every meal counts

A bad or mediocre meal is more than just an unpleasant taste, it is an unnecessary negation of life's pleasures. It is a wasted chance to refine our tastes, learn about the world, and share a rewarding experience. Virtually every locale—whether it's Nicaragua, the local suburban strip malls, or an apparently inscrutable Asian-American supermarket—offers some good meals at a cheap price, if only we can decipher their codes and discover the signals for distinguishing good from bad. In discussing how and why every meal counts, certain questions are crucial. How do I choose restaurants? How do I shop for groceries? Do cookbooks really help?

2. Good food is often cheap food

Who has the patience, the time, and the money to take most meals in fancy restaurants? Hardly anyone. But I do want to make my life richer in discovery, especially when it comes to the very human, very basic, and very primeval pleasures of food. I also want to do so as cheaply as possible, precisely because food is not the only good thing in life.

Junk food is cheap, and to a lot of people it tastes good, but junk food doesn't much improve or refine our taste. It gets boring very quickly, and it isn't good for our health or for the environment. Junk food is an attack on the idea of the world as an information-rich treasure, full of surprises and hidden gems and pathways for new learning. Junk food is a dead end.

Furthermore, we don't need junk food because better and cheaper food can be found close to home. In my immediate area—Northern Virginia, Maryland, and Washington, D.C.—my half dozen or so favorite restaurants all offer first-rate meals for fifteen dollars or less, though sometimes of course I decide to spend more. I've been writing restaurant reviews for twenty years, and at the end of the day I prefer their best fifteen-dollar offerings to a typical two-hundred-dollar meal at Michel Richard's fancy Citronelle in Georgetown. These favorite restaurants serve diverse items, ranging from Sichuan dan dan noodles to French Époisses cheeseburgers to red salmon curry to Ethiopian raw beef with chilies and dry cottage cheese. But they all have one thing in common: Their on-site owners and chefs are devoted to food they love to prepare.

It is possible to find this same dedication around the world. The best barbecue cooks of Texas are highly skilled applied scientists; you can find chili ecstasy in Albuquerque diners and sometimes even in pharmacies; and the region in Italy with the fewest Michelin-starred restaurants—Sicily—has some of the best, most surprising, and also cheapest food in Europe. There is a strong commitment to quality seafood at New Zealand fish 'n' chips shops, even if they charge you less than ten dollars for the takeaway experience of carrying out the wrap. In none of these cases do the restaurants expect that their customers are operating with expense accounts. More and more, Paris has a lot of the worst and most expensive food in France.

3. Be innovative as a consumer

Once you have some understanding of the economics that underlie what and how we eat, the power of each of us as individual consumers to improve upon the national and international economy becomes clear.

Typical incomes in America, and in many of the other wealthy countries of the world, have stagnated since about 1973. Could the way we eat help us, at least partially, transcend this sorry state?

We think of innovations as coming from entrepreneurs; and we think of innovations in terms of major life changes, such as electricity, flush toilets, and automobiles—and these do represent very real improvements. Maybe today some of us are still expecting a jet pack, a flying car, or workable robots to ease our household chores, but we'll probably be waiting for a while. Even with the marvelous Internet, the modern world hasn't offered the same quantity of life-changing alternations that were experienced by my grandmother, who was born in 1905. So in an era where technological progress has slowed from its 1870–1970 peak, we need to look to a broader concept of innovation. Being a better and wiser consumer is one way we can bring more progress into our lives and so fight back against "the great stagnation" I have written about elsewhere.

This is a book about food and eating, but it's not just a book about food and eating. Broader issues are at stake. Our attitudes toward food have a lot to do with our attitudes toward life and also toward ourselves. In the eighteenth century, James Boswell defined man as "a cooking animal"—so a foodie is a person interested in playing up one of the essential features of his or her humanity.

Do you remember those stories, from antiquity, of the Romans who vomited so that they might start again on a new feast? That represented a pretty special attitude toward food and enjoyment, although not one you'll find represented in this book.

Some commentators have viewed food as a means of social and political control. Charles Fourier, the nineteenth century French Utopian socialist, saw gastronomy as a pure science, and one that required elite culinary judges and juries to bring about the requisite "harmony." Fourier thought that sex and food should be the dual bases of control for the new social order, which he called "gastrosophy." Good behavior would be rewarded, by the guardians, with lots of food and sex and in that manner socialism would create incentives for economic cooperation and production. Fourier saw the Aristotelian virtue of moderation as an abomination. He predicted the future would bring five meals a day plus two snacks, all with delicious food. Men will be seven feet tall, digestion will be easy, and life expectancy will reach 144 years.

That's another food vision you won't find here. I like the optimism but I worry about the use of food as a mechanism for control. In fact this book is one way to take some control *away* from political elites or food elites. Most of all, my vision is about encouraging the individual diner and empowering him or her with some skills of pattern recognition and innovation.

I believe that people can do a lot better in life by cutting through some socially engineered illusions. Most of all, figure out when a food presentation or sale is about the taste of the food or when the food presentation is about something else, like acquiring higher social status or feeling good about yourself. For a few years running Noma, in Copenhagen, has been judged the world's best restaurant, but my meal there bored me (fortunately I was not paying). You can avoid a lot of so-so expensive restaurants by making sure you're paying for good taste rather than for social illusion. (Of course, you can invert some of my recommendations and read this as a manual of how, at the expense of better food, to buy higher social status.) I've focused on food, but there's nothing special about food markets in this regard; in many areas of life understanding is a powerful tool for getting what you really want.

I also view wise eating as a way to limit inequality. In the United States, it's often the case that wealthy people eat better than does the middle class or upper middle class. It doesn't have to be this way and I'm explaining how, even on a modest income, you can eat and enjoy some of the tastiest food in the world.

Ultimately, I hope these pages will show that becoming a better consumer of food can literally revolutionize the world.

An Economic Approach to Good Food

As a professional economist, I see food as the result of capitalist supply and demand. Whether it's the restaurant or the supermarket or the kitchen-supply shop, it's hard to think of a sector that is more commercialized and more replete with entrepreneurship and innovation. It is all monetized. If we care about food, we have to care about economic reasoning. The novel idea of this book is that knowing some dry scientific economics helps make every meal count in a deeply human way and it helps you realize—counterintuitively—that a lot of the best food is cheap rather than expensive.

Throughout, to find better eating, I will use this economic principle: *Food is a product of economic supply and demand, so try to figure out where the supplies are fresh, the suppliers are creative, and the demanders are informed.*

Most food writings are not much concerned with economics, but the early history of my discipline is for the most part a theory of food production and distribution. Early economies were built upon agriculture and of course they still are in the world's poorer countries. Adam Smith, who wrote *The Wealth of Nations* in 1776, was the father of modern economics and some of his best pedagogic examples had to do with the grain trade. Frédéric Bastiat, a leading nineteenth century French economist who remains in print to this day, focused on explaining how it is that Paris gets fed, even though no central planner sees to this fact. I'm bringing my own profession back to its historic roots.

Before we can understand how people are beginning to put things right, we need to understand how matters went wrong in the first place.

2

How American Food
Got Bad

The trajectory of food in America had a long arc through some big black spots. We have a Cheez Whiz culture. Bad food from McDonald's and Hostess Twinkies to Velveeta and Lucky Charms seems to be everywhere. Good & Plenty has always been more about the Plenty than the Good.

In the early 1960s, Holiday Inn served 80 percent of its food from frozen packages, shipped out from a central Chicago commissary. Most of its restaurants required only a single cook and a single dishwasher. Tad's, a well-known steak chain at the time, started a new branch of restaurants called Tad's 30 Varieties of Meals. They served frozen dinners of chicken, scallops, steak, and potatoes. The dinners were wrapped in plastic and diners would defrost them in microwave ovens next to each table, without shame. Or much taste.

There's a standard explanation for why American food became so bad, and you will hear it from foodies, you will find it in a lot of food histories, and it is cited by Michael Pollan. This story, quite simply, is that American food got commercialized. More precisely, this country commercialized its food supply network so rapidly and so thoroughly that taste got lost in all the efficiencies. We became the country of shipped food, frozen food, canned food, and the large agricultural corporation. We lost our earlier and purer food ways in the quest for profit and ease. Agribusiness corrupted our chance to buy everything in cozy, local markets and to chat with nearby farmers, like a good locavore should.

I'd like to set the record straight. Any objective observer will find plenty of excess and low quality in American agribusiness and indeed that is what you would expect from such a ubiquitous commercial force. But a closer look at the history shows that commercialization wasn't nearly as much at fault for the low quality of a lot of American food as most people believe. The biggest reasons American food turned out so bad have been overlooked.

The commercial success of, say, Doritos doesn't explain how things got so bad overall. Politicians and legislators are much more central to the story of our culinary problems than is usually let on. The political war on alcohol in the early decades of the twentieth century shut down legions of top-quality restaurants for decades. Then, wham, World War II shoved America into a trough of high-volume, low-quality junk. This historic one-two punch stunted the growth of quality restaurants when the rest of the U.S. culture was booming. Perhaps even more important, the war against immigration, which started in the 1920s, kept American food away from its best and most fruitful innovators for decades, precisely at the time when commercialization was gathering momentum. Given the power of these three social forces, it's no wonder that a lot of our food was so bad.

Later in the century, it took decades for American food habits to adapt to the two-income family and the dominance of television as a way of spending time. At first those trends were bad for food quality, at least until we learned how to turn them to our advantage; the frozen TV dinner came long before The Food Network. Americans thus experienced a century-long perfect storm of bad news for good food.

That storm came at the time when refrigeration and trucking were becoming more important and American food supply chains—the distance, time, and number of steps between harvest and consumption—were growing longer. The rise of mass transportation, mass marketing, and mass food preservation techniques helped American food markets expand at a rapid clip through the twentieth century. Farmers could grow lettuce in southern California and sell it in Maine. Yet the mix was biased—unnecessarily biased—against good and diverse foodstuffs. In large part that bias stemmed from unwise laws and in large part it stemmed from some accidental social forces, which required some time for us to adjust to.

It could have been different. The commercialization of food markets isn't the big villain because the mediocre American food phenomenon was *highly contingent* on particular circumstances of time and place—and also on some pretty stupid laws.

But there is an even bigger misunderstanding of what happened in the twentieth century based on two oversights. First, more people ate well than ever before. Today the American poor are more likely to be obese than starving. Even the mass mobilization of the Second World War, and the accompanying constraints on resources, did not prevent most Americans from eating meat, albeit lower quality meat, on a regular basis. In practical terms, these gains were far more important than the ugliness of junk food.

Second, we exaggerate how bad American food is, just as was done with British food a generation or so ago. The twentieth-century U.S. culinary scene was by no means totally dim. The French appreciated our salads and our better hamburgers. The Midwest and the South were full of fresh vegetables, and California agriculture ushered in year-round produce. Texas beef and barbecue flourished, and New Orleans extended its signature Creole and Cajun cuisines. The United States was one of the best places in the world to eat a steak, and on the coasts fresh seafood was plentiful.

Foreigners have had a skewed picture. The further away a foreign country, the less likely they will see the fresh foods of the United States. The less likely they will see the barbecue or taste the fresh corn of the Midwest or sample the vegetables that are commonplace throughout much of the year in Alabama. The foreigners will, however, be familiar with our canned, prepackaged, and frozen items, namely everything we are good at shipping. Americans see less of the prepackaged foods of Europe, if only because Europe has less expertise in transporting food for long distances. Our European food memories are of wine, cured ham, and fresh strawberries; the Europeans get from us McDonald's and frozen pizza. So while some of their criticisms of American food culture are correct, those criticisms also are not balanced.

And when European tourists show up in the United States, a lot of them don't have cars, don't sample the suburbs, don't understand a lot of our ethnic foods, and in general they are pretty clueless about how to find good food here. They wander around cities such as Boston and San Francisco and expect that good food, in the forms they are used to finding in their European homes, will simply bite them in the ankle. That isn't how it works.

That said, I do accept that there has been a lot more low-quality food in this country than ever should have been the case. Let's now turn to why, looking at our rather unique history, starting with the legal prohibition of alcohol.

The Prohibition Tsunami

After numerous false starts, it's pretty clear that the wine bar is here to stay. Customers like the idea of tasting before they drink, they like the idea of wine as something casual, and they like the appetizer-size portions of food that most wine bars serve. Wine bars feel like cozy, nice places to socialize. My favorite local wine bar is a Moroccan tapas place in McLean, Virginia, and I don't think it would be there if not for the profits from the drinks. The wine bar also has boosted tapas. The link between good wine and good food runs deep. A lot of restaurants, especially of the fancy kind, make more than half of their profits from selling drinks.

That political war on alcohol I mentioned above culminated in the banning of public sales of alcohol in 1920. The era of Prohibition that followed forced a lot of good restaurants either to break the law or go out of business. The puritanical American attitudes toward alcohol, as codified in the law, are a major reason why our food and our dining stayed backward for so long.

While the Eighteenth Amendment outlawed the public consumption and sale of alcohol across the United States, the stingy legal tolerance of alcohol has a much longer history in this country. Before World War I, twenty-six states already had enacted restrictions on its public sale, mostly in the South and in the West. Prohibition in Kansas began as early as 1881. Even if a state was not dry, particular localities often were. In California by 1914, dry towns included Berkeley, Santa Barbara, Long Beach, Pasadena, Pomona, Redlands, Riverside, and much of Los Angeles County. The dry movement also won victories in the Northeast; for instance, by 1908, 90 out of the 168 towns in Connecticut were dry. Prohibition of alcohol was a bigger and longer experiment than many people realize.

National Prohibition brought catastrophe to most good restaurants, especially the fancy and the expensive ones. One commentator of the time referred to a "gastronomic holocaust." A British visitor noted "the wholesale assassination of the charm and pleasure of dining . . . practically every restaurant is a sepulcher." *The Saturday Evening Post* argued that American gastronomy had been destroyed. These problems, which already happened in the dry states, now infested the entire country, including America's dining capital, New York City. Journalist Herbert Asbury wrote: "For a long time dining in New York was a grim business."

In New York, the famous Delmonico's shut its doors in 1924, unable to make money without alcohol sales. Other notable restaurants to close—for similar reasons—included Rector's, Shanley's, the Ted Lewis Club, the Boardwalk, the Little Club, the Monte Carlo Club, Murray's Roman Gardens, Thomas Healy's Golden Glades, Reisenweber's, Jack's, Sherry's, and Mouquin's, considered the best French restaurant in New York at the time. Many of these establishments were raided and busted for having alcohol on the premises. In other cases top hotels shut down (their bars had been important sources of income), taking their restaurants with them, or the hotels discontinued or neglected their restaurants.

Part of the problem was government corruption. Formerly legitimate restaurants that decided to serve alcohol suddenly had to operate outside the law and compete with mob-run rivals. The less reputable establishments used the law, and corrupt police, to close up their competitors. If a restaurant drew too many of your customers, you, as a competitor, could report it for breaching Prohibition. The surviving places were the best at bribery, corruption, and legal connections, not good cooking. The more profitable the restaurant, the higher the bribe one would be expected to pay. A typical New York City speakeasy had regular bribery costs of about four hundred dollars a month, which if we adjust for inflation would be roughly equal to about ten times that sum today. This did not include periodic payments, in terms of food, drink, or otherwise to visiting policemen.

Expensive, high-quality food was hurt the most. In addition to the loss of profits on drinks, no public restaurant could use a sauce with wine. French restaurants were almost completely abandoned, as this was before nouvelle cuisine and related movements made wine-based sauces less central to fine cooking. Most French chefs in the United States were walking the streets, looking for work, or they took a steamship back home.

From 1919 to 1929 the number of restaurants in the United States tripled, most of all to meet the demands of a rapidly growing consumer society. After all, these were boom years. But most of these locales emphasized speed and convenience more than the quality of the food. Diners—which do not rely on alcohol sales for their profitability— became more popular. Soda fountains, ice cream parlors, and candy shops also flourished. For instance, Broadway in New York City changed from a theater and restaurant center to cheap food and retail outlets. Suddenly it was full of hot-dog and hamburger shops, chop suey restaurants, candy stores and drugstores, penny arcades, and speakeasies, all harbingers of the new food world to come.

Prohibition also made restaurants more child-friendly. Family life became more convenient, but the quality of food suffered. Most children prefer bland, predictable food, and, as I'll discuss in more detail below, American adults have been especially willing to cater to the food preferences of their kids. Prohibition, by letting more kids into restaurants, gave them greater influence over American restaurant food. To this day, the United States has a higher drinking age than does most of Europe and those restrictions are usually enforced in restaurants. This encourages restaurants to supply food that does not require the accompaniment of wine. In Europe it is far more common to serve some wine or beer to a sixteen-year-old at the table and then expect the kid to eat like an adult. Americans ratcheted their standards down while the Europeans kept theirs high.

Returning to the 1920s, alcohol consumption was driven underground to the speakeasy or to private homes. Often the speakeasies served food, but observers have reported the quality as poor and the prices as high. The incentives militated against good food. A speakeasy was keen to keep a low public profile, which made it hard to develop a long-term reputation for culinary innovation. Restricting the clientele to known persons limited the incentive to draw others in with good food, and instead emphasized social or business ties. Furthermore speakeasies faced a risk of being prosecuted and shut down. Short-time horizons meant that the owners had little incentive to make long-term investments in quality products. Why build up a top (illegal) restaurant when you could be put out of business any moment? One study of New York City remarked that "these raids . . . did serve the purpose of closing most of the places where good food could be bought."

Illegal drinking also tended to avoid wine, which is hard to transport, store, and market. Instead drinkers chose cheap spirits, but those drinks do less to enhance the taste of quality food. Furthermore, these drink preferences persisted after the end of Prohibition. Even through the 1940s, it was common for Americans to drink whiskey, not wine, with fine food. Per capita alcohol consumption did not reattain its pre-Prohibition levels until 1973, and so Prohibition cast a long historical shadow.

Prohibition ended in 1933, but that was in the middle of the Great Depression. It was not an auspicious time for restaurant openings. One estimate from the time suggests that culinary recovery began in New York City six years after Prohibition ended. Another estimate cites 1941 for the first great post-Prohibition restaurant, Le Pavillon in New York City. At this time, 1939, the United States was shortly to enter the Second World War, which dealt another blow to quality food.

World War II pushed America further along the spectrum of convenient, low-quality food by encouraging prepackaged foods and fast food restaurants. Restaurant openings boomed during the war, but they were of a particular sort. The war put six million women into the work force for the first time and most of these women were married and had children. Many husbands were off fighting the war and over 10 percent of the U.S. population enlisted in the armed services. When it came to food, speed and convenience were at a premium. Families demanded foodstuffs that were cheap and could be eaten on the go. This gave an additional push to diners, malt shops, fast food, burger joints, and cafeterias. The roots of 1950s and 1960s food can be found during the earlier wartime experience and the destruction of fine dining during Prohibition.

Wartime rationing and scarcity made high-quality ingredients and careful cooking distant priorities. For instance, 60 percent of U.S. Choice grade cuts of beef were reserved for wartime use, so more and more people ate mass-produced chicken. Canned Spam, which became especially popular, typified the American response to the war. Spam was easy to store, quick to serve, and offered plenty of fat and salt. Fresh vegetables and fruits were often not available, given the diversion of labor, resources, and transportation facilities into the war effort. Coffee, butter, cheese, fats, oils, and most of all sugar were all extremely restricted.

During the war, Americans ate less sugar and less pork, but calorie consumption remained robust. In fact beef consumption *rose* and reached a new peak in 1943. After all the adjustments were made to the new scarcities, quality suffered more readily than quantity. Maintaining high levels of meat consumption became a status symbol during the war and Americans thought of themselves as the land that never had to do without, even during a titanic struggle. Yet the adjustments required to maintain this posture pushed America further down the road of readily available but low-quality foodstuffs.

Unlike Europe, the United States had an intact industrial and agricultural base and also greater distances between farms and cities. Industrially canned goods were an important way of adjusting to the war. The shipment of foodstuffs abroad—whether to soldiers or for wartime foreign aid—gave a big boost to the American canning industry and it was then simple to direct the new canning facilities to serve the home market too.

So, while the quality of American meat went down, Americans were able to get through the war maintaining high levels of meat consumption, at least compared to most of Europe.

The responses to the Second World War show how differently food transport networks had evolved in the United States and Europe. Most European economies were deeply affected by the war, more so than the United States. Throughout much of Europe, war meant that many foodstuffs simply were not to be had. People ate less. They also resorted more to local production, garden production, barter with local farmers, and home preservation of foods. In extreme cases people would eat the family pets or stray animals. These responses lowered the quality of European food, but they did not shunt Europe onto a convenience-oriented, quantity-emphasizing, low-quality food track during the postwar period. Europe did not have the factory capacity to shift into mass food production; if anything, the wartime responses to crisis solidified the European tendency to resort to local ingredients, at the same time the United States was turning to long-distance transportation. Ironically, because Europe suffered *more,* its food tasted better.

Even after the negative shocks of war and national Prohibition were over, American dining still was not left free to grow and improve. Many state and county liquor laws continued for decades after these events. Texas allowed the sale of alcohol in restaurants only in 1971. A restaurant boom followed.

Many counties still have dry laws. While the exact numbers fluctuate, of the 120 counties of Kentucky, 55 are dry and 35 more have partial restrictions on alcohol. Of the 254 counties in Texas, 74 are completely dry; more than half of the counties in Arkansas are dry. It is estimated that about eighteen million Americans live in dry areas. This overregulation has shackled innovation and also reflects broader and anti-alcohol attitudes. The United States did not really focus on wine, or wine as a complement to good food, until the 1970s or later.

Manna from Immigrants

Everyone is heartened by stories of immigrants who come to America and make good, but I am especially delighted by stories of immigrants who improve our food culture.

There is a new restaurant, about twenty minutes from my home, and the sign—in Korean only—says Pyongyang Soondae. That's right, Pyongyang, the capital of North Korea.

The proprietor is Ma Young-Ae, a charming North Korean woman who wears an apron, decorated with cats and hearts, and greets all of her customers with a big smile and a hello. She was delighted to see me, even if her English was not up to all of my questions about the food.

Like many Korean-American success stories, her workday stretches from about 9:30 in the morning to 10:30 at night, and most of that time is dedicated to keeping up the quality in her restaurant. Yet only ten years ago she was working for North Korea's Ministry of Public Security, busting drug smugglers, namely those who were trading with China without the approval of the government (the government itself is involved in the trade).

Today she's a devout Christian with Bible quotations on the wall of her restaurant and an implacable political opponent of the North Korean regime; sometimes she travels to the United Nations to lead protests against it.

She once spent a month in a North Korean prison and was interrogated for filing false reports and for possibly being a Christian. She was released but shortly thereafter found herself in political trouble again.

She fled the country, crossing the Chinese border and leaving behind her husband, but she was caught, put in prison again, tortured, and beaten repeatedly with an ashtray, the scars from which are still visible. Finally she was able to flee the country with forged papers, and she made her way to South Korea, backed by bribes along the way and aided by some family and political connections. She later came to the United States on the grounds of political asylum and now she is cooking in northern Virginia to the delight and acclaim of the region's foodies.

Her restaurant serves pork liver and intestines, but also some of the best sausage, with some of the freshest pepper, I have had. There is a cold soup of buckwheat noodles with cucumbers, and there are dumplings of pheasant meat. There are at least forty Korean restaurants in the general area, but this isn't like the others. It's usually better and at the very least it's always different.

In addition to cooking, Ma plays music (piano, accordion, and *yanggeum*, a stringed instrument with bamboo sticks), sings Korean folktales, speaks and sings at Korean churches, and watches TV shows about the FBI. She donates part of the revenue of the restaurant to refugee aid and ongoing efforts against the North Korean regime. She also still receives death threats.

I call Ma's cooking North Korean food but I also call it *American food*. Without Ma, my culinary life would be poorer and so would America's.

What's striking is that cuisines rely on immigration to varying degrees. French food has drawn upon international influences, but it has not in recent times been much influenced by immigrants to France. Paris has many good North African restaurants, but had there been no Algerian immigrants, Parisian food still would be a world leader, and probably it would have taken a broadly similar path up through the current day. French cooks have focused on refining preexisting national and regional ideas, or in the case of nouvelle cuisine, they have thinned sauces and focused on pure ingredients. There hasn't been that much of a mingling of ideas, at least not in recent times. If anything, the evolution of classic French cuisine was originally a *reaction against* earlier Arabic influences, most of all by taking sugar, cinnamon, and honey out of their prominent place in the main courses and segregating them into the desserts. You won't often see Moroccan bistillah pie in French haute cuisine.

Italy had low levels of immigration for much of the twentieth century, but like France it has focused on refining preexisting materials, techniques, and recipes. Immigration to Italy has been rising more recently, but an Italy without recent immigration still would have excellent food. It would be harder to hire restaurant waiters, and thus harder to keep a restaurant going, but the content of the food wouldn't be so different. Sicilian food is often North African in its inspirations and in its prominent use of orange, mint, and other herbs. But those influences are from centuries ago, not from recent arrivals.

In contrast, American food *is* immigrant food. Many of our best food ideas came from immigrants or in some cases from African slaves. The New York deli blended numerous influences from Eastern Europe, the hamburger evolved from German meat cooking, American pizza is a remixed Italian idea, and barbecue probably came from the Caribbean and Mexico. The so-called "ethnic" cuisines now dominate our cities and suburbs. Fusion cuisines draw on European, Latin, Asian, and now African influences. California "Napa Valley" cooking is one of the most international styles that can be found.

American food is immigrant food translated into a new physical, economic, and agricultural environment. As such, it is continually moving in new directions and bubbling over with innovative and sometimes improbable ideas. Only in America would you find a Cajun-Thai restaurant or dozens of New York City restaurants blending Cuban and Chinese food. American food was never based on refining the quality of static recipes and thus it is potentially vulnerable to losing its sources of ongoing inspiration, namely if immigration dries up, as it did for the middle part of the twentieth century.

When it comes to food, the United States is extremely good at supplying cheap raw materials, cheap transportation, cheap marketing, and access to a large market of wealthy customers. In most parts of the country, land is plentiful. American food is, in part, what results when we explore many combinations of these inputs, including ethnically diverse cooks from around the world. I would even say this: Our long supply chains—usually thought of in terms of cross-country trucking hauls— also include our ability to attract immigrants from far away.

Chinese food in America is not as good as in Sichuan province, but Sichuan province does not offer comparably diverse food options across the board. American food, and much of the trade-oriented, market-oriented Anglo world, is moving toward this "next best" status for many ethnic cuisines. No *one* of these cuisines is American food, but there is something strongly American about the combination of all those food choices in one locale. In many areas of life, America has been about perfecting diversity and choice, rather than about perfecting any single style. So if immigration restrictions limit the number of food choices, they are striking at the greatest qualities of American food.

Up through the 1920s, the United States was largely an open nation for immigrant arrivals. Land was to be had, it was easy to find a job, the class system was open and flexible (for most whites), and American cities absorbed millions of newcomers. It's not surprising that recent immigrants formed so much of the U.S. population. From 1820 to 1920, the United States took in about thirty million Europeans. Yet this source of ideas and experimentation was choked off by immigration policy. In 1921, the Emergency Quota Act enacted the first ceiling on the number of immigrants admitted per year; restrictions were tightened in 1924 and for the next forty years the United States was largely closed to legal foreign immigration on a large scale.

These immigration restrictions hurt American food and they came at broadly the same time as Prohibition, the Great Depression, and World War II. To consider the suffocating effect of immigration limits alone, imagine how your current dining scene would suffer if you were cut off from the food products of Chinese, Indian, Vietnamese, Thai, and Mexican immigrants, not to mention all the other groups, from Bolivians to Ethiopians, depending of course on where you live. Not only would these varied and delicious foods be much harder to find, but the competitive pressures on mainstream American restaurants would be weaker. By the middle of the twentieth century, eaters in the United States had lived in that world for about fifty years. The effect was inferior and blander food.

Stopping the flow of new immigrants also damaged the culinary value of older, already established immigrants. Earlier immigrants were cut off from the food ideas from back home. Chinatowns dried up, Italian districts turned mainstream, and Greek immigrants opened diners with only a moderate Greek influence; you'll see souvlaki on these menus but not much more from the homeland. Previous immigrants lost touch with their roots and moved closer to mainstream American eating habits. Social identification with one's ethnic group made less sense when that group was shrinking in numbers. While this may have been good for national unity, it was bad for American food. Immigrants sought normality and acculturation. Spicy or garlicky foods were seen as signs of lower-class status and habits to be overcome. Cut off from their roots, isolated pockets of immigrants were seduced by the promise of American household ease. They started buying canned goods, bottled ketchup, and later frozen dinners and microwaves. Sometimes they pursued these trends in excess, to show they were "real Americans." Cooking from the "home country" was limited to special holidays or large Sunday family dinners. Some ethnic styles persisted but they ossified in form: If you visit an old-style German restaurant in Pennsylvania you'll find plenty of heavy meat dishes, with lots on the plate, but few of the flavorful subtleties you can find if you visit southern Germany.

The American dining scene was insular. Duncan Hines was arguably the leading restaurant critic in the United States in the 1940s. He made his first trip to Europe only in 1948, reporting back that the United States enjoyed the world's finest cuisine. In his view, the only competitors for this designation were the English, who had excellent roast beef.

Immigration restrictions were not relaxed until 1965, when the Hart-Cellar Act abolished national-origin quotas; the Act went into formal effect in 1968 and there was further delay in getting people to come and to open up successful restaurants. Nonetheless, over the next ten years, 4.7 million immigrants were admitted. This was much larger than the 2.5 million admitted in the 1950s, nearly five times the one million of the 1940s, and a full order of magnitude greater than the half million of the 1930s. The coming of age of food in the United States, in the 1970s and 1980s, owed much to this change in immigration policy.

The American restaurant scene responded to the wave of newcomers, albeit with a lag. In 1960 the United States had over six thousand Chinese restaurants. In the 1960s, the Chinese population of the United States increased by 84 percent, largely through immigration. The number of Chinese restaurants rose steadily, and eventually their quality and diversity grew too.

The American Southwest shows just how much immigration restrictions damaged American food. Despite all the immigration restrictions enacted into law, Mexican immigration to the Southwest was largely uncontrolled until the 1970s or later. Although the restrictive laws from the 1920s were supposed to apply to Mexicans, the enforcement was lax. Mexicans therefore moved into Texas, Arizona, and New Mexico in large numbers throughout the twentieth century, even when other sources of national immigration were slow. Mexican dishes already had been prominent in these areas, but continuing immigration kept the traditions alive. Tex-Mex food evolved into a new variety of Mexican food, with unique Texan, New Mexican, and California variants. All this happened well before the immigration blossoming of the 1970s. The various excellent chilies of New Mexico, for instance, have been a popular ingredient since the early history of that territory.

What Kids and Television Have Wrought

During the twentieth century, the structure of the American family also tipped the balance away from quality foods.

Food habits start in the family. That is where we learn what to eat, how to eat, and how to value food. While a palate can be retrained, most people keep the food tastes of their childhood. It is no accident that so many Chinese will eat sea cucumber for the feeling of smoothness, that so many Mexicans do not mind the spiciness of chilies, and that so many

Argentines have a taste for kidneys and intestines. They grew up with the stuff. Many Americans treat Wonder Bread as a normal taste, but few Germans will, as they are expecting harder and stronger-tasting breads.

Through a series of social accidents, the structure of the twentieth-century American family, when combined with the new technologies of the time, discouraged quality food. Television viewing, working mothers, and spoiled children all combined to dumb down American culinary tastes.

Amy Chua's recent book *Battle Hymn of the Tiger Mother* explained that Asian kids are so successful in engineering and the sciences because of an approach to parenting that includes limiting kids' TV time, forcing them to practice a musical instrument such as the violin, even calling one's children "garbage" when they don't meet expectations. Whatever you think of this as a parenting method, strict parenting is better for a country's food than is permissive parenting. When the kids are in charge, food quality is bound to go downhill and that has been a big part of the problem with American food.

Recent immigrants aside, Americans spoil and cater to their children more than do other countries. We buy them more toys, read more books about how to bring them up, and give them larger allowances to spend. Dr. Spock's best-selling 1946 book told parents to cater to the needs of their children flexibly. Europeans often express their amazement at the child-centered nature of U.S. culture, how much we are always running to please the little tykes, and how little respect we give our elderly.

We also spoil our children by catering to their food preferences, but this damages dining quality for everyone. American parents produce, buy, cook, and present food that is blander, simpler, and sweeter, and in part that is because the kiddies are in charge. Children love sweets, French fries, unornamented meats, and snacks. Since it is easier to cook for the whole family, American food followed this simpler, blander path. You simply cannot count on children to monitor the quality of food. Few children will complain that the vegetables are not fresh, that the sauce is under-seasoned, or that the fish is overcooked.

In France, in contrast, the wishes of children, whether for food or otherwise, are more frequently ignored. The kids are simply expected to eat what the adults feed them. A lot of American food is, quite simply, food for children in a literal sense. It's just that we all happen to eat it.

If you've brought the kids to McDonald's, for that fun plastic play house, or for the Chicken McNuggets, odds are you are going to eat there too, whether you like it or not. Many fast food outlets target their marketing at children, hoping that parents will be dragged in as well. Burger King and McDonald's run extensive marketing programs aimed at children and offer brightly colored playgrounds. These franchises are implicit baby-sitters, since the children often run off to play while the parents sit, eat, and talk. Fast food restaurants still cluster around high schools; they are three to four times more likely to be located near a high school than would otherwise be expected, given the locations of those high schools. Furthermore, the United States is still a much younger society, demographically, than is Japan or most of Europe.

Parents also give their kids bigger allowances in the United States than in other countries of the world. In part the United States is a relatively wealthy country and in part Americans are, for whatever reasons, more willing to cater to children. Of course children spend a lot of their allowance money on candy, fast food, and snacks. This shapes their tastes and gives them some food autonomy, relative to their peers in other countries, who are typically more dependent on the food chosen by their parents. The result is a lot of bad food and a lot of sweet, bland food.

For instance, children have been the driving force behind the prominence of doughnut chains in the United States. In 1962, which arguably is one of the nadir years for American food, 59 percent of U.S. households had children; 91 percent of those families bought doughnuts regularly, as compared to 74 percent of the families without children. Doughnuts are extremely sweet, they come in bright colors, and they contain lots of additives. They are the snob's culinary nightmare, and their popularity is not surprising in such a child-centered culture.

Fast food restaurants did not prosper in Western Europe until American social trends—albeit in weaker form—reached the continent. This includes the dual-income family, suburban commuting, a workday with no lengthy lunch break at home, widespread advertising, and greater purchasing power for children. McDonald's did not enter the Italian market until the relatively late date of 1984 and it still is not prominent there.

The tube is also responsible for a lot of the bad eating habits in this country. Television became popular in the United States more quickly than in Europe. The American love affair with TV took off in the 1950s and viewing rose through the 1980s. By 1955, two-thirds of all American households had TV sets. In most of Europe, this process happened two decades later. This is one reason why America, and not Europe, has been the vanguard of many low-quality food trends.

Television encouraged the consumption of food that was quick to eat and prepare. Think about the 1970s for instance. Soap operas ran all afternoon. Reruns already had started at five o'clock, the evening news was shown at six, and prime-time shows began at eight. The "TV cost" of preparing a time-consuming meal was high. Furthermore most of the family would not want to sit around the table and savor multiple courses. More commonly, one parent, or perhaps a teenage child, would prepare something quick, heat up a frozen dinner, or order out for food delivery.

In my childhood, many of my favorite shows—including *Star Trek* and *I Dream of Jeannie*—were shown in reruns precisely at dinnertime in the critical five-to-seven P.M. slots. By seven thirty or eight, new sitcoms were under way. I was anxious to see Captain Kirk and so I required little more than a hamburger and perhaps French fries. My mother obliged; but I would have fought any approach that tied me to the dinner table for an hour. I learned how to heat frozen French fries, how to order out for "Chicken Delight," and how to cook a simple hamburger. My culinary tastes were formed during these years, and they were not much modified until a stint living in Germany in my early twenties.

The entry of women into the work force pushed food in similar "ready to eat" directions. In 1940, 8.6 percent of married American women with children held jobs. By 1948, the figure had risen to 26 percent, and by 1991 it was 66.8 percent. One early Jell-O pamphlet was persuasive: "Why should any woman stand for hours over a hot fire, mixing compounds to make people ill, when in two minutes, with an expense of ten cents, she can produce such attractive desserts?"

Chain and fast food restaurants grew rapidly during this period, mostly to economize on the time and effort of the parents. By 1975, housewives were working thirty-two fewer hours a week preparing meals and cleaning up, on average, than their counterparts from 1910. A lot of this time saved was liberation from drudgery, and who wants that back? Still, it meant that prepackaged food was replacing hand preparation of fresh raw ingredients. The rising divorce rate forced many women out into the workplace and further cemented these trends.

Entrepreneurs stepped forward to provide TV-friendly and latchkey-friendly foods. The microwave oven was patented in 1945 and marketed for commercial use in 1947. In 1955 a microwave still cost $1,295 but by 1967 a countertop model could be had for $495. Today a perfectly acceptable microwave can sell for as little as fifty dollars.

In 1954 Swanson marketed the first nationally available "TV dinner," which consisted of turkey with cornbread dressing and gravy, sweet potatoes, and buttered peas. The Swanson executive who thought of the serving drew upon his wartime "mess" experience; he had once consumed a similar meal on a rainy battlefield in Okinawa. Many subsequent Swanson recipes were developed by bacteriologists rather than chefs; it was difficult to figure out which foodstuffs would withstand the rigors of the production process and the subsequent preservation; those factors became more important than the taste of the food. Frozen and pre-prepared foods also had compartmentalized trays to make it easier to eat the food without a table underneath and without looking at the meal. Later the folding TV table-tray kept the food from falling into one's lap.

Pizza took off in the United States only in the 1950s. A pie or two could feed everyone, so it fit well with family life. An order was easy to transport in the car. Above all else, pizza is good for eating in front of the television. It is easily reheated, can be ordered for delivery, and can be eaten by hand from a plate without needing much in the way of a table or utensils. For a busy family, it is quick to clean up and throw away.

Television encouraged the purchase of food that can be eaten in one's lap or from a big bag or bowl. In addition to pizza, this also favored pre-packaged, easy-to-handle snack foods such as cookies, potato chips, French fries, and wrapped candy. It disfavored fresh foods with easily spilled sauces and broths. The problem wasn't agribusiness per se, it's that consumers were not innovating enough, in part because TV was distracting them.

The centrality of television in American life also drove a national market in advertising and this made food more homogeneous. The national networks had most of the popular programs and that further shifted the balance of influence in food markets. National advertising means that the product must be saleable to large numbers of people, as it is not worth buying network airtime for niche or specialty items. The result was that nationally advertised products tended to be bland and popular in flavor; they appealed to a "least common denominator" among American eaters. This favored national brands, which are the same everywhere, and made it harder for niche foods to get a hearing. The advertisement had to feature a single product or a consistent product line, as repetition and consistency of message are paramount to market-ing. What better way to reach people than to advertise on a popular show such as the evening news or *I Love Lucy*? Kraft Cheese would find this profitable, but your local organic grocer would not.

As with the stultifying effects of Prohibition, the effects of these causes have often lasted longer than the restrictions themselves. Culi-nary excellence is hard to start up again once it is destroyed, cooking knowledge in the home is lost, and a network of wonderful restaurants cannot be created overnight. Excellent restaurants require customers who know the difference and care enough to pay for it. When so many restaurants have been mediocre for decades, or altogether absent, it is hard to suddenly rebuild a clientele that appreciates quality. American diners, and home cooks, became accustomed to looking for convenience and the tried-and-true. Furthermore most top chefs are trained by other, older chefs, and it is hard to get the training chain started again.

To sum up, a number of contingent historical factors have pushed American food supply networks toward convenience rather than quality:

laws and our politicians, our children, and our acquiescence to these forces. Agribusiness does have a greedy quest for profit, so it will support both positive and negative food trends, when consumers are demanding them. It may appear that agribusiness is at fault, but they are the builders of the platform rather than the main shapers of the content. We need to think first about . . . ourselves.

A good place to strike back, to begin a new food revolution, is in the aisle of the supermarket, perhaps behind one of those shopping trolleys designed to conveniently trap and soothe demanding toddlers. What are the ways to turn America's unusual food markets in your favor? The aisles of the American supermarket reflect a lot of what went wrong, so improving the supermarket experience is one natural way to cement your credentials as an everyday foodie.

3

Revolutionizing the
Supermarket Experience

Most of us are pretty familiar with the traditional American supermarket, maybe too familiar. The Safeway or Wegmans or local corner market all supply a lot of convenient foodstuffs—and a lot of those middle aisles are full of things that are only a rough approximation of food—but that very convenience can make the modern American supermarket a rut. The deadening hand of routine takes over our shopping lives: we know what we want, where to find it, when to get it, and what to do with it when we bring it home. These mindless habits can be the biggest obstacles to discovering new regions of the food universe.

Abstaining from your standard routine for a week or so and your natural ability as an innovator flourishes. An innovating consumer has a profound effect on the marketplace and the whole food economy. After all, maybe the mainstream American supermarket, for all of its conveniences, isn't actually the best way to sell—or buy—food. At the very least, maybe it's not the best way *all the time*.

With that thought in mind, I conducted an experiment. For a mere month, I would refrain from consuming food from mainstream supermarkets and instead choose—exclusively—a particular ethnic supermarket, in this case a Chinese/Asian supermarket called Great Wall. A month may not sound like long, but my goal was to show how quickly adaptation can or cannot take place, not to challenge my ability to endure food I might not like.

Full disclosure: I still traveled to other cities, and ate in restaurants, so the supermarkets never completely dominated my food life, but that's the same way I use my local Whole Foods. I would go "cold turkey" on traditional American supermarkets and for every day out of town I had to do an extra day shopping at the specified ethnic market.

The idea behind this experiment? As noted above, my economic approach:

Food is a product of economic supply and demand, so try to figure out where the supplies are fresh, the suppliers are creative, and the demanders are informed.

When it comes to ethnic markets, most of the shoppers really are very well informed. Most of the shoppers come from cultures—including China—where food preparation receives a lot more attention than in the United States. These shoppers also are largely immigrants or children of immigrants. Either they come from cultures where most food prices are lower than in the United States, or the immigrants have lower incomes themselves, or both.

It seemed natural to select what is probably the world's oldest and perhaps most sophisticated food culture, namely Chinese.

The Great Wall

Great Wall Supermarket is located in Merrifield, Virginia, about a twenty-minute drive outside of Washington, D.C., in an upper-middle-class suburban area in Fairfax County, with plenty of Chinese immigrants. The Chinese-owned store has ten long aisles, along with some side spaces, and it is set in a low-rent strip mall dominated by a very large Latino thrift market.

The most daunting task in Great Wall is finding something. At first, even though I had been there numerous times before, and I am relatively familiar with Chinese cuisine (by Western standards at least), it could take me twenty minutes to find just one or two items. It felt like walking into a labyrinth, even with my savvy stepdaughter helping out.

Many of the jars are in Chinese characters, with the English lettering very small, hard to find, not always in the same place on the jar, and often facing away from the viewer. So if you are told "aisle eight, in the middle, on the right side," it is a help but not a solution. You're still confronted with an array of many difficult-to-distinguish jars. Even if you know something about Chinese food, "Bean Sauce" comes in a number of different colors and kinds and the store has dozens of versions of soy sauce. Once I moved beyond the highly visible items, such as the meats, virtually every time I stumbled to find what I wanted, at least at first.

The dried goods and candy items are hardest to search. Not everything has an English language label. Often I don't know exactly what I am looking for, if only because the name of something in a book or cookbook doesn't correspond exactly to the name on the package. Is *"ya cai"* the same as "pickle mustard vegetable" or, in other words, "pickled mustard green"? I still don't know for sure, although I think so, and that's assuming I can find the English inscription at all. And when I entered those aisles, I sometimes had the feeling that people were staring at me and thinking: What does he want here? I learned quickly how much I am dependent on background cultural knowledge and simple rules of thumb.

I decided to ask Rong Rong. Rong Rong is a Chinese graduate student at my university, studying for a Ph.D. in economics, and originally from a region near Shanghai. Rong Rong has a diminutive frame and a friendly manner and she is possibly the sharpest student in her cohort. And Rong Rong told me to try the double mushroom soy sauce, which she claims tastes just like what her mother serves in China.

I asked Rong Rong if she has trouble finding items in Great Wall. The answer was a simple no, although she did admit to being confused in a local chain, the Giant supermarkets, even though she has lived in the

United States for almost four years. She found the Giant cereal aisles to be the hardest to master; and even though her English is very good she cannot read all of the labels nearly as fast as I can, or recognize from a glance what a foodstuff is going to taste like.

Another obstacle in using the Great Wall is asking for directions to sought-after items. By all appearances, the staff works hard and, unlike in a Safeway, finding a store employee on the floor is not difficult. The problem is that virtually all of the workers are Spanish-speaking, most likely from El Salvador, with varying abilities in English. I am fortunate to speak Spanish, but this is not always much help. Some of the words for Chinese grocery items I don't know in Spanish, but more commonly there is not a good translation. *"Salsa dulce de los frijoles"* doesn't carry the same connotation as "sweet bean sauce" and requesting it did not get me to where I wanted to go. *"Dulce y agrio"* does map directly into "sweet and sour," but that easy translation is the exception rather than the rule: It's not easy to find out the Spanish word for pickled fresh bamboo shoots. In most cases the Latino staff knows neither the English or Chinese words for what is on their shelves. Entering the store is like being robbed of part of one's linguistic facilities. Another Chinese graduate economics student, Siyu Wang, noted that the prevalence of Spanish among the store's workers was one of her biggest surprises when she first visited Great Wall.

There are some Chinese staff in the store, including most of the cashiers, but their English is limited and I have no Chinese. One strategy that does work, when it can be applied, is to bring a Chinese cookbook with the Chinese characters for the desired items. Show the relevant character to someone who works in the store. If you can find a Chinese employee, they will then lead you directly and enthusiastically to exactly the right point.

Mostly, I learned where things were by walking down all of the plausible aisles and then looking in places that seemed logical. Over time, that worked better as I learned the supermarket. With each visit, I increasingly divided the store into "parts I use" and "parts I don't use." The parts I used included the produce, the meats and fish and tofu, and the spices and the sauces, plus the frozen goods, most of all the dumplings, and the large piles of different noodles, dried and fresh. I didn't do much with the American goods, the Latino goods, the bags of dried fish, the cans of condensed milk, the Asian sweets, or the cookware.

A further difficulty is that the store takes less care than does a mainstream U.S. supermarket to put the most important items at eye level. There are also fewer highly visible corner displays and promotions and the overall organization of the store is much more cluttered than is a Giant or a Safeway, much less a Whole Foods.

The final obstacle to searches is getting one's cart down the aisle. The main aisles fit two carts sideways, barely; and usually at least one of those lanes is taken by a cart, and sometimes both are taken by either a cart or a person. It's hard to get down the aisles and even harder to do so with one's own cart. That discourages looking and it also discourages browsing. My initial tendency was to search the empty aisles, if only because I know I can get down them and back without much delay. This is not obviously the best strategy and arguably it led me to spend too much time looking at the highly durable items, which are purchased less frequently by the other customers (thus the emptier aisles). Overall, I felt far less mobile than in a typical American supermarket, even if I left my cart behind in a parked position, as I usually needed to do.

I also started going later at night, and avoiding the weekends, to circumvent these problems. Later Rong Rong remarked to me that the non-Chinese patrons are most visible at night, because they are intent on avoiding the crush of visitors during the day on the weekends. She finds the weekend the most convenient time to visit, because that is when she has more time and is more likely to be cooking something special. The crowds do not bother her, and by Chinese standards they are unremarkable (Siyu Wang agreed).

In general many of the patrons are not so mobile, although for different reasons than cited above. It is common to see a woman spending a solid minute or two inspecting the quality of a pineapple, thereby blocking that portion of the aisle. The customers who seek green peas go through the bin pea by pea, no matter how long it takes. A woman became entranced picking out the best garlic chives and a man asked for sales help in selecting the best clams—by what standard he judged them I am not sure. No one was much enamored of the "shovel" or "scoop" technique for filling a plastic bag with food.

The immobility of these customers in turn further limited my mobility; I often was waiting for someone to get out of the way. I wanted to grab what I needed and get home. In contrast, this was all thoroughly inconvenient.

Six Varieties of Bok Choy

So much for the process of shopping, what about the contents of the Great Wall?

The most striking difference, other than having lots of Chinese food, is how much of the store was devoted to greens. Once you push your cart through the door, that's the first thing you see, and you see lots of it. They are fresh, cheap, and it is a more attractive selection than you will find in any other supermarket in the area. The greens are the store's signature achievement and once you have tried them you know you will always have reason to come back. Even the other local Chinese supermarkets do not compare on this score. Great Wall deals with special farms in New Jersey, New Mexico, and Texas to keep the supply flowing.

The greens are also the store's "loss leader," namely what brings customers in the door to purchase other, higher-margin items, even if the loss leader does not itself make money. In a U.S. grocery store, the loss leaders are more likely to be standards, such as milk, or whichever prices are advertised prominently in the circular or on the web. That's what gets people to come.

The selection of greens in Great Wall includes Chinese garlic chives, sweet potato vines, baby Chinese broccoli, chrysanthemum greens, snow peas, green beans, baby red amaranth, Malaman spinach, yam tips, white shen choy tips, baby yo choy tips, and many others. Where else can you get six or more varieties of bok choy? Most of the greens are in large piles, they look very fresh, and they are attended to frequently by staff. My dominant impression of the store is one of seeing rows of endless greens, broadly similar in appearance, and not being sure which ones to buy, but they all turned out to be tasty and easy to cook, if only by steaming.

You also can find the U.S. supermarket standards of cabbage, broccoli, spinach, green peppers, kohlrabi, leeks, cauliflower, and squash, among other vegetables, so you don't have to give up any mainstream American favorites at Great Wall. The quality of these items is also above average and the prices are much lower. For a comparison, at Great Wall green peppers are $0.99 a pound, but at a nearby Safeway they are $5.99 a pound, six times more. The quality at Great Wall is just as good. Green beans are $1.49 a pound at Great Wall, $2.99 a pound at Safeway, and if anything I prefer them at Great Wall. If I am buying a bunch of different vegetables or greens, I am still shocked when the cashier tells me how low the bill is.

The greens are also the busiest part of the store. Often mainstream supermarkets put the most coveted and commonly bought items in corners or on the back wall (think dairy), to force long walks and thus to stimulate impulse purchases along the way. Great Wall puts the greens up front. Everyone comes in and immediately stops to look around at the greens. The traffic jam of carts starts right away, most of all on weekends.

Once I started shopping at Great Wall, I quickly began to eat more greens and also I began to enjoy them more. I never had to tell myself it would ward off cancer, make the earth a better place, help me lose weight, or ease animal cruelty. I wanted to eat the greens and the purchases felt virtually free of charge, given the low prices. I could try any new and unknown green without investing much money in it. There wasn't much of a learning curve: I made this entire shift to eating more greens by my second or third visit of the shopping experiment. If nothing else, I would steam some greens whenever I was making dumplings. Each time I visited, the main question was which green I would try next, and whether I could remember the ones I had already sampled, and often I could not. Every single one of these leaps into the dark was delicious; that I was not once disappointed is remarkable.

It was just this kind of lopsided reward that got me thinking about the need for a new kind of food revolution and how it can be accomplished.

The nearby fruits were also good, although they cannot compare to the greens. Great Wall has better than average grapes, standard American fruits at lower prices, and a touch of exotica, such as durian and rambutan when available.

Fresh and Smelly

The second notable section of Great Wall is the seafood, which has a far more extensive choice than would a mainstream U.S. supermarket. On one day I counted fifty-one separate bins for distinct seafood items, including crabs, clams, octopuses, mussels, and fish. The seafood section is crammed to accommodate this variety, with fish tanks running both below the main counter and also on the wall behind the heads of the workers. Just about all of the space in this section is used to store and present creatures, living and dead. The final impression is one of a cornucopia of items that are too bony, with too many scales, or too reeking of the sea to satisfy most American appetites. I asked Rong Rong about the fish and she expressed some disappointment, at least compared to China. She is used to live fish, swimming in tanks, and the displayed dead fish she didn't always find tasty when she tried to cook them.

In contrast to many of my fellow Americans, I enjoy and indeed often prefer whole fish, especially if accompanied by a good sauce. But at Great Wall too many of the fish need to be scaled, or the fish would yield a ratio of flesh to bone that is inefficiently low for a typical American appetite. There are some filets of fish but most of the produce is whole, bones and eyes and all. It is a splendid section for constructing a seafood stock, but I never got the hang of how to convert the dozens of fish choices into easy-to-make, easy-to-eat meals. Bringing home a bunch of small whole mackerel made me long for the good canned product at Whole Foods; eating a steamed small mackerel with chopsticks isn't that much fun for me. I like the taste, it just feels like too much work.

Most of the shrimp are still in their shells. The octopus and squid and mussels all look like they were just pulled out of the ocean, eyes, tentacles, everything. There is no attempt to make them look easier to cook or easier to eat than they are, rather the premise is that it should look and smell exactly like what it is. There are also live frogs, turtles, and eels in tanks for sale as food. There is also a big pile of disgusting-looking jellyfish, including one bin that purports to present just the head of the creature. (According to answers.com, jellyfish do not even have heads.) Sometimes not-yet-dead fish have been pulled out of the tank and they are flopping around on the ice, but no one seems to notice. "Striped pangasius bladder" was the most unusual seafood item I found there.

The seafood section emits a strong smell, much stronger than a mainstream American supermarket would find desirable. The scent serves as advertising to Chinese customers but it puts off many potential non-Chinese customers. My wife and stepdaughter object to this smell and it is one reason why they do not like to accompany me to Great Wall. At first they will cite pragmatic reasons why we should not go there, but if I continue the debate, sooner or later they come back to the smell, which I believe is their real concern. In the online reviews at Yelp.com, the smell of the fish and meats comes in for repeated criticism from reviewers who, from the photos, appear to be non-Chinese. Not everyone was comfortable with seeing so many fish swimming in crowded tanks, or having to scale the fish themselves at home. "Why is seafood located so near produce?" was one complaint. The seafood section is the easiest part of the store to find, the greens by the entrance aside, because it is on the back wall, next to the greens, and because it emits such a characteristic smell. You don't have to ask anyone how to get there. Personally, the smell never bothered me and I even found it a convenient navigational aid.

In the meat section, there are many kinds of beef. One popular item is the flank steak, tasty and cheap but chewy, and there are also short ribs, brisket, and various organs, some wrapped in plastic and some behind a counter. Rong Rong remarked that the display of the meats reminded her of China and this was one of her favorite aspects of shopping at Great Wall.

Most of the meat section is devoted to variants of pork, including organs and ears and feet; and there is also a large clump of fresh pork fat, a useful commodity for many kinds of cooking not just Chinese. The "beef pizzles" are I believe frozen penises. Unlike in one of the local Vietnamese supermarkets, I never saw pork uterus. Moving along the row, there are chicken feet and duck tongues and plenty of smoked meats such as smoked chicken and duck, including in ready-to-cook form. Along the top of the entire meat section is a long and varied selection of different kinds of "balls," including fish balls, meatballs, and "fish balls rugby shape." In the far corner of the store, the meat section merges with the on-site restaurant (more on that later) and there is a butcher selling whole, hanging ducks; this is a very popular section and on weekends there is often a line.

I thought I would spend a lot of time eating pork belly bought in the store, but no. Great Wall does sell pork belly but not in thinly sliced form, rather in thick rolls. I tried it once but gave up in frustration because it wasn't easy for me to slice the meat evenly or thinly. Once again, Great Wall assumed its customers had a real facility with handling food products and preparing them for convenient consumption. Pork belly is one of my favorite Chinese dishes (sautéed with chilies, ginger, cinnamon stick, soy sauce, and anise star, for instance), but that meal had to wait until I was freed from my obligation to shop at Great Wall. Great Wall sold me on the greens idea, and it also got me to cook more, but I never was tempted to learn a lot of new skills of food cleaning, scaling, slicing, and preparation.

I also found I spent a lot more time making stocks: chicken stocks, beef stocks, and fish and seafood stocks. The spare animal parts are readily available and very cheap. More than half of my cooked meals, from this store, were based on some kind of stock or another, and this is one reason why the quality of our dinners went up. Making a stock went from "a hassle but maybe worth it" to "a no-brainer." After a few weeks, I took the idea of a fresh stock virtually for granted, which I never had done before.

Items in Great Wall were usually totally fresh or completely dried or frozen. For my shopping and cooking, I was most interested in the fresh items, but diligence was required. The fish and the seafood are not intended to be kept in the fridge for two days, then cooked; the fish are meant to be cooked that evening.

Great Wall made no attempt to cover up how much of its products were frozen; and in fact the word "frozen" was prominently displayed on many signs, like a boast. In mainstream supermarkets, most U.S. customers like the idea of "fresh food," even if it, such as the fish, was typically previously frozen. There is a pretense of fresh maintained to various degrees because people do not wish to hear about what is being frozen, and they like seeing the food in a thawed state. I did not find such a pretense in Great Wall.

Most of the frozen products in a mainstream U.S. supermarket are set off in a separate "frozen foods" section, where it is packaged, labeled, and ready for some kind of mechanical reheating. Frozen macaroni and cheese, frozen pizza, or frozen buffalo wings are staples of my local Safeway. In Great Wall, a lot of the frozen items were plastic-covered fish, meats, or seafood, in bins or piles with very little in the way of packaging or branding. You can pick up a wrapped frozen fish, put it in your cart, and move on to the next item. It's not ready to stick in the microwave. Rather, what you have purchased is a frozen fish for which you then must puzzle out a use and preparation. The closest equivalent to Stouffer's might be the "mung bean and taro frozen popsicles."

In Great Wall there is no shortage of unusual items. An entire half of an aisle is devoted to teas of various kinds, with a few cereals thrown in. The two most unusual I spotted were Kung Fu Tea and Menopuse [*sic*] Tea.

I made a visit to Great Wall with two Singaporean friends, and I asked them what I should try, requesting that they pick out some mix of the iconic and what I might actually enjoy. They picked out for me Baked Shrimp Flavored Chips and LongXuSu, a slightly sweet powder, sometimes called Dragon Beard Candy. Both were okay, but neither would be for me a real source of diet-breaking temptation.

My consumption of snack food plummeted. Is it that I don't like Chinese snacks or that I was too incompetent to find the good ones? It doesn't matter. Typically I munch on cheese and chocolate and crackers, but I wasn't going to incorporate salty Chinese shrimp chips into my life the same way. I consider them well described by that ambiguous phrase "an acquired taste." Virtually all of the food I ate from Great Wall was fresh. I liked it better and it was also easier to identify and find.

In terms of ethnicity, Great Wall is more than just a Chinese market. The sauces and spices on hand allow the visitor to cook many major dishes of Vietnamese cuisine and Thai cuisine; in the latter case it has the area's best supply of fresh lemon grass and plenty of cheap coconut milk ($1.19 rather than $2.49 at Whole Foods). It is less useful for Korean and Japanese cuisines, which in part may be due to the large Korean H Mart a few blocks away, but still they have a sauce for marinating bul-gogi and large jars of kimchee.

The Latino part of the store is put in the aisle specified for "American goods," which might have been better labeled "Latin American goods." The aisle offers lots of beans and lots of Goya products. I never saw an Asian buying these items. If you see non-Chinese shoppers at Great Wall, most likely they are Latino and, in my immediate D.C. area, likely to be a recent immigrant from El Salvador (most of all), Guatemala, or Honduras. In addition to the Latino offerings, in this "American" aisle, there are canned goods, Pop-Tarts, and lots of space for Pringles potato chips. Without warning, the American section stops and suddenly there is "organic adzuki," a bean product used to make sweet Asian desserts.

You could use Great Wall to make meat, beans, and rice, but you cannot replicate traditional American shopping, cooking, and dining with this aisle. Most of all, you cannot get cheese in the store, as they offer only a very small selection of two processed spreads. There is plenty of milk, however, including a noticeable section for non-lactose milk (many Chinese are lactose-intolerant).

The frequency of shopping ended up as one of the most pronounced features of my experiment. I found myself returning to the store more often than I usually go food shopping. Great Wall had plenty of items that are durable, such as root vegetables or frozen fish, but those are not what I tended to buy. I was each time lured toward the fresh goods, and so the idea of "stocking up" for three or four dinners never worked out, given what I wanted to eat. My trips to the store were pretty much on a one meal–one trip basis. That's what happens when your meals are regularly fresh. But I didn't always feel like getting into the car, so I skipped a few meals because of the morning hour or because of traffic. Those were the only meals I skipped all year.

Checkout

The checkout experience was distinctly non-American and Rong Rong reports that it is done very much as in China. I was not usually smiled at nor was I told to have a nice day. Yet overall I like the service. The items were scanned rapidly and I never experienced a difficult time or a delay. Everyone was keen to get on with his or her business (though they may have taken half an hour to choose their seafood), so I never saw a customer in front of me strike up a conversation with a cashier about the new coupons from the newspaper, the weather, why the swiped credit card had been canceled, or whether the avocado sale would run for another three days. Silence was the norm, and I found this aspect of the store to be an improvement. What appears to be a dauntingly long line at the checkout is more manageable than it looks.

There was one time when a cashier spoke to me. I was buying "red bean ice cream popsicle sticks," and she held up the box, looked up at me, and said "Yum, yum" and smiled.

There was no systematic display of junk food by the checkout stands, although there was an attempt to stimulate impulse purchases. Beside each stand there is a pile of something: At one register it is cheap chewing gum; on one typical day other impulse purchases I saw were dried persimmons, buns, dates, rice noodles, and crackers, all placed in informal-looking piles by the cashier stands.

Once you've paid for the groceries, customers may be tempted to grab a bite to eat. Great Wall has a restaurant against the left wall, which is run by a separate entrepreneur. A few years ago the restaurant offered some simple noodle dishes and a small buffet. It recently expanded to a larger menu, including dim sum in the morning and a much larger buffet. On the wall is written, *Tastee Chinese Food*, although it is not clear if that is the name of the restaurant or promotional copy.

Most of their food I don't like. It's greasy and rarely fine; I once used the phrase "too authentic" in one of my online reviews of the place. The cafeteria-style food sits under a lamp. There is too much emphasis on noodles, without them being special or unusual. The cooked vegetables are limp and sometimes sit in the infamous "brown sauce." They don't have the spicy Sichuan dishes that I favor, and I find that Cantonese cuisine—which comprises most of the menu—needs to be done at a higher standard to be effective. Tastee reminds me of the lesser Chinese restaurants I have seen in Asia, which I suppose is part of the point. On weekends the place is packed, but the Chinese I spoke with all confirmed that they don't consider the quality to be outstanding and many will call it outright lousy. The place is renowned for its low prices.

Their best offering is probably the dim sum, which they serve mornings and tends to be fresher. Of the traditional cooked dishes, the tofu does better than the vegetables and noodles sitting out on the buffet. One okay option is to order some noodles cooked fresh rather than from the buffet. The pork with tofu dish is pretty good.

The restaurant opens at around nine A.M. or slightly thereafter, and at that time it is easy to meet some non-Chinese in the supermarket. A number of local non-Chinese individuals—it would not be stretching too far to call them derelicts—go to Tastee in the morning for the very cheap baked goods, such as a large bun with pork and sugar for $1.50. It's good. I was dressed down that day (who dresses up for nine A.M supermarket dim sum?), so when they saw me in line for the bread I received a number of knowing smiles, indicating a shared understanding of a camaraderie in bad luck and desperate times. It is the cheapest good breakfast I can think of in the area.

The Take Home

I asked Rong Rong what she found indispensable at Great Wall and she responded with this list:

1. Fresh bamboo shoots, not those in cans

2. Black chickens (they are really black)

3. Tiger-skin cake

4. Noodlefishes (related to smelts)

5. Duck feet

Siyu Wang expressed support for the duck feet, the cheap snow beans, the cherries, and the Sichuan sauces (she is from Sichuan province). For her it was a relief and a surprise to find so much Chinese food in the United States, even though she doesn't think the quality usually matches up to China. She had heard about Great Wall supermarket while still in China but nonetheless hadn't quite thought it would deliver on so much authenticity. She describes Great Wall as being like the previous generation of supermarkets in China and remarked how they play old, corny Chinese songs on the loudspeaker, like her mother and father might listen to, comparing these supermarkets' appeal to that of Jackie Chan's.

So what are the results of my shopping at Great Wall for a month-long experiment?

- You can, at the same time, significantly lower your supermarket bills and eat a healthier diet. This requires spending more time in the shopping process itself, but it doesn't require additional effort beyond that. Once you get yourself into the right supermarket, it is self-enforcing.

- If you're lacking vegetables and greens in your diet, or don't find them sufficiently cheap and convenient, a Chinese market can solve those problems for you. It really is possible to have a world—an incentive-compatible, economically functioning world—where greens receive much more attention. Great Wall is proof that it works.

- When it comes to non-fresh supermarket purchases, I realized more how much of our behavior is due to habit and simply knowing what to do and how to find our favorite snacks. I have found that one of the best ways to discover new foods and recipes is to force myself out of my familiar food habitats, and Great Wall was perfect for that. The labyrinth was good for my diet and good for my taste buds.

- Breakfast is the meal that changed the most. Cereal was replaced by rice dishes, congees, greens, and dumplings. Shopping at Great Wall forced me to confront a food world where breakfast is one of the most important cooking decisions, rather than a routine to take for granted. I realized how much I had been neglecting what is perhaps the most important meal of the day.

- Even if you cook and eat a lot of Chinese food, as I have done for years, you still are probably pretty far away from "the real Chinese food experience." Shopping at a Chinese supermarket won't get you all the way there, but it will bring you one big pleasing step closer.

- On the down side, I found the cycle of always buying "fresh" to be a little exhausting in terms of time and trouble. That's one thing restaurants are good for—namely, that we can get fresh food without doing all of the legwork ourselves. And I certainly like eating out.

Putting that all together, the closing segment of one Yelp.com review of Great Wall struck me as close to my own impressions:

"Is everything as fresh as I want? No. Could the actual store be in better shape? Yes. Would I come back? Absolutely. Pair a trip to the Great Wall with some Bon Chon [Korean] chicken and you have the makings of a great afternoon in the suburbs."

Months after the experiment ended, I'm still going back on a regular basis. I'm still eating more greens, more dumplings, and using easy-to-make stocks to a greater degree. Those lessons have stuck with me. Perhaps most importantly, I'm a lot more skeptical about the other supermarkets I visit. I don't take their core features, or their defects, for granted. I am much more likely to experiment with different supermarkets—not just Great Wall—and I think more critically about all of my food choices.

And, did I mention that I really like to eat out? We need a new chapter for this topic.

4

The Rules for Finding
a Good Place to Eat

"I went to a hospital cafeteria the other day and ate a fantastic lunch." No you didn't.

Hospital cafeterias are not profit centers for hospitals nor significant elements in their overall reputation. No one ever said, "Take me to the Mayo clinic for my bypass—my visiting relatives love the food!" The cafeteria just has to be good enough not to cause too many complaints, if that.

Hospitals have a more or less captive audience of visitors for their cafeteria offerings. If you're waiting for someone in the emergency room, or coming out of surgery, you won't go for a long walk for a sharper curry. And maybe your mind isn't on food in the first place. In response, hospitals don't take much care in making their food good, even though they have lots of business, lots of customers, and lots of revenue. It's not about the money: Hospitals don't have the *incentive* to make the food good.

How far can we extend this simple line of reasoning to articulate some general principles for how to find good food—and, again, without spending enormous sums of money?

We thus return to economics. Economists, when they seek to understand how stuff of all kinds gets made, typically postulate what is called a "production function." A production function describes output (in this case, food) as the result of applying raw ingredients like fish or fruit, capital, labor, and land. That's a starting framework for understanding where quality food comes from, so let's go through each of these commonsense categories and see what kinds of principles we can develop for making every meal count.

Raw Ingredients

As already discussed, you cannot take high-quality raw ingredients for granted in the United States. There are plenty of first-rate ingredients in good American restaurants but in general they are not cheap. You have to pay for the fish to be flown in, the game to be hunted and delivered, and the fresh vegetables and artisan cheeses to be cultivated by hand. The American restaurants with excellent fresh ingredients—the ones good enough to serve naked on a plate—commonly cost fifty dollars and up for dinner.

New York's Masa is commonly regarded as one of the best restaurants in the United States and it is arguably the best sushi place. The chef-owner has hired a personal fish shopper in the Tsukiji fish market in Tokyo and that shopper rushes the fish to the airport to take a direct flight to New York City, namely JAL 006. Once the fish clears customs, a van driver calls Masa and tells them what time the catch will be arriving. The basic prix fixe dinner at Masa goes for $450.

If you're willing and able to pay, that's great—go for it. But if you want a very good cheap meal, you need to realize you are not living in Tokyo, Puebla, Mexico, or in a small Sicilian village. Good ingredients don't fall from the sky, at least not in Chicago, New York, or most parts of American suburbia. Someone has to put together a tasty concoction, because the basic capital goods—which include raw materials—don't stand up so well on their own, at least not in most parts of the United States.

Avoid dishes that are *ingredients-intensive*. Raw ingredients in America—vegetables, butter, bread, meats, and so on—are below world standards. Even most underdeveloped countries have better raw ingredients than we do, at least if you have a U.S. income to spend there, and often even if one doesn't. Ordering the plain eggplant salad in Turkey may be a great idea, but it is usually a mistake in Northern Virginia. Opt for dishes with sauces and complex mixes of ingredients. Go for dishes that are *composition-intensive*.

If you're in a poor country, you will likely encounter lots of fresh ingredients, even if there's less diversity or lower standards of safety and sanitation. The restaurant is maybe fifteen minutes away from the farm and they receive fresh deliveries just about every day. If they're not used to having refrigeration, the perishable foodstuffs will be *extremely* fresh. In Haiti and Thailand, I've seen fishermen on their boats pulling out the fish or conch from the sea while I am eating the morning catch for lunch. It doesn't need an amazing sauce or an innovative preparation to be superb.

For most American city dwellers and suburbanites, this is *not the world we live in* on a daily basis. The best option is buying prepared food from people who can put together *sufficiently good* raw ingredients in an interesting way. The United States is a country where the human beings are extremely creative but the tomatoes are not extraordinarily fresh. Grilled sardines on bread are amazing in Portugal—and pretty cheap—but in Peoria you should look for something else.

Although the United States does not have the best raw ingredients when it comes to foodstuffs, we have some of the best raw ingredients when it comes to human talent. That's because we are a nation of immigrants, relatively commercial, and the country is an attractive setting for smart and ambitious people. It's no accident that the United States wins about 39 percent of all Nobel Prizes. You'll find a lot of talent here when it comes to dining, and that is further reason to look for dishes that are composition-intensive rather than ingredients-intensive. That's playing to American strengths.

Let's say I am in a Bolivian restaurant in suburban America. There's a good chance I will ask for the silpancho, a specialty of the Cochabamba region. There is a plain steak in the dish, but it's not just sitting out there on the plate. Underneath are rice and potatoes, and piled on top is scrambled egg, tomatoes, onions, and, on the side, green chili sauce. The sauce is not to be missed. The steak does not have to be that good for the overall meal to be delicious. If I don't feel like steak, I might order the peanut (*mani*) soup. That usually contains a mix of ingredients like peas, pasta, beef stock, potatoes or other South American tubers, beef on the bone, onion, tomato, carrots, and parsley, all depending on the recipe of course. It is best when there's lots of pasta floating in the soup. Pasta floating with purple potato and beef stock— the novel composition of ingredients is a kind of poetry.

Some raw ingredients travel well, such as dried chili peppers and seed-based spices. If I buy dried ancho chili peppers from Mexico, or New Mexico, weeks or months or maybe years may pass between the farming of the product and its use in my kitchen or in a restaurant. In the meantime, the product is losing very little value and freshness. You take the ancho peppers, fry them in some canola oil for a few minutes, rehydrate them in water for thirty minutes, and puree them with water into a pasty liquid. It's a superb ingredient in many dishes, from a chip dip (add pureed white onion and tomatillos to the blend) to Mexican molé sauces.

A lot of spicy foods travel relatively well to the United States. But trying to replicate Bresson chicken, Turkish eggplant, or Hong Kong scallops is going to be much, much harder because those ingredients are harder to preserve across long journeys. They have to be refrigerated or frozen and they arrive battered and somewhat tasteless, unless you pay to have them flown in and handled by specialists; then we're back to the expensive restaurants with fine raw ingredients.

Raw materials are the most obvious form of capital to an everyday foodie, but the relevance of capital does not stop there.

Hospital Food Bad—Casino Food Good?

Another way to judge restaurants, or dining locales more generally, is to think about the cross-subsidies they enjoy or, as the case may be, fail to enjoy. "Cross-subsidy" is a technical term in economics, but it is straightforward enough. Does a commercial establishment receive a positive or negative boost from the surrounding circumstances of its production?

Some Las Vegas casinos offer good restaurants and good food to get you to gamble in their establishment; you could say that the gambling is subsidizing the food. The very best Las Vegas restaurants are located well behind the casinos and slot machines, not in front of them. The hope is that people will stop and gamble on their way to and from the good food. So if you're in a Vegas casino, don't eat at the first place right by the entrance, unless of course your gambling addiction will destroy you on your way to first-class Chinese food. Recently authentic Chinese food has appeared in Vegas casinos, because they are hoping to draw in Chinese gamblers. Vegas attracted Japanese customers in the 1980s with similar initiatives, by catering to what they wanted to eat and also how they wanted to gamble. In essence the overall business plan is subsidizing the chicken with rice.

The idea of the cross-subsidy applies in a broad variety of settings. In the old days, Parisian restaurants located themselves near butchers so as to receive choice cuts, entrails, and innards quickly and easily. Mexican food stalls (*comedores*) draw upon the cooking expertise of grandmas, honed over decades of family cooking, and they do not have to train their chefs or pay them very much. Those are all examples of cross-subsidies—the food provider is getting something important on the cheap and subsequent competition forces them to share some of those gains with happy customers.

When prices of air flights were held artificially high by law, before deregulation in the 1970s, airline food was often excellent. They served lobster to attract more customers, and they knew they could make up for the lobster by charging the higher regulated fare they were forced to charge. Prices were so high that flying was, for the most part, the province of the wealthy rather than a common American experience, as it is today. By law, there was no way to attract more customers by lowering the price of the flight. So the desire to compete for high-fare passengers forced the airlines to make the service as good as possible and that included delicious food.

Today, we have bargain flights and usually the food is pretty lame. Most passengers aren't willing to pay for the higher quality, at least not outside of business and first class. Furthermore it's not easy to keep items fresh in airplane cabins. I am glad that flying is so much cheaper, but I've learned that if I want to eat well on a plane, I need to bring my own food. If the food is starting to get a little better again, it's because the airlines are charging more for it, which gives them a reason to attract customers. You now have a hope of adequate yogurts, cheeses, and snack bars. But the simple fact that you must pay by credit card rather than cash (which you may prefer to use) is clear evidence that airlines are still not set up to feed you well.

Since most plane trips are short, or involve waits and connections, markets have adjusted by putting the good food in the airport rather than in the airplane. You don't want to be buying steak from Delta anyway. Food in U.S. airports used to be below the level of fast food. Now at a U.S. airport you might eat in a Ruth's Chris, in a decent wine bar, or maybe order some sushi, all reasonable options even if they are not your favorites or peaks of their respective genres. Dallas airport has okay barbecue, the Cincinnati airport has Gold Star Chili, and Heathrow in London has excellent if pricey smoked salmon. Airports have stopped treating food as secondary to their main operations and they have realized that people are willing to pay more for better selection. Increasingly, I hear of people who drive to airports to eat out (if the food is outside the security gate) or people who arrive at the airport early to enjoy a meal or stick around the airport to eat before catching a cab to their final destination. I've done the latter myself; I thought the Wolfgang Puck pizza at Chicago's O'Hare airport was probably better and quicker than what I plausibly could find on a ride between the airport and Beloit, Wisconsin, where I was scheduled to give a talk.

The vending machine shows you what food looks like when there is no cross-subsidy. When you are buying food from a vending machine, it is a relatively pure transaction. You give up the money; you get the food. There's no décor, no service, no ancillary products, no nothing, other than the swap of specified assets. And what do we know about food from vending machines? It's reliable but it's hardly ever special. Not even in Tokyo, which is the world center for sophisticated and high-class vending machines. It's common to buy noodles out of a vending machine in Japan, but you're purchasing convenience, not taste.

Eat *and* Drink?

Restaurants make a lot of their money off the drinks. In essence, they are supplying food as a kind of window dressing to lure customers in for some other purpose, namely high-priced liquids. It might seem that if you don't buy the drinks, and don't mind settling for plain tap water, you can't lose. However, these restaurants produce the kinds of food that will appeal to people drinking alcohol, such as rich red meats, which appeal less to water drinkers.

It can get very complicated analyzing precisely just how much money an establishment makes off its drinks—say, sodas. Often it's hard to tell exactly which costs of the restaurant are associated with the Coca-Cola since, for instance, the waiter who carries the Coke performs many other functions as well (what percentage of his salary gets apportioned to the cost of the Coke carry?). Still, you pay $2.50 for the drink, and it seems that the Coke itself costs the restaurant less than twenty cents. That's a pretty high markup. A markup on a beer can run up to 500 percent.

For finer restaurants, the markup on wine might run about two and a half to three times the underlying wholesale price, although with a great deal of variation across restaurants, depending on their clientele, décor, and sheer ruthlessness. That means a hundred-dollar wine bottle (wholesale) will be sold at $250 or more and the waiter's wage won't make up for that difference. A wine store might sell the same for about $140.

Not all of this is pure profit, as wines involve glassware costs, breakage, and storage costs, plus staff to handle and serve the wine. A very fancy restaurant also might have $1 million in value tied up in its wine cellar. It has been estimated that Daniel restaurant in New York has $800,000 of wine stored. From a business point of view that's another relevant cost. If you love drinking, by all means pony up; but if your drink is just an impulse purchase, maybe give it a second thought. Is it really worth it?

High prices for drinks are often a form of price discrimination, an economic term which refers to the extraction of additional money from the people willing to pay more for the product. For instance it's price discrimination when a movie theater offers discounts to senior citizens. The cinema realizes that a certain group in their customer base (senior citizens) will see more of their movie offerings if they give them a special price. The rest of the customer base isn't so price sensitive, so the cinema "discriminates" against them.

Here's how the restaurant story runs. It is easier to find out and remember the price for the major items, such as the main courses, than the prices of all the minor items, including the drinks. The market for dining therefore has (at least) two kinds of buyers. The first kind is highly price-sensitive and takes the time to shop around for bargains; this includes remembering how much the drinks cost.

The second set of buyers is less price-sensitive and more inclined to pay the bill without remembering how much the drinks added on. These customers pay more attention to upfront costs—the main items on the menu—than to delayed costs, such as the final tally with the drinks. A lot of these people are pretty wealthy and a lot of them are prone to spend a lot of money. In any case, high prices for drinks will induce some of the latter customers to spend more money, while the more price-sensitive customers concentrate their buying on the better-bargain, lower-margin items—namely, the food and not the drink—and thus they are not scared away from the restaurant.

In essence, *the wealthy and the myopic are the friend and supporter of the non-drinking gourmand.* By paying the markup on the drinks, certain customers make quality food cheaper and more available than it otherwise would be. They are, without really knowing it, helping out the other customers, including yours truly.

Looking back in history, formerly you could take advantage of this cross-subsidy far more than is possible today. For instance nineteenth century saloons took the drinks cross-subsidy to an extreme by offering, literally, a free lunch to their customers. Once food supply became liberated from local farmers and hunters, such free lunches became common. The hope, of course, was that they would make the money back on the drinks. An 1899 survey of 634 saloons in Minneapolis found that the free lunches were "elaborate" in 3 saloons, "excellent" in 8, "good" in 50, "fair" in 88, "poor" in 77, and the rest provided no free lunch whatsoever. A 1901 survey of 115 Chicago saloons found that "nearly all" offered free lunches; Chicago was especially known for the practice. At first it was a rigorous code of honor that the eater must also buy drinks. But over time "free lunch freeloaders" became increasingly common, thereby rendering the deal increasingly unworkable from the restaurant's point of view. By 1910 the free lunch practice was criticized for presenting unsanitary food (as more people take advantage of this kind of offer, the quality of the food has to be lowered if the saloon is to stay in business). By the time war came to America in 1917, the practice was considered wasteful and was pretty much abandoned. Even so, the practice of using food to sell drinks lives on, simply not in such extreme form. Peanuts anyone?

The mix of cheaper food and more expensive drinks is good news for some of us, but there are at least two caveats.

First, the markup on drinks is in part a fee for using the table so long and also it is a way to charge for the décor of the restaurant. Restaurants do not just sell food, they also provide table space. Yet they do not charge explicitly for table space. They do not set an egg timer on the table to charge by the minute and thus encourage rapid turnover. Being a hardy economist, I wouldn't mind such a system, but I expect it would make most people too nervous. But a high markup for drinks serves some of the same purpose, albeit invisibly; and in essence it charges people for use of the space without making them hear that egg timer ticking. I'm sure you've noticed that many restaurants make a big point of trying to get you to order more drinks. It's hard to just sit there and order nothing when they keep on asking you to spend more money and everyone else is doing the same. Don't think you're immune to this pressure. So, in practical terms, I would say this: You're only benefiting from the cross-subsidy if you go light on the initial drink order and plan on leaving the table promptly. If you're looking to save money on very good food, don't hang out in the place you consume it. Scram.

I've also noticed that restaurants with wonderful views or innovative décor charge an especially high amount for the drinks. When I was a kid my dad would take me up to Windows on the World, a restaurant on the top of the World Trade Center. The drinks in such places are often out-rageously expensive, but customers are paying for the view. Good food is not likely in such locations because the drinks are the main profit center and a lot of the customers will come in any case. You won't usually find food bargains and beautiful views in the same place.

At some restaurants the drinks don't have much of a markup at all. Chinese restaurants, for instance, serve pretty cheap drinks and Coke, as they are usually hoping to make their money on the food and by bringing in large Chinese families to their major tables. Those people, on average, just don't drink that much Coke or Pepsi. So if you like Coca-Cola at all, the time to get it is with Chinese food, when it is much cheaper and it is not being used to extract extra revenue from spend-thrifts. More broadly, if the customers in a restaurant are elderly non-Americans from countries where Coke is a relatively recent innovation, the Coke is probably going to be cheap. That is to say, it won't be a vehicle for price discrimination.

Of course not every Chinese restaurant has cheap Coke, because not every Chinese restaurant is marketing its product toward traditional Chinese. If you go to a yuppie-oriented, socially oriented P.F. Chang's, you're back to the higher price for the soft drink. In my local China Star restaurant, which attracts a largely Chinese clientele, a Coke costs $1.00, circa 2010, with free refills. In the P.F. Chang's, also in Fairfax, a Coke costs $2.50. You'll also find sauvignon blanc there.

Why Popcorn Is a Bad Deal and Starbucks Coffee Isn't

If you visit a lot of different food venues, it's amazing how often you'll see this cross-subsidy idea pop up.

Cross-subsidies help explain why the food is so often so bad in movie theaters. The food subsidizes the movies and not the other way around. Movies are an especially good deal and the food in movie theaters is an especially bad deal. There's a little bit of history to this story and here's how it goes.

Popcorn entered American movie theaters in the 1930s in the midst of the Great Depression. Popcorn sales kept many theaters afloat that otherwise might not have survived. By the late 1940s, virtually all movie theaters had poppers. By 1945, half of all U.S. popcorn was consumed in movie theaters; and a 1949 survey indicated that 60 percent of all moviegoers spent money on snacks. Popcorn and sodas quickly obtained the reputation of being high-margin items. Over time, theater owners stimulated demand by loading their popcorns with larger amounts of fat, salt, and oils; this stopped only during the "popcorn health scare" of the mid-1990s, but still the offerings are pretty bad for your health.

There's no special tricky way to get a good deal on movie theater food, but I would give the case more attention if this were a book on how to find cross-subsidies for good movies. Look for a big popcorn bar!

It's even worse if you think about the economics of the movie business. Today's theaters send back most of the ticket revenue to the studio. On a typical opening weekend—the most important event in the history of the movie—possibly up to 90 percent of the ticket receipts go back to the moviemakers and overall about half of the ticket receipts go to the moviemakers. And this is a logical distribution of the proceeds. The studios made the movie, which is hard to "get right"; plus they must pay for costly advertising, and this requires a lot of compensation for crowd-pleasing, popular movies. Theaters in contrast make a lot of their money from selling popcorn. The popcorn revenues are not sent back to the moviemaker at all.

The incentive of the movie theater is to charge a low price for the movie, and a high price for the popcorn. The low movie price lures in viewers/eaters and the theater doesn't much miss out on the movie revenue anyway. In return, they make the popcorn relatively expensive. Since low quality is another way of creating a high net markup, the taste of the popcorn and other concession stand items usually isn't so gourmet.

To make it all worse, who goes to the movies anyway? It's mostly people under thirty years old, and even then it's a lot of teenagers and younger kids too. As I've indicated, that's not usually the group with the best taste in food, especially in the United States.

If you want to eat well in a movie theater, your best shot is to go to an "indie" theater, which shows foreign films, offbeat movies, and attracts an older and more mature audience, all of which point to better taste in food. Furthermore, compared to traditional multiplexes, indie theaters keep a higher proportion of their ticket revenue. An indie theater might keep up to half of the ticket receipts and that means they view you as a moviegoer rather than as a popcorn-consuming machine. I'm hardly pushing indie movie theaters as the place to eat, but at least there's a chance you'll find a sandwich, some hummus, or—who knows?—maybe even a plain, ordinary apple. It's not about the profit margin on the food; it's about trying to get the mature crowd to come back for the movie on a repeated basis.

You'll also find useful cross-subsidies in Starbucks, especially if you love their kind of coffee. In its early years the chain revolutionized coffee consumption in the United States. Even Starbucks haters usually will admit the brew was stronger and better than most of the competitors at the time that the chain rose to prominence. But over time, the expansion of the chain required greater attention to sales volume and high profit margins. Plain coffee was not enough to keep so many outlets going, so sweeter beverages were marketed too. Today the store specializes in sweet, milk-based beverages, many of which are associated with the coffee idea in some indirect manner or other. We're now in a setting where the quality and above all the availability of this coffee is subsidized by the milk and the sugar. The Starbucks "coffee image," and perhaps coffee smell, provide a new portal for selling sweet beverages to people. That means if you love that brand of coffee, Starbucks is an especially good deal, due to the favorable cross-subsidy. If you like milk and sugar, however, you're paying through the nose—in part to prop up the coffeelike infrastructure of the store—and maybe you should consider mixing the two at home for the desired effect. Just a whole lot cheaper.

So far we have been looking at capital in the business of food. Let's now turn our attention to those who actually make the food.

How to Exploit Restaurant Workers

First, quality food is cheaper when there is cheap labor available to cook it. In a relatively wealthy country like the United States that can be hard to find. We have a high level of labor productivity, there is a legal minimum wage, and in a lot of parts of the country even illegal immigrant labor earns more than the legal minimum. Still, the one obvious example of cheap labor is in family-owned, family-run Asian restaurants. Family members will work in the kitchen or as waiters and they will be paid relatively little or sometimes nothing at all. Sometimes they're expected to do the work as part of their contribution to the family. The upshot is that these restaurants tend to offer good food buys.

The polar opposite case is when you see a restaurant replete with expensive labor. There's a valet parking attendant, a woman to take your coat, a wine maître d', a floor manager, a team of waiters, a manager to greet you, and so on. The ability to afford those laborers is a sign of financial success for the restaurant. If you go for instance to the Palm, a fancy steakhouse chain with restaurants across the United States and in

AN ECONOMIST GETS LUNCH

Mexico City, you can see a lot of people at work. Everyone is scurrying around and you have the feeling they put a lot of time and effort into coordinating the large staff. Customers enjoy the restaurant and they attract a lot of famous celebrities and politicians. I've enjoyed the three meals I've had at the Palm, but I worry about what I am paying for. All other things equal, I like quality service, but only when I am steered toward better items on the menu or when I reap some other concrete benefit rather than just feeling fancy. I'm not sure what I am getting from the service at the Palm. I feel I understand the menu already (steak, lobster, etc.), and it seems to me that the staff members are there to make the customers feel special and powerful and important. I visit the Palm, and I immediately think of cigars.

Another way to think about labor in restaurants is to get the most out of the labor they offer, namely the waitstaff. Maybe you can't find cheaper waiters and thus cheaper food, but you can learn how to use the waitstaff to your advantage.

One of the most important strategies in dining is asking the waiter or waitress what to get. It is important to phrase the question properly. Think about the waiter's incentives. Waiters often have an incentive to push a high-margin item or to market a standard dish, which the kitchen has prepared in large numbers that evening. This is true not only at expensive restaurants but is true *especially* at some kinds of expensive restaurants, in particular those that serve lots of tourists or non-regular or somewhat ill-informed customers.

So don't just ask the waiter "What should I get?" The waiter will likely direct you to the most high-margin item on the menu, and even more likely to want to get rid of you quickly so as to move on to his next task. The waiter probably thinks you are no smarter, in culinary terms, than the average face he hasn't seen before. He will tend to remember his most stupid customers and this will lead him to associate you with them. As a default, walk into a restaurant expecting the waiter or waitress to have an insulting assessment of you, no matter how polite he or she may seem on the surface. They are used to idiots and they are used to people who don't tip as well as they ought to, and for all they know you are one of them.

I go at them pointedly. Even scurrilous waiters want a tip and they will relent in pushing their weak dishes if you stand up for yourself and signal your commitment to making every meal count.

One way to proceed is to ask the waiter "What is best?" I am then happiest when the waiter does not hesitate to tell me what is best. "The venison with the spaetzle is best, sir," is the sort of answer that warms my heart. I get more nervous when the waiter responds: "All of our menu items are good." Another problem is when you hear: "Best? That depends on what you like. It's hard for me to say." Those responses are signs of cowardly or underinformed waiters, not used to dealing with demanding foodies. The bottom line is that these waiters have never been given firm instructions by a quality boss or chef, or those instructions have been summarily forgotten. It's a bad sign for the whole restaurant.

Sometimes you need to refer to "signature dishes." Or mention being a serious foodie who travels long distances to find wonderful meals. If none of that works you might try asking—politely—if there is anyone else who can help you.

At fancy and expensive restaurants ($50 and up for a dinner is an imperfect benchmark for this category) there is a simple procedure, which I outlined in my book *Discover Your Inner Economist*. Look at the menu and ask yourself: "Which of these items am I least likely to want to order?" Or "which of these sounds the least appetizing"? Then order that item.

The logic is simple. At a fancy restaurant the menu is well thought out. The time and attention of the kitchen are scarce. An item won't be on the menu unless there is a good reason for its presence. If it sounds bad, it probably tastes especially good.

Many popular-sounding items can be just slightly below the menu's average quality. For instance, you should be careful not to get too enthusiastic about roast chicken, especially if you are in a restaurant that, like virtually all restaurants, does not specialize in roast chicken. The problem is that roast chicken is too often simply okay. I can cook reasonably good (and sometimes excellent) roast chicken. The result is excess familiarity, and so many people will order roast chicken to experience the familiar. Fried calamari is usually fine in elegant restaurants, but rarely is it wonderful.

In plain language: order the ugly and order the unknown. In a fancy restaurant, order the item you are least likely to think you want. There are two caveats for this rule. First, I know the spicy pig's blood and tripe stew isn't for everyone (even though it makes a fine piece of a broader, multi-course meal). I will get to more specific advice on Asian restaurants in this regard in a later chapter. Second, and more important, if you like roast chicken every night, this won't work—just order the roast chicken!

Why Great City Centers Are Bad for Food

If a restaurant cannot cover its rent, it is not long for this world. Over half of all restaurants close in the first three years of operation, so this is not a small problem. You can lay off kitchen staff when times get tough, or substitute the cheaper tilapia for the fancier and scarcer Chilean sea bass. But rent is what economists call a fixed cost, meaning that you have to pay it every month no matter how many customers walk through the door or no matter what ingredients you are serving. It is the ultimate reality test a restaurant must face. Even if a restaurant entrepreneur buys the land and building, turning monthly rent into zero, that just means he is paying the equivalent of rent up front and it doesn't much change the basics of the problem.

The rent constrains what kind of business is possible in a given space. High-rent activities include chain clothing stores, Starbucks, the Disney Shop, and Tiffany's jewelry. An upscale mall is full of high-rent stores. A high-rent store typically attracts a large number of paying customers per hour, charges high markup on its goods, or both. Otherwise there is no way to make the rent payments every month. Low-rent activities include Dollar Stores, antique and secondhand shops, and the local Chinese restaurant in the suburban strip mall. A lot of low-rent places are ugly, but still they might have good food and they are especially likely to have cheap food that isn't junk food.

There is a lot of awesome food in high-rent districts, but it tends to have awesomely high prices as well.

Manhattan restaurants locate in high-rent districts to be near very wealthy customers. Of the four three-star New York City restaurants listed in the 2011 Michelin guide (Le Bernardin, Per Se, Daniel, and Jean-Georges), all four are in a thin strip of midtown Manhattan, not too far from Lincoln Center. These restaurants are near the homes of millionaires and billionaires, and adjoining the central tourist, theater, and shopping areas of Manhattan. Of a total number of forty-one restaurants bestowed with stars, only three of those places are in the boroughs outside Manhattan, even though those regions of the city have much greater space and population.

Most fine restaurants are in high-rent areas, but most restaurants in high-rent areas are far from fine. Manhattan and other large urban areas are full of T.G.I Friday's, Hard Rock Café, and so on—name your list of villains. These locales stay in business by generating volume, which means they don't usually take too many chances. Paris is full of middling-level or even mediocre bistros, even in the tonier neighborhoods. Again, if the place is not Michelin-recognized at a high level of quality, they are probably trying to get by on quantity. If they don't turn a lot of tables, they can't keep on paying the rent.

In many cases the food is linked to a brand name—such as Hard Rock Café—or to a well-known generic designation, such as deli food, pizza, or bagels, which also serves a kind of branding function. Large numbers of customers visit these restaurants in search of a well-known, predictable product and associated image. Their prices are not outrageous, but if they lose the volume they will have to shut down. Basically these are the places I say should be avoided.

It has become increasingly difficult to maintain quirky ethnic restaurants in midtown Manhattan. The expensive *haute* Chinese, Latino, and fusion restaurants are flourishing, but the cheaper good ethnic places are being pushed to the lower-rent fringes. Most of the important new, cheap ethnic restaurants serving everything from Colombian food to classic Italian are burgeoning in Queens, Brooklyn, and the Bronx. Chinatown in Flushing, Queens, is deliciously hectic. It is also possible to find good, cheap ethnic food on the far West Side of midtown Manhattan; this remains an underpriced location, as are the deeper and more distant parts of the East Village. It is difficult to find such food in the major, midtown parts of Park Avenue and overall, in New York City, the expensive areas are encroaching on the quirky. The collapse of the real estate bubble slowed down this trend but did not halt it.

Manhattan avenues tend to be higher-rent than locations on the streets. Given the long, thin shape of the island, the north-south avenues carry more vehicular and foot traffic. A Fifth Avenue spot will be seen by most city residents and visitors at some point or another. A shop front on Thirty-ninth Street will be seen more by neighborhood locals or by people who work in the area. Only a few broad cross streets, such as Eighty-sixth, Fifty-seventh, or Fourteenth take on the economic properties of the up-and-down avenues, and that is because they carry so much traffic. If you are stuck in midtown, and you want good, cheap ethnic food, try the streets before the avenues. Opt for narrow passageways rather than broad ones. That neat Korean place can make ends meet on Thirty-fifth, but it would not survive on Fifth Avenue. In other words, no matter where you are, turning just a bit off the main drag can yield a better meal for the money.

The key to understanding the current evolution of dining in the United States is that rents (on average) have been rising over the last thirty or so years—well, until the collapse of the real estate bubble. But even the financial crisis has not overturned the longer-run trend. The expensive places are costing more and more. That is part of a pattern of growing tourism, falling rates of violent crime, and the general growth of commercial activity. The ethnic foods found in the middle of high-rent cities are becoming more upscale. The cheap, experimental, and low-décor ethnic foods are moving to the geographic fringes. The same is happening in London, Paris, Berlin, and even Mexico City, among other major urban areas that are seeing growth. And just as high rents push out quirky food, so do they push out quirky culture, including clubbing scenes and offbeat art galleries, which also are moving to the peripheries of major cities. Whether or not you like that trend, it's a development you have to understand and, to some extent, work around.

One upshot of this is that the recent Great Recession has been good for a lot of foodies. Rents are stable or falling rather than rising and so unusual eateries have a better chance of staying close to city centers. We'll see how long this trend lasts, but in the meantime flat rents are slowing down the process of culinary dispersion to the suburbs and fringe areas of cities.

Now let's turn to low-rent meals. My favorites.

One good way to find a tasty and cheap meal is to seek out low-rent areas near higher-rent customers. In Los Angeles, eat Mexican food in East Los Angeles or Asian food in Koreatown. There are better food buys in East Hollywood than West Hollywood, where the movie stars live. Thai food in northeast Hollywood is especially delicious. If I am flying into LaGuardia airport, I stop in Flushing—the Chinatown of Queens— on my cab ride to or from Manhattan. That's probably the best concentration of Chinese food in the United States.

Most of all, I love exploring the U.S. suburbs for first-rate ethnic food. It's pretty common to consider these suburbs a cultural wasteland, but I am very happy searching for food in Orange County, California, the area near San Jose, northern Virginia, or Maryland near D.C., the ugly parts of New Jersey, Somerville, Massachusetts, the outer reaches of Houston, and many other areas I have enjoyed. I don't always pre-Google to the best place and I don't keep on tapping on my iPhone. I drive around and keep my eyes open for dining establishments likely to follow the economic rules for good, innovative, and affordable food.

The larger the number of restaurants serving the same ethnic cuisine in a given area, the more likely the food they serve is good. Why? Restaurants that are competing against each other can't rest on their laurels. They are appealing to an informed customer base; and they can participate in a well-developed supply chain for key ingredients. In other words, a town that has only a single Indian restaurant probably does not have a very good Indian restaurant. In Houston this strategy will lead you to Mexican and Vietnamese food, in parts of Michigan it will lead you to Lebanese and Arabic, in Monterey Park, California, it will lead you to Chinese and Taiwanese; and in my home base of Fairfax County, it means that the Bolivian, Peruvian, and El Salvadoran offerings are a much better bet than the local Mexican food. Competition works.

Stand-alone restaurants along with those in suburban strip malls pay less rent. Of these, the establishments located in suburbs that have lots of recent immigrants have the best food. Most ethnic restaurants in the United States seek low-rent locations. They're marketing to people who care about the quality and kind of food, most of all; and many of those people come to this country with relatively low incomes. They're not mostly looking to date or pay for fancy, frilly, or "cool" locations.

If I am in a hitherto unknown part of the United States, the region has immigrants, and I am looking to eat, I head away from the center of town. I look for the strip malls. The best strip malls, for food, are usually those without Wal-Mart, Best Buy, or other big-box stores. Large anchor stores bring high rents and large crowds, which are typically not the right combination for interesting ethnic food.

The ultimate low-rent venue is the food truck. New York City, Portland, Oregon, and Austin, Texas, have started allowing food trucks to sell their wares, and it has greatly improved food in those cities. No longer is street food a bad pretzel or fatty hot dog; food trucks bring diners authentic Mexican tacos, homemade sausages, dim sum, Vietnamese bánh mi sandwiches, and hundreds of other delicacies. One of the most famous food trucks, Los Angeles Kogi (@kobibbq on Twitter is how you track it), specializes in Korean-Latin fusion food, such as their Kogi Kimchi Quesadilla, which mixes spicy, garlicky Korean cabbage with Mexican cheese and a flour burrito. It's also fairly quick food for when you don't have the time, or perhaps the money, for a more socially elaborate sit-down meal.

My favorite local food truck is Las Delicias, which parks on Route 50, Arlington Boulevard, Falls Church (near my house), every Sunday afternoon, and serves Bolivian specialties from the Cochabamba region. This includes peanut soup and a dish called charque, which blends thick white cheese, dry, salty and twisted beef jerky, and a Bolivian white corn. To my palate, it is better than the area's Bolivian restaurants. The city near me, Washington, D.C., allows food trucks but with trepidation; and it is frequently threatening to crack down on them and put them out of business. That's the nature of bureaucracy. And local restaurants don't want the competition, thus they lobby for restrictions. There is one set of street food vendors in D.C., in Adams Morgan at Columbia and 18th Streets, serving El Salvadoran, Mexican, Puerto Rican dishes. The food is excellent, but again the city is reluctant to allow the idea to spread.

If we wanted to improve American food, and make it much cheaper, I have a suggestion: Let's deregulate the food trucks and the other street vendors, provided they can show enough responsibility to get an open-to-all license competition. Many cities already have moved down this path and it's been good for the consumers and good for the food truck merchants, and it is not the case that people are keeling over with salmonella. The next food revolution in the United States is likely to be a mobile one and it will be advertised on Google and Twitter, not through fancy commercials during Super Bowl Sunday. That's how the low-rent food of the future is going to work.

Low-rent food venues can experiment at relatively low risk. If a food idea does not work out, the proprietor is not left with an expensive building, fancy décor, or a long-term lease. A strip mall restaurant or a food truck is more likely to try daring ideas than is a restaurant in a large shopping mall. The shopping mall restaurant pays a higher rent and it has invested more in décor. It will try to attract a large number of customers, which usually means predictable, mainstream food. Lower rents also mean that more people can try their hand at starting a restaurant and marketing the family cooking. The people with the best, most creative, most innovative cooking ideas are not always the people with the most money. Very often they end up in dumpier locales, where they gradually improve real estate values.

It is common to see good ethnic restaurants grouped with midlevel or junky retail outlets, and often the best food trucks are in quite inconspicuous locales. When it comes to a food truck, or a restaurant run by immigrants, look around at the street scene. Do you see something ugly?

Poor construction? Broken plastic signage? A five-and-dime store? Maybe an abandoned car? If so, crack a quiet smile, walk in the door, and order.

Welcome to the glamorous world of good food.

The Social Element in Eating Well

Finally, economics isn't just about how labor costs and capital costs and rent add up, there is also a significant human or "behavioral" element in our choices, as it is now called in the branch of behavioral economics. Human beings are fundamentally social creatures. We copy the social cues of others or sometimes we deliberately do something different to set ourselves apart from the crowd.

When it comes to the social element in good dining, my first advice is this: *Be meta-rational,* to borrow a word from decision theory. Meta-rationality means recognizing your limitations and realizing that very often the best information is in the hands of other people. Even if you've memorized all the food books you own, there is still plenty about food that remains a mystery. Recognize when other people know better and do not be afraid to ask which course of action is best. But ask in a smart way. When you're looking for a good meal, some knowledge of social science is often more useful than is a knowledge of food.

If you need to ask where to eat, start by finding people who themselves love good food and who take pride in food. Ask a person between 35 and 55 years old for a tip, as that is a group especially likely to be eating out a lot at good places and having a lot of experience with food. Look for someone who is prosperous or middle class but not necessarily very rich. Ask people who are geographically mobile in their professions and thus accustomed to eating out and collecting information about food. Ask a fireman for a good, cheap local place; drive to the fire station if you have to, or call them. Ask a cabdriver. I have found that regional textbook salespeople—who are traveling and dining out all the time— are a good source of food information. If you ask someone for a food tip, and their eyes don't light up with excitement, ignore them.

If you're asking Google, put a "smart" word into your search query. "Best restaurants Washington" will yield lots of information, arguably too much information, and it will serve up a lot of bad restaurants too. That's a least-common-denominator search query. Google something more specific instead, like "best Indian restaurants Washington," even if you don't want Indian food. You'll get more reliable, more finely grained, and better informed sources about food, and you can peruse those sources for their non-Indian recommendations. Google "Washington best cauliflower dish," even if you don't want cauliflower. Get away from Google for the masses.

If you're reading online reviews, don't be too put off by negative reviews per se; any place that takes chances will have its detractors. Instead, focus on the positive reviews. How long are they? How smart and committed do they sound? If so, give it a try.

Finally, not all of us are good at judging unknown restaurants, but most of us are good at judging people. If you are looking to judge a restaurant, and can't find anyone reliable to ask, my suggestion is to take a look at who goes there. This is another way of mastering the efficient use of readily available social information, a common theme in economic reasoning.

When I'm out looking for food, one of my fears is to come across a restaurant where the people are laughing and smiling and appearing very sociable. There are many restaurants like this in downtown Washington, D.C., Manhattan, and in many other cities. It looks like everyone is having fun. That's when I run the other way. Don't get me wrong. There is nothing wrong with having fun, but it's not the same thing as good food. So many restaurants "get by"—and charge reasonably high prices—by creating social scenes for drinking, dating, and carousing. They're not using the food to draw in their customers. Very often the food in these places is "not bad" because the restaurant needs to maintain a trendy image. They will serve some kind of overpriced fusion cuisine, sponsored by a famous or semi-famous chef who is usually absent from the premises. There are worse places to eat, but if I'm spending my own money I'll usually give it a pass.

If you are going to visit such restaurants, go in the first four to six months of their operation, though not the first two weeks when they are still working out the kinks in their kitchen routine. Very often such restaurants take great care to get good reviews at their opening; and because they are sponsored by a famous chef, they will be reviewed quickly. The famous chef, or some competent delegate, will be on hand early in the history of the restaurant to make sure it gets good reviews from sophisticated food critics and smart food bloggers. Then everyone will want to go there and then the place will become established as a major social scene. The laughing and the smiling will set in. Beware! That's when you need to stop going. Cut loose and don't look back.

When Richard Sandoval's Zengo opened in Washington, D.C., in 2005, it was a special place. They offered some excellent Latin-Asian fusion food, including sashimi, crisp empanadas, and charred wonton tuna tacos. The décor was cool and the place had a cosmopolitan vibe. It was opening in the newly revitalized part of Washington, D.C., right next to a major sports arena. I said to my wife: If you like this place, we need to go often, now. Soon it will be ruined. Circa 2011, Zengo is still around and it is okay. But I wouldn't spend my own money there, and that has been the case for the last few years. The proprietor, Sandoval, spends his time at other ventures, the place can ride off its bar scene, and the most innovative dishes no longer taste so fresh. This review on Zagat .com says it all:

> "One of my favorite places in DC—awesome lounge, great décor, and food is delicious."

At least they got the order straight and put the food last. Beware any restaurant, which, like Zengo, each year does a mass e-mail blitz for Mother's Day. Remember, this is a book about finding the best food, at the best prices, and not about the décor, which at Zengos is still lovely.

One thing I've noticed, in the last ten years, is that the life cycle of trendy restaurants has been accelerating. It used to be you had a year or two before an interesting restaurant would become a venue for happy faces, joyous socializing, and culinary decline. These days it seems to be six months or less. The problem may be that the Internet helps a reputation become established, and spread, very quickly. So if you find a new trendy place you like, visit repeatedly—now—and don't wait. Soon the restaurant you love will be gone; of course in less trendy places you don't have this problem.

I also start to worry if the women in a restaurant seem to be beautiful in the trendy "eye candy" sense, as they are at Zengo. For me that's another danger sign. I ask myself: "Why should this place have such women?" The point is not that beautiful women have bad taste in food; as a group they will have good and bad taste just like other groups. Instead, the problem is that when you see a cluster of beautiful women, a lot of men will go to the restaurant, whether or not the place serves excellent food. And that allows them to cut back on the quality of the food.

It is often best when the people in a restaurant look a little serious or even downright grim. You don't want to see sour expressions or disgust on the faces of the diners. But you do want to see a certain seriousness of purpose. No matter what the price range of the restaurant, you want to see that the people who are eating there mean business.

Pull out a mirror and try eating some really good food. How much are you smiling? How happy and sociable do you look? Not as much as you might think.

I recall visiting Sabitzer, a fine and now-defunct Munich restaurant, with my friend Kevin Grier in the early 1990s. This was the day after Easter Sunday and we were one of only two tables of customers. At the other table sat a French family and they seemed, dare I say it, *pissed off* the entire time they sat there. They sneered every time a course was brought out, ate without apparent joy, and at some point I started wondering how we looked to them. It was one of the better meals of my life at that point, and they consumed every morsel on the plate just as we did. It was at that moment when I realized that joyous customers are not in every way a good sign.

In a lot of restaurants, it is a propitious omen if the diners are screaming at each other and appear to be fighting and pursuing blood feuds. It's a sign they are regular customers and that they feel at home in the restaurant. It's a sign they go there a lot. Few people show up at a strange restaurant and behave that way, but they might do so in a place where they know the proprietor and staff. A lot of Chinese restaurants are full of screaming Chinese patrons—don't ask me if it's fighting, I have no idea—but it is a sign I want to be there too.

There are many applications of this principle of judging restaurants by their clientele. Probably most of you know that if you are walking in Florence, and you see a restaurant full of guidebook-clutching British tourists, catching an early dinner at six P.M., you need to run the other way. I'm saying that this logic can be expanded to cover many other cases. I have another maxim and it is this: *Quality customers are often more important for a restaurant than is a quality chef.*

Of course restaurant owners know they are judged by their clientele, and so they make concerted efforts to cultivate the sort of customers who will support their business plan. When McDonald's first started to expand, in the 1950s, it took great pains to be a "family restaurant." Ray Kroc designed the restaurants to discourage teenage loitering. He didn't want the outlets to be too comfortable or too "cool." He didn't want the restaurants to have pinball or newspaper boxes or telephone booths or candy and cigarette machines or to look like teenage trouble spots. He wanted rapid turnover and he wanted people to come and go in the normal course of their day. McDonald's thus made its designs deliberately antisocial, the opposite of today's Starbucks. At the time, it was well known that teenage loitering had helped make many drive-ins unprofitable. McDonald's is a family restaurant and it looks and feels the same way. Dunkin' Donuts once introduced a new hot sandwich and called it a panini, changing the name to "stuffed melt" after customers complained the other name was too fancy.

Like most other commodities, eating is a social experience. It isn't just about the nutrition, calories, and taste, so people seek out social environments that fit them and please them. That's your entry point for figuring out the "code" of what a restaurant is trying to do.

Whether we like it or not, there is a "long-run equilibrium"—to cite an economics phrase—when it comes to restaurants. That means simply that the quality of restaurants can usually be judged by the kind of customers they attract and by a number of other static features. Attempts to buck those regularities usually fail. If you are visiting a restaurant for the first time, and considering walking through the door, ask yourself a very simple question: "Are these people like me in the sense of having my attitude toward food?" If so, you probably have a good match. If not, it's time to run the other way. Leaving may feel a little bad, but sitting there and suffering through the food-and-clientele mismatch will seem worse. And since you'll probably end up talking about the experience, you're doing the proprietor a favor by never developing a bad history with his restaurant's food.

5

Barbecue: The Greatest Slow Food of All

O kay, I like ethnic food, but I'm also an American. I was born in New Jersey, but nonetheless later in life I acquired a real taste for barbecue. That is to say, I like meat cooked in:

1. An open pit—The original and historic barbecue technique that cooks food buried in the ground and over a spit, or in a free-standing structure in the open air.

2. The classic barbecue pit—This is usually made out of bricks, and cooks the meat with wood using a live fire and no electrical devices. These are sometimes (misleadingly; they are not literally open as in #1) called open pits.

And to a lesser extent, sometimes I like:

3. The mechanized barbecue pit—Slabs of meat are tucked into a mechanized device, which slow cooks them in a mechanically controlled fashion. A mechanized pit may use wood, gas, or other sources of heat. Hybrid

mechanized pits—increasingly common—will use gas to heat the wood, which then cooks the food.

All those forms differ from backyard or porch barbecue—more appropriately called grilling—which cooks meat quickly at high temperatures. One estimate suggests that Americans grill over flame an impressive 2.9 billion times a year, but fast, mean grilling generally doesn't produce food as good as good old slow barbecue. Arthur Bryant's Barbecue in Kansas City cooks its baby back ribs for ten hours, its briskets for twelve hours, and its pork shoulders for sixteen hours. One restaurant from Memphis is known for cooking its pork shoulders for thirty-six hours. The central elements of classic barbecue are smoke, slow cooking, and low temperatures.

I walked into Lonnie Ray's BBQ, in Harrisburg, Missouri, after about half an hour drive from Columbia. The place had all the marks of excellent barbecue: It was in a small town, it enjoyed strong word-of-mouth (a local, in fact—a textbook sales representative with whom I was working had driven me there), the restaurant itself was small, and the other customers gave off a distinct air of the vernacular.

The barbecue, which was a mix of regional styles, was excellent. I was, however, impressed by the proprietor of Lonnie Ray's: Mike Whitely (he named his restaurant after his father). Mike came over to talk to me once I asked a few questions about the nature of the place where I was eating. The chatty but focused Mike was not shy and he launched immediately into scientific discourse. He asked me what I liked about the barbecue, what I didn't like, and where else I had eaten barbecue. Such talk can sound like fishing for praise, or a chance to boast, but he really wanted to learn more about the craft of barbecue and improve his product. And so we quickly launched into a lengthy discussion of different styles, different restaurants, and how barbecue is done around the world. Most of all, he was interested in hearing about barbecue in central Mexico. Mike had an attitude of inquiry and self-criticism that should be the envy of virtually any scientist.

You might expect Mike to be an uneducated yokel, but he has a psychology degree from the University of Missouri, and has worked as a youth counselor. He cooks food in his spare time for his own enjoyment, and does some catering for extra cash. He became intrigued by the potential of teamwork as a teenager when he saw how it worked in a friend's family-run Chinese restaurant. He saw the family taking pride in the food, in their food traditions, and he learned how they worked together to pluck chickens. Might it not be possible to apply such cooperative techniques to other cuisines as well?

Barbecue is a market segment obsessed with quality, teamwork, and continual improvement. At its peaks, it is arguably America's best—and cheapest—restaurant food. If there's any American food that approaches the status of a religion with its partisans, it's this method of slowly cooking meats, with saintly sides. Aficionados will travel hours for better barbecue and then passionately debate which pit master and which style is the most heavenly. Few food areas come closer to this idea of the holy quest. There's something real behind all this devotion. It is one key component of the kind of food revolution we need.

How does the best of American barbecue end up being so good? Furthermore, if barbecue can be so tasty, why isn't there good barbecue everywhere? The sad truth is that my home area of northern Virginia has only slim pickings and so my research has taken me around this country and across the border into Mexico.

Some foods seem to be able to migrate, to cross mountains and oceans, and some do not. Take any classic French recipe, of the kind you might find served in a very nice country inn, in France. It can involve twenty or thirty critical ingredients, including local herbs and spices. The meats should be free range or otherwise custom grown. The sauces often require quality wines. The relevant cooking techniques are, by global standards, hard to teach to would-be chefs. The breads, butters, cheeses, and pâtés require specialized skills to produce. Within France, cuisine tends to be regional rather than national. Yet it is possible to replicate that classic French recipe all over the world. You have probably had great coq au vin, if you are interested, wherever you are. It's common for Germany to have very good French restaurants, cheaper than those in Paris and often quite good. My most memorable meal in Rio de Janeiro involved nine courses of French food. For all of the French hesitancy to embrace cultural globalization, French chefs have produced a globalized cuisine, albeit with country-specific variants. It sells for a high enough price that restaurants will incur considerable expense to recreate some version of French finery.

But quality barbecue is available in only a limited number of regions and countries: in the United States, namely, Texas, parts of the American South, parts of Missouri and Illinois, and Hawaii, which has a public barbecue tradition usually done with roast pig; in other countries, central Mexico, most of Jamaica, which has great barbecue, and I've been told in northern Africa, in the desert regions, where the barbecued lamb or goat is spectacular if you hit upon the right tribe and festival.

Maori barbecue—*hangi*—is done for weddings and feasts and is buried in the ground for a long time until it has a very smoky flavor. Every now and then you'll find a New Zealand restaurant that serves it or maybe a Maori place that offers hangi takeout, but it's hardly an established restaurant tradition. The two times I tried hangi there I wasn't impressed. Maybe, like a lot of things, it is better at a family picnic or wedding.

Overall, barbecue restaurants outside of a few core places usually disappoint. We may be reminded in a nostalgic way of real barbecue, but it isn't the real thing. Barbecue is a passageway to an earlier food era, a time when production was personal, artisanal, and depended on being in the right time at the right place. When *Texas Monthly* magazine proclaimed Snow's BBQ in Lexington, Texas, to be the best barbecue in America, no one complained that the place is open Saturday mornings only. Instead, that was a sign of culinary status. When you walk into Smitty's Market in Lockhart, Texas, it is a point of pride that the barbecue fires spill out onto the floor, right next to where you order your meal. "Don't trip," I told my wife before we entered the place. In one possibly apocryphal account, they offer free barbecue to keep the fire chief and the insurance inspector in support of their enterprise.

That said, barbecue is also a highly commercialized development, dependent on modern American consumer society and on big business—most of all, the meat trade. It does not fit the classic European story of basing the best foods on the finest raw ingredients. The meats are not always of the highest quality—that's one reason why they need to be cooked for so long—and often the cooking technique matters more than the vintage. Many of the best barbecue sauces are composed from mass-produced ingredients commonly available in the modern American supermarket. The use of long but efficient food supply chains helps make barbecue so affordable. Barbecue markets itself as artisanal, but it is equally adept at blending in the influences of mass commercial society.

Barbecue also offers the promise of a more or less pure American food art, untainted by fancy dining or urban snobbery. The scrawled menu, the shack, and the discarded cookers strewn around the backyard no longer represent the modern barbecue reality, but they don't feel so far away. Texans in their macho way disdain sauce altogether. It's all about the quality of the meat and the rub.

Here are some basic observations about good old slow barbecue:

- The best barbecue places open early in the morning.

- Eat barbecue in towns of less than 50,000 people.

- Good ribs, unlike good brisket, are available in many locales.

Understanding what underlies these three observations is an insight into where just about all idiosyncratic culinary creativity comes from.

Early Traditions and Rule-making Amateurs

The word "barbecue" comes from the Spanish *barbacoa,* which dates back to a 1526 Spanish book on the Indians of the New World. The term referred to a Caribbean technique of cooking food by skewering meat on sticks and roasting it slowly over a dug pit. The Taino word *babracot* referred to the framework of sticks that make up the barbecue grill. Jamaican jerk pit barbecue has a direct link to this early tradition, but indigenous Mexicans claim they also were cooking barbacoa before the Spanish conquest. Probably we'll never know which group had the idea first.

The first (non-Indian) American barbecue appears to date from the 1660s in North Carolina; slaves may have brought the technique from the Caribbean. It seems that barbecue was popular because its core ingredients fit into the colonial lifestyle. Pigs were plentiful. Vinegar, which is still part of North Carolina barbecue sauces, served as a natural bactericide. Peppers contributed vitamin C to protect against scurvy and other diseases. Slow cooking at low temperatures made it less likely that the wooden barbecue rack would go up in flames. It has been speculated that fine chopping of the meat was introduced to help individuals with bad teeth. Note that tomato was not eaten much at the time and it did not find its way into the early sauces.

In Texas, barbecue spread in the nineteenth century as a traditional means of feeding large groups of people. A sheep, goat, pig, or steer would be cooked in an open pit for up to twenty-four hours. Civic events held barbecues. A Sam Houston political rally from 1860 was called Great American Barbecue. Sometimes the word "barbecue" was used to refer to political rallies, rather than to the food itself.

Barbecue crossed over from churches and political rallies into small stands, barbecue shacks, and restaurants in the very early 1900s. The growth of disposable incomes, dining out, and the consumer revolution of the 1920s—all economic forces—encouraged commercial barbecue to expand. The advent of cars made it possible to open rural restaurants of many kinds, including barbecue, because now more customers could get to them. Unlike in a Chinatown, most of the customers are not walking to their meal or taking public transportation. Often in the 1920s the phrase "barbecue stand" was used as a general reference to roadside eateries. The consumer revolution of American society made the side dishes easier as well: ingredients for sauces could be found in supermarkets and the new availability of manufactured bread made it easier to serve barbecue sandwiches. Basically the blossoming of barbecue into public restaurants was part of the broader consumer revolution in early twentieth-century America.

But barbecue never really became fast food or junk food. The Pig Stand company expanded barbecue to over a hundred outlets in the 1930s, but the number of restaurants shrank to almost nothing during the 1940s. Luther's reached sixty-three stores in the mid-1980s, but by the 1990s had retrenched to twenty stores. A Cincinnati radio preacher named Reverend Deuteronomy Skaggs once proclaimed, "If God had meant for Cincinnati to have barbecue, He'd a give it to us a long time ago." Barry Farber, the New York radio star, in 1977 believed that barbecue would take over the food world. He opened a barbecue restaurant in Times Square, believing that barbecue would be "the next pizza." Both the restaurant and Farber's broader plans failed. The closest thing to quality, mass market barbecue are some of the meats at Chipotle, and they are cooked by sous vide, which I'll discuss at the end of this chapter.

Barbecue developed regional artful traditions. In most of the southeast, barbecue means pork, often a whole hog or pork shoulder roast. Pulled pork is common in the South and parts of the Midwest, but it is otherwise difficult to find in authentic form. Pork ribs are a staple in Chicago. Texas barbecue emphasizes brisket, sausage, pork ribs, and sometimes beef ribs, especially in West Texas. Other regional traditions involve goat (southern Texas), mutton (western Kentucky) and barbecued snouts (East St. Louis).

Eastern North Carolina barbecue differs from that found further west in the state. The East is more likely to barbecue the whole pig, the West will do the shoulder. More recently, the East has switched more rapidly to gas and electricity in modern commercial cookers. The traditional eastern sauce contains no tomatoes but uses vinegar, pepper, cayenne, and salt. The western sauce will add ketchup and Worcestershire. The eastern barbecue tends to be drier, some argue because the pork is chopped more finely by machine. The East also uses Brunswick stew, originally made with squirrel but now usually with chicken, tomatoes, potatoes, onions, corn, and lima beans, among other ingredients.

Barbecued potatoes are popular in the east as well. Coleslaw in western North Carolina is usually red and is crunchier as well. While Highway 1 often served as a rough dividing line for differing barbecue styles, these distinctions are blurring with time.

But why does this matter? Barbecue is about local creativity.

Even after commercialization, barbecue resisted turning into junk food, and has retained strong ties to its amateur roots. In a given year, over six million Americans attend more than five hundred barbecue contests. The Memphis competition, usually the nation's largest, might bring up to three hundred teams and about eighty thousand spectators. This intense interest often takes over people's leisure time or even their entire lives.

In earlier times, the barbecue masters often were the amateurs who have succeeded and worked their way up through the ranks. Still, for all the achievements in this field, wherever you have great barbecue, you also have mediocre barbecue. Trial and error is going to mean a lot of error. Often barbecue masters got started by cooking for their church, for a political rally, or for their friends. The popularity of the food induces some of the better cooks to start restaurants and perfect their products through experimentation on a larger audience of customers. The best establishments rise to the top and, in the process, train staff who often go on to open their own barbecue restaurants.

Nelson Head, perhaps the best barbecue master in the Washington, D.C., metropolitan area, grew up in Birmingham and ate barbecue from his early childhood days. He started in real estate but later decided to enter the restaurant business. He learned barbecue from a well-known pit master before starting his own restaurant. He experimented with restaurants in Washington, D.C., before moving to his current location in Woodbridge, Virginia, right off the interstate and with easy access to truckers and tourists. And like so many other barbecue proprietors, he has that calm, reasoned air of a man used to thinking and talking in terms of rigorous applied science.

As we might expect from non-chained, amateur products, barbecue restaurants often have idiosyncratic names. Like Bubba's. Other well-known barbecue outlets have been called Fat Willy's Hawg House (Rockville, South Carolina), Dr. Hogly Wogly's (Tyler, Texas), or Bubbalou's Bodacious Bar-B-Que (Orlando, Florida). These names represent deliberate decisions to personalize the product, to identify it with an artisan, and to accept standards of quality outside of formal dining canons. Even the spelling of barbecue is not the same across many of these restaurants, the ultimate rebellion against homogenizing cultural trends.

A Big Fire Before Breakfast

This is why barbecue is what it is.

In rural Texas a classic barbecue pit is no longer strictly open, as defined above, but rather the term refers to long (10- to 20-foot) brick compartments that cook meats using wood. Metal gratings hold the meats up, a chimney disposes of the smoke, and a large woodpile is nearby. Often the fires are concentrated at the ends of the compartments, so that the meat is cooked by indirect heat—but, still, imagine a wood pile as big as a car, on fire. Typically such pits were made by hand, decades ago, rather than purchased in ready-made form. Classic barbecue pits in the American South are more likely built into walls and aboveground, but they rely on essentially the same cooking process.

Classic pits work best when someone watches for all or much of the night. This person ideally sleeps near that big fire, awakening periodically to stir it or to make sure nothing has caught fire that wasn't supposed to. Not all pits are monitored so closely, but then the owners incur greater risk or they must shut down some or all of the pits at night, thereby limiting the long cooking times and thus the quality of the product.

Using a draw and flue, the pit master gets the air entering the pit and the smoke leaving it. Just lighting the fire properly is an acquired skill. Then the meat must be turned, the temperature must be sampled, the fire must be lit, maintained, or restoked, as conditions dictate. The wood doesn't always burn the same way each time. The pit master must regulate the temperature by making ongoing adjustments in the pit conditions, such as adding more wood or poking around in the pit. An open pit is difficult to run and takes years of practice and training. This is a style of cooking that involves high labor costs and is not conducive to assembly line methods of production, as one might find in a McDonald's or Applebee's.

Doughnut shops, which are usually nationally chained (Tim Hortons is the classic Canadian suburban landmark), are based on the opposite principles. The equipment is standardized and not very expensive or difficult to learn. The typical restaurant is fairly small, franchising is easy, and a huge fire is not required in the adjacent room to serve a doughnut. Doughnut shops often rely on a national brand to provide image for the shop, like Dunkin' Donuts, whereas barbecue revels in its local, regional, or idiosyncratic image. Doughnuts are about mass production and distribution. They are about snacks that are available in uniform quality around the clock. A powerful fire doesn't fit that kind of food.

From the beginning, many of the very best barbecue places have opened early in the morning. Classic pit barbecue starts cooking the food the night before and the next day the proprietors try to sell this food as rapidly as possible. A very high quality barbecue restaurant therefore tends to open early—even in the 7 to 9 A.M. range—and hopes to sell much of its product by the middle of lunchtime. The food is ready from its overnight processing and it will only lose freshness as the day progresses.

Given that the food must be sold in large batches, lunchtime is the obvious market target. In rural America, lunchtime is very often a much bigger food audience than dinnertime anyway. People are out at their jobs, in their cars, looking for a big meal, and they haven't yet settled into the house routine with the kids. So the proprietor synchronizes a batch of meats to be ready early in the day. Given the risk of uncertain daily demand, the restaurant is willing to sell before lunchtime, to make sure it takes in as much business as possible. The restaurant is less willing to extend these same sales through late in the evening. High-quality barbecue restaurants are committed to making every meal meet a certain level of quality. They do not wish to sell inferior food much later in the day, so it's not unusual for a quality barbecue restaurant to close by two thirty or three.

Along with bunched selling, the best barbecue restaurants often run out of their best meats at some point in the day. It is common to show up—perhaps no later than one o'clock P.M.—and be told that ribs or shoulder or brisket are no longer available. This encourages the crowd to come early. A popular barbecue restaurant is often full by noon or earlier, whereas many other restaurants hit their peak time around one or a little after.

Another factor favors early opening hours, namely that the proprietor must tend to the meats early in the morning. So why not open up as well? The top barbecue spots in Lockhart, Texas, open between seven and ten in the morning. Many locals or tourists will stop in for breakfast, often ordering the sausage, which is the first dish ready in the morning. In the case of Kreuz Market or Smitty's, the butcher running the pits simply chops off some meat for you; early opening does not require an extensive staff of waitresses or a lot of preparation. You take your meat to the table and you pick it up with your fingers; the napkins are already there.

The slow cooking times limit the ability of a barbecue pit to meet surges in demand. Suburbanites often seek immediacy, as evidenced by the popularity of fast food. If Applebee's does not have enough chicken sandwiches ready, it does not take them long to make more. Similarly, most ethnic restaurants in the United States are open all day long and offer ready-to-serve food, usually in less than ten minutes time. But the best barbecue restaurants tend to run out of their best dishes as the day runs on. Rather than periodically frustrate its best customers, a barbecue restaurant is more likely to close, and open, early. At the very least they will simply be out of some of the best dishes.

Memphis barbecue does not tend to open early or close early. Barbecue restaurants there commonly open at 11:30 or 12 noon, which is the norm for the town. But Memphis barbecue centers around pork ribs, which brings us to another critical distinction. It is possible to cook ribs for a dozen hours or more, and end up with a delicious product, but decent-quality ribs can be produced in as little as ninety minutes. Good beef brisket, in contrast, requires eight to twelve hours or more. Barbecued ribs are much easier to handle than a whole hog and they are easier to cook by machine rather than using a classic pit. They take less time, less space, and less fuel. The major Memphis barbecue restaurants also use mechanical rather than classic pits. In other words, they've been liberated from some of the traditional constraints, albeit at the risk of losing some of the artisanal qualities of the finest barbecue. The result has been that barbecued ribs have spread across America in a way that other barbecue forms have not. The restaurant Tony Roma's—to provide one example of many—offers quality ribs in the form of an expensive but polished chain restaurant.

In North Carolina, the barbecue has found a disturbing solution to the problem of barbecue freshness. Most barbecue restaurants in North Carolina open early, but now more out of tradition than economics. The food is cooked in advance and then either frozen or placed in a heater. Sometimes the food sits for as long as a week; Lexington Barbecue #1 proudly tells the customer that the food never sits longer than overnight, and yet neither I nor my traveling companion were impressed to hear that. Sometimes today's mix and last night's are thrown together and served for lunch. These restaurants never run out of their best product, but their best product is less impressive in the first place. The economics for this decision are obvious, and they illustrate just how uneconomical true barbecue art can be. North Carolina barbecue restaurants do not close early, do not run out of food, and can serve their customers extremely quickly. So if you're asking me to weigh in on this classic dispute—North Carolina vs. Texas barbecue—I have to rule against North Carolina, precisely for these reasons.

Barbecue Paradise

Sad to say, the best barbecue region in the world is probably not the United States. You can understand a lot about the economics of classic barbecue pits if you go south of the border.

In rural Mexico still some of the oldest barbecue traditions are alive and well. Commonly a family will have a goat or pig barbecued for a special occasion such as a wedding or birthday. For the underground barbecue, rural Mexicans dig a hole in the ground and build a fire in a stone-lined pit. The meat is then wrapped, often in maguey leaves, and placed on the fire. The hole is covered with damp earth and the food is allowed to cook. The well-known Mexican dish cochinita pibil, which you can find in some of the better Mexican restaurants in the United States, refers to barbecued pig in a pit. *Pib* is the Mayan word for pit barbecue, although our Mexican restaurants serve bastardized versions of the dish with the pork wrapped in banana leaves and cooked in ovens.

In San Agustin Oapan, the small Mexican village where I have done fieldwork (for other projects), the villagers cook the meat by burning hard sugarcane, the kind with "hearts" inside. It is claimed that wood would break apart during the cooking process and this may reflect the limited wood choices available to the villagers. Some rural Mexicans use charcoal for cooking, but throw onion, garlic, chilies, or oregano on the coals for seasoning.

The best-known barbecue master in San Agustin Oapan is Angel Dominguez, who is also a noted maker of pottery from the clay by the village riverbank. If you walk over to Angel's house to visit, either you will find him sitting in a hammock, simply smiling, working at his sewing machine, or you will be told that he is out tending his watermelons by the riverbank. He is known as a village eccentric, in part because otherwise both the pottery and the sewing are the exclusive province of the village women. He always responds with a slow lisp, but his fierce burning eyes betray his dedication to his creative arts. When he feels like it and needs a few extra pesos, Angel does brilliant work shaping his pottery and then cooking it underground, using pre-Columbian methods and all-natural materials from around the village. If he doesn't feel like it, offers of money will not spur his efforts. And if you leave him money as an advance on the work, it is simply treated as a gift.

Having learned the skills of using and controlling underground fire, he naturally stepped into a position as village barbecue master. He cooks goat meat and pig meat for village ceremonies, such as fiestas and weddings, simply by burying the wrapped meat with a burning fire and tending it to make sure the fire is neither too strong nor too weak. The animal comes right from the village and it is slaughtered by hand right before it is cooked, for some of the freshest goat flavor I have enjoyed.

If you ask Angel, he has no idea that such a thing as commercial barbecue exists. For him, barbecue, like his traditional pottery, is an ancient way of the village and an art that can be mastered by only a few people.

Most mid- to large-size Mexican cities, at least in central Mexico, have numerous barbecue outlets, often on the outskirts of town rather than in the immediate center. The very best would not meet traditional definitions of a restaurant and I might add that they are also very cheap, serving spectacular meals for often less than five dollars. The food is served outside, or perhaps under a tent covering or awning. The barbecue meat is cooked in a pit, traditional style, usually completely outside the city and in the neighboring countryside. The meats range from mutton to beef to pork, the head and stomach are treated as well, and often the pit is lined with maguey leaves. While the barbacoa is cooking, a metal pan collects its meaty juices, which are served as barbacoa consommé, a kind of side soup accompanying the taco in which the meat is wrapped. Fiery sauces are optional additions to the tacos.

The meat from the countryside is ready early in the morning, at which time it is shipped by truck to the barbecue restaurants. The restaurants open between 9 and 10 A.M., at which point they serve barbecue for breakfast. Cooking the meat in rural or more remote areas makes catastrophic fires and loss of life less likely. Classic Mexican barbecue of this kind is most prominent in the states of Hidalgo, Tlaxcala, and Mexico but you also can find it in Morelos, Guerrero, and possibly in other locales that I have not visited. The Mexican hinterlands where the meat is cooked are not densely inhabited and not much regulated by the government. If there is any problem with the police, a bribe can be paid. Barbecue cooking, in the classic open- or dug-pit manner, proceeds unhindered and the art is alive and well like nowhere else in the world.

If you'd like the name of just one place, try Cucina Económica

"Lupita," about ninety minutes north of Mexico City, near the town of San Juan del Río, in the state of Querétaro. There isn't really an address or phone, but rather it is designated at "Carretera [highway] Galindo Amealco, Kilometer 3." On the back of their business card is a chromo-lithograph of John Paul II and a quotation about justice, peace, and love. They are only open weekends and the barbecue runs out sometime by the middle of lunch, after which they serve only delicious quesadillas. Get there early. It's basically a covered shelter on the side of the road, but on the weekend they come along and put out chairs, tables, and the cooking equipment and they are ready to go. It's run by an elderly Mexican woman, named Lupita, who requires some convincing that an American visitor can handle the spicy sauce for the barbecue. This is how barbecue is meant to be cooked and there are hundreds of places like this, scattered around Central Mexico. If you are into barbecue pilgrimages, these kinds of places should be your first stop.

It's not just at Lupita's. In Mexico, once the fresh meat runs out, the restaurants close. This can happen as early as one o'clock in the afternoon. The limited hours are one reason why these eating places do not invest more in costs of décor and presentation. A few barbecue establishments will stay open later in the day. Either they are serving a less fresh or inferior product, or they receive a second shipment of meat during the day. Even these restaurants, however, might close as early as seven P.M.

Less fresh forms of barbecue can be found in Mexico as well. Barbecue is served in more mainstream Mexican restaurants, but there the meats are often frozen and later thawed. These restaurants do not have delivery problems, but as in most of North Carolina, this efficiency is obtained at the expense of quality.

Mexicans also cook meats—especially pork—*al pastor* in yet another version of the barbecue arts. A meat is skewered and then roasted slowly on a vertical spit, with the coals to one side. Pork *al pastor*—a kind of mini-barbecue—might cook all day long. A similar technique is found in Greek and Turkish gyro cooking, and the inspiration comes from Arabic food culture. In Mexico, the gyro method of cooking was first used in the 1930s, when Lebanese immigrants came to the city of

Puebla, a longstanding center of Mexican cuisine. It's now about as Mexican as you can get and it is more closely identified with Mexican food, to most outsiders, than is the more classic tradition of Mexican barbacoa.

Mechanized Barbecue vs. the Human Touch

Homo sapiens all cooked with fire at one point or another. Everything was a little smoky. Barbecue in one broad sense did conquer the world once. It just turned into a whole lot of different cooking methods.

Just as there are coexisting barbecue traditions in Mexico, diversity exists in American methods. Instead of firing up open or indoor pits, many U.S. barbecue restaurants cook with easily controllable mechanical technologies. The staff can cook the barbecue overnight, resting secure that the temperature and cooking speed are taken care of by machine. No one need stay in the restaurant to monitor the cooking. Training an individual to turn on a machine is much easier than training him to work a classic fire pit. By lunchtime or earlier the meat will be ready in a quite predictable fashion.

Mechanical barbecue pits come in differing forms, but typically the cooking process tucks slabs of meat into a multilevel vertical machine. The meats are exposed to a regulated source of heat, which can result from wood, gas, or charcoal. Of these three options, wood has the highest status and offers the best taste but is also the most costly. Gas has the lowest status but is the cheapest. One quality advantage—but not cost advantage—of the classic pits is simply that they make a gas flame impossible. Owners of mechanical pits face the temptation to substitute gas for wood or charcoal. And if wood is used, whether in a mechanical or classic pit, the temptation is to cook a batch of barbecue every few days and reheat the product, rather than spend more money on wood each day.

Barbecue also can be cooked in a smoker, constructed from 500-gallon metal propane or furnace oil tanks, and fitted with racks for holding the meat. A simple smoker can cost $1,500, while the more elaborate devices run up to $10,000 or more. Again, the meat is placed on a metal rack a few feet above the heat. The heat is kept low and never flames. The meat is cooked through slowly by both the heat and the smoke. Sources of heat may include gas, electric, liquid smoke, pressure cookers, airtight ovens, and even microwaves.

The mechanical pits, however much they offend the purist, boosted the barbecue revival of the mid-1970s and 1980s. It was now easier to run a barbecue restaurant, to franchise, or even to start a chain. Barbecue spread to new locales, including to Manhattan. Most major metropolitan areas now have numerous barbecue restaurants, typically all using mechanical pits. In the Washington, D.C., area, there are easily fifteen places or more to buy barbecue, although not at the quality levels found in Texas or the deeper South. Whatever its aesthetic or culinary drawbacks, mechanical pit barbecue is much more mobile than classic pit barbecue. If nothing else, it has introduced people to the idea of barbecue and made them curious about the real thing.

For most mechanized pits, local regulators are not a huge issue. A quality mechanical pit typically will not allow the meat or fat drippings— both flammable—to come into contact with fire. The pits also shut down automatically, and emit signals if the temperature exceeds a certain level. An accomplished maker of mechanical pits already has prepared documentation about how the pit performs smoke removal, it has private sector certification of its quality and safety, and it satisfies legal safety standards. The pits will have gone through consumer product testing services and will have all the needed certificates. None of this is true for the classic pit and of course not for the older open pit. Not surprisingly, sellers of mechanical pits, in their marketing, stress the much lower risk of fire and the greater ease of satisfying the regulators.

Memphis Championship Barbecue, owned and run by "Barbecue King" Mike Mills, in Las Vegas (now three branches in one city), is typical of where the barbecue sector is at in most locales. The interior is spotless, the staff is professional, the look is corporate, and the trappings refer to the history of barbecue. Their mechanical pit produces large amounts of meat every day at relatively low labor cost. The original home base was Mike's two barbecue restaurants in southern Illinois; Mike is considered a master of classic techniques, but his expansions rely more heavily on technology. Memphis Championship Barbecue has opened several branches in Las Vegas and it runs a catering business.

As mechanized barbecue has spread, regional traditions are weakening. Beef barbecue now can be found readily in the Carolinas, and pork barbecue can be found in Texas. Barbecue restaurants outside the major centers tend to offer barbecue dishes from across the country. Willlard's, a barbecue restaurant in Northern Virginia, offers Kansas City, Texas, St. Louis, and Carolina styles of barbecue, and markets them explicitly as such in an attempt to provide one-stop barbecue shopping. Like many other new barbecue restaurants, they offer nostalgia for barbecue as a whole, rather than any single tradition. Many of their customers come from these barbecue locales, but no one locale supplies enough customers to induce complete specialization.

It is a longstanding debate among barbecue fans how much is lost by moving to mechanical pits. A little bit of economics, however, helps resolve this issue. Let us start with two facts. First, many of the famous barbecue restaurants, especially in the South, have moved to mechanized pits. While some would argue these restaurants have become somewhat worse, they remain excellent by common consensus. Nonetheless, restaurants with a classic pit tend to be much better, on average, than restaurants with a mechanical pit.

Barbecue purists object that gas gives the meat a distinctive gassy flavor. Wilber Shirley, a renowned pit master, argues that the positioning of the meat matters. Classic pit wood cooking puts the fire underneath. As fat from the meat drips onto the fire, the heat is moderated. This may make the meat softer. Furthermore, the fat has more time to make the meat more flavorful, which is important for brisket. Other partisans argue that wood cooking is more irregular, since the temperature cannot be controlled precisely. Every classic or open pit meal is a bit different, which may allow pit cooking to hit higher peaks, whether or not it has a higher average quality. Classic wood cooking offers a unique smoked flavor, which varies with the kind of wood used. Some say sauces may cover up this taste, some say they don't.

They're missing the real point: It isn't just about the fire or its absence. It is more important to consider what statisticians call a "selection effect"—namely, that the classic pit restaurants differ systematically in a number of ways. A classic pit restaurant is more likely to be artisanal, is more likely to employ well-trained and highly experienced labor, and is less likely to be corporate. Most of all a classic pit restaurant is more likely to have an on-the-site proprietor with many years of experience. At the very least a highly trusted associate will be there. It is harder to put the classic pit on automatic pilot. This raises restaurant costs, but it ensures that the overall level of quality monitoring—not just for the pit— remains high. The costs of messing up in a classic pit are a local tragedy, maybe burning down the town, not just a few unsatisfied customers. So someone is always watching, usually the owner, and this has a positive effect on overall food and restaurant quality.

Mechanical pit restaurants are usually more corporate; and because of the larger number of customers they can serve, they are more likely to make money by cutting corners. The classic pit restaurant therefore has a lot of quality advantages, which don't come from the use of the pit itself, even though the use of the pit is what brings about these advantages, such as the on-site proprietor.

The classic pit restaurant produces on a small scale, is more likely in a rural area, and relies on regular customers who are dedicated to the idea of barbecue. A mechanical pit restaurant—which can be more easily set in cities or suburbs—will more likely follow trends or attract uninformed, casual visitors. While more and more tourists are seeking out classic pit restaurants, even in distant or obscure locales, these individuals tend to be well informed about quality barbecue.

Classic pit barbecue restaurants will find it difficult to make many shortcuts, even if they might wish to in the abstract. They are forced to be of higher average quality than the mechanical pit restaurants. At the same time, the very best mechanical pit restaurants, if they are truly committed to quality, can be very good indeed.

Lexington, North Carolina, offers a partially controlled experiment. Of the twenty or so barbecue establishments in town, only a few have kept the classic pit technique. As Lexington restaurants switched to mechanical pits over the last twenty years, they did not systematically lose their customers. The Lexington barbecue tradition remains popular. It is rumored that some North Carolina restaurants keep a faux woodpile to fool outsiders, but this is hard to verify. Barbecue purists object strenuously to the mechanical pits, sometimes to the point of denying them the word "barbecue." It is sometimes said that the deviants cook roast pork designed to look like barbecue. But I hold no prejudice against mechanical pits in Lexington. The sauce on the pork is typically strong and can obscure the method of cooking used. Furthermore the product from the classic pits is not typically delivered fresh on the plate. It can be a little dry, from having sat around or from refrigeration. It is not always piping hot, since reheating would dry it out too much. When it comes to Lexington, modern technologies and economic efficiencies have limited the quality of *both* the classic and mechanical pit products.

Most Americans who barbecue at home (or grill, for that matter) use gas technology. The griller needs only to push some buttons or move some dials. In contrast to the cooking times for classic barbecue (8–12 hours), gas allows for rapid cooking if desired. Gas cooking also avoids the need for barbecue coals and lighter fluid, both of which are costly and can be difficult to manipulate. Gas grilling at home has changed consumer tastes for the product. People now expect barbecue to taste somewhat gassy. It is seen as no great sin—or noticed—if chain restaurants cook their barbecuelike entrees with gas.

Korean barbecue shows a similar history of gas technology displacing classic wood-burning techniques, especially in the cities and suburbs. Classic Korean barbecue also uses wood to cook meats for a long period of time, typically over an open fire. Charcoal making is an art—oak stumps will be baked for days to prepare the cooking medium. This technique remains in use in the countryside, but most Korean cooks now use gas, for reasons of convenience, safety, and economics. Koreans have developed a wide variety of ingenious mechanical devices for cooking meat, and these have come to define Korean cuisine. Korean wood cooking persists as a rural and artisanal art, and sadly it is something I have never experienced in anything like its authentic form.

Some barbecue establishments are becoming more like doughnut shops, especially if they are located in major cities. Health, fire, and safety codes have made classic barbecue pits more difficult to maintain. Truly open, outdoor cooking pits, for commercial purposes, are illegal in most counties of the United States. Tin roofs, screened porches, and other facades help circumvent such laws, but the open pit is in any case no longer profitable at the restaurant level. It is simply too hard to cook large quantities of meat in manageable fashion with this technology.

The older classic pits were built without a uniform design, often by founders of the restaurant, rather than meeting standardized corporate or legal specifications. This makes it harder to please the regulators and the insurance agents. As America has become wealthier, and more safety-conscious, fewer municipalities have been willing to tolerate non-mechanized barbecue pits. Remaining classic pits are typically in open, rural areas, and that limits the spread and scalability of barbecue.

It would be difficult to place a classic barbecue restaurant in either a strip mall or a shopping mall. The smoker and pit would interfere with the other shops and so the stand-alone nature of classic barbecue raises real estate costs. Even in Texas, North Carolina, and other barbecue-rich areas, the very best barbecue tends to be found in rural areas, again in roadside, stand-alone restaurants. That's why a lot of the best American barbecue is found in towns of 50,000 people or less and even then we often should look on the outskirts of town, not in the immediate center. Barbecue does best in low-rent settings with lax regulations.

Smoke disposal is another problem. Many municipalities object to the streams of smoke issued from wood-burning pits. It is not uncommon for part of a barbecue-rich small town to smell like barbecue smoke. The rise of environmentalism has caused many people to complain about the ambient effects of barbecue smoke and barbecue proprietors often speak of the local environmentalists as their enemies.

Blue Smoke, one of the primary barbecue restaurants in Manhattan, had to jump through considerable hoops to open. The approval process took almost a year and involved delay, uncertainty, and the costs of proving to regulators that the restaurant would be safe. The most serious problem was showing the regulators that the restaurant had a good way of getting rid of its smoke. Blue Smoke survives by catering to an exclusive and well-heeled clientele, which seeks the novelty of classic barbecue in Manhattan and is willing to spend a fair amount of money on drinks. Most barbecue restaurants, which operate on a relatively small and cheap scale, would not survive such obstacles.

Classic pit barbecue cannot flourish in such restricted environments. Employment prospects for pit masters decline, customer tastes grow accustomed to other methods, and it is harder for pit-cooking techniques to stay alive and spread. Classic pit barbecue must be a living art if it is not to die out.

Even in rural areas regulatory constraints are starting to bite. Across southern Texas—especially in and near San Antonio—cow's head barbecue traditionally was made on Sundays by Mexican-Americans. In earlier times the dish was cooked in open pits for ten to twelve hours, but health codes have eliminated this practice in all but the most out of the way locales. For instance government regulations in Laredo, Texas, require steam pressure cookers for barbecued calf's head, in lieu of the traditional buried pit. The stainless steel, steam-pressure tubs cost more and the result is that a few wholesale distributors have replaced the earlier system of independent, amateur production and experimentation. The cookers, the need for gas plumbing, and concomitant insurance regulations have raised the costs of cooking and centralized supply. Barbecue fans argue that the steam technique is not nearly as good as underground cooking. Sadly, the goat's head tradition is dwindling. The last time I went to San Antonio (2009) and asked the hotel concierge about goat's head barbecue, he didn't know what I was talking about. Over time this barbecue tradition may die out altogether, at least in the United States.

Cooking in a truly open pit, in the United States, is most common in Hawaii, but even here the tradition is vanishing. Traditional barbecue requires buying a whole pig, refrigerating it, finding a place to dig the pit, and preparing the accompanying dishes. It is not unusual for a whole pig barbecue to be prepared by as much as a year in advance. Even though the Hawaii government offers a relatively favorable legal environment for pig roasts, the practical difficulties remain. It is increasingly common to prepare smaller pig parts in the oven, using liquid smoke to approximate (poorly) the classic barbecue smoky flavor.

Why America Is Good at Sauce

We must note that barbecue is about the sauce and the side dishes almost as much as the meat. In Texas the sauce is less important than elsewhere (it is sometimes absent altogether), and consists of ketchup, water, vinegar, and meat drippings. St. Louis sauce is sharper and tomato-based. The eastern part of North Carolina uses a clear vinegar sauce, while the western part of the state reddens the sauce with ketchup. A mustard rub is used in southern North Carolina, and this "mustard region" runs through South Carolina, Georgia, Alabama, and parts of Mississippi. Columbia, South Carolina, is the center of the mustard style. Parts of North Carolina and Kentucky use a thin sauce with a Worcestershire-like taste. In the American protectorate of Guam, barbecue is made with a finadene sauce of onion, soy, and vinegar.

Regardless of region, a barbecue sauce or powder has many possible ingredients. These include commercially prepared barbecue spices and sauces, basil, cayenne, celery seed, cilantro, cinnamon, cumin, curry powder, fennel seed, garlic (usually granulated), ginger powder, horseradish powder, jalapeño powder, mustard powder, onion, oregano, parsley, red pepper flakes, sage, tarragon, thyme, and white pepper, just to provide a few examples. Beer, Pepsi, and Worcestershire sauce also turn up now and then. Barbecue chefs have experimented with controversial spices such as allspice, bay leaf, cloves, lemon zest, and marjoram.

Barbecue sauces and spices are often kept secret. They have developed by trial-and-error, within a broader setting of friendly yet intense competition. Amateurs try out new recipes all the time, playing out their mad scientist dreams. Most of the new ideas fail, and we never see or taste them, but the better ones end up in restaurants and they also influence the sauces of others. The classic recipes came before the cookbooks and first circulated in the amateur realm. A large number of sauce permutations were needed to hit upon the successful use of Miracle Whip in one barbecue sauce; one cook cautions you not to use mayonnaise instead. Whether or not they are pulling your leg is not the point. Good sauces tend to cluster where many people try their hand at inventing new barbecue and barbecue sauces.

Barbecue sauces have never relied on locally produced foodstuffs. Most barbecue ingredients can be found in the grocery store and they are available at a national level and often they come from the ugliest sides of American food culture. Mustard, ketchup, and vinegar are paramount in importance, depending on the regional tradition. They are storable rather than fresh; in fact some barbecue cooks are proud of using prepackaged and powdered spices rather than fresh spices. Often the onion and garlic are granulated and the ginger is dried and powdered, the opposite of what a Chinese or Indian cook would prefer. It is not ingredient availability that limits the spread of barbecue sauces, but rather knowing the right combinations. In this regard, barbecue sauces perfectly fit the paradigm of what American cuisine is good at.

The best barbecue sauces cannot be sold nationally. To be canned, bottled, and sold across state lines, as part of the national food nexus, the mixes would require additional regulatory approval. In order not to spoil, the sauces would have to add preservatives and chemicals to keep the sauce good for a long time. In addition to requiring regulatory approval, the manufacturer faces liability problems if the sauce rots after a week or two. The best barbecue sauces therefore are found locally and are not distributed nationally. Heinz marketed the first barbecue sauce nationally in 1948, but a lot of classic barbecue fans look down on such mass-produced products. Furthermore, barbecue sauces made in large batches tend to be less tasty than sauces made in small batches; the small batch makes it easier to control and measure the quality.

Side orders also make some barbecue restaurants better than others. The Southeast is most likely to serve coleslaw and hush puppies. Rice and hash are found in South Carolina and eastern Georgia; the hash is usually a stew made from pork and pork organs. Parts of Virginia and eastern North Carolina often serve Brunswick stew, which can contain game, corn, lima beans, potatoes, and tomatoes, in varying combinations. In earlier times, Brunswick stew was made with the meat of the squirrel. Texas barbecue restaurants might serve potato salad, red beans with cumin, or even sauerkraut or Wonder Bread.

None of these dishes require unique regional inputs, but some of them (not Wonder Bread) are nonetheless hard to replicate on a national level, most of all because national marketing requires preservatives. The side dishes will be freshest and most unique when the barbecue restaurant is run on an artisanal basis by an on-site proprietor. High quality side dishes thus are found together with classic pits, even though the quality of two inputs is more or less logically independent. The sauces and sides of barbecue therefore provide distinct reasons—tied to the artisanal nature of true pit cooking—why the best barbecue does not spread far and wide.

Where There Is No Smoke

Most of the legal problems from spreading the joys of real barbecue come from the smoke. From environmentalists in Washington State to Manhattan apartment dwellers, people don't like to breathe it in much at all. Nonetheless the demand for smoked foods is growing, even if those are not barbecue foods in the traditional sense. It's easy enough to order high-quality smoked meats over the Internet and have them delivered by FedEx or UPS. The upshot is that quality and availability of smoked salmon are higher in the United States than ever before, even if you don't get those meals from classic barbecue restaurants.

The idea of slow cooking at low temperatures is assuming a central role in American haute cuisine, although more and more it is separated from smoked flavor. New machines are capturing some of the best features of the classic barbecue pit and bringing them into top restaurants and even into some of our homes.

The technique of *sous vide* (French for "slow vacuum") enables large quantities of quality food to be prepared by slow cooking techniques. The food is first put into an airtight plastic bag and cooked in a precisely controlled water bath at a low temperature. The water and the bag, in essence, substitute for the pit. If done properly, it will taste fresh and delicious. If necessary, the food can be frozen and later thawed by simmering.

Sous vide replicates some features of barbecue cooking, albeit by other means. The water in the bag helps the food heat evenly, which substitutes for fidgeting with the meat and turning it in the pit. The bag seals in the juices, much as the confines of a barbecue pit and the low temperatures prevent the meat from drying out. Sous vide machines offer the special bonuses of allowing for strict and exact cooking instructions. An assistant need only heat the bag at a certain temperature for a certain amount of time. In an age of absentee celebrity chefs, this assures a predictable taste. That said, sous vide fails to replicate the smoked taste of barbecue and the crispy textures.

Costco sells lamb shanks (with rosemary and mint sauce) in sous vide form; Wegmans and Safeway offer sous vide items in their prepared foods department. Sous vide is now common in top restaurants and good sous vide machines are being brought into homes for five hundred dollars or less.

Consider barbecue as a series of bundled and potentially separable features, rather than a single take-it-or-leave-it package, and many features of barbecue appear to be spreading quite readily.

Barbecuelike ideas also are spreading through ethnic foods. Some Cuban and Filipino restaurants will, with advance notice, barbecue a whole pig for customers in the native style. The traditional Indian tandoor oven cooks food over charcoal (some versions use gas) at high temperatures. Brazilian *churrasco* cooks meat on skewers over an open flame; churrascarias can be found in most major cities and suburban areas in the United States. One of the most popular restaurants in downtown Memphis is Texas de Brazil. It is a small leap from barbecue to this concept and their meats are of good quality. Not surprisingly, they emphasize rib dishes more than other churrascarias might in other parts of the country. In downtown San Antonio there is a large branch of Fogo de Chao, another churrascaria, and again the question arises whether this should be considered a deviant form of barbecue. The original inspirations for these dishes, stemming from rural Argentina and Brazil, are close to traditional barbecue in their methods.

The purist may object that some of these developments are not "real barbecue," but that is misguided. In 1999 Lockhart, Texas, was voted by the Texas State Legislature as the barbecue capital of Texas. Foodies love the place. Yet Lockhart cooking does not always use low temperatures for long periods of time. Lockhart barbecue cooks quality meats in a classic pit, but often quickly at high temperatures, especially for the sausage and the beef shoulder. Lockhart barbecue has Germanic origins, blended in with a bit of Mexico, like the region itself, which is full of German-named towns.

In parts of Kentucky they barbecue mutton. Baltimore has a version of barbecue, known as "pit beef." Unlike most barbecue, the beef is grilled rather than smoked. In addition, the beef is rare (well done is more common in the barbecue world), and the cut is top round rather than brisket. The meat is sliced thin before cooking, another exception to usual practice, which typically cooks meat in large chunks. Finally, the tradition uses horseradish sauce as the core condiment, with raw white onion on top as well. Many of these outlets are located on one particular road—namely, Pulaski Highway—right next to what appears to be houses of prostitution and disreputable dance clubs. This too counts as barbecue, at least according to most partisans, yet it again raises the question of authenticity and whether barbecue is not, at least partly, a state of mind.

The lesson about food is that the most predictable and the most orderly outcomes are always not the best. They are just easier to describe. Fads are orderly. Food carts and fires aren't. Feeding the world could be a delicious mess, full of diverse favors and sometimes good old-fashioned smoke.

6

The Asian Elephant
in the Room

Most of the world's people live in Asia and most of the world's food *is* Asian food so it makes sense to turn our attention to it, with a focus on how it is served here in the United States. Asian food is a big part of our quest to better understand how good food can be had and what can get in the way.

Asian cultures have a special love of food; they build socializing around meals rather than treating food as something to be gobbled while doing something else. On visits to Hong Kong or Singapore you are likely to hear enthusiastic advice about where to find the best places to eat. Food in these places is like the weather, a topic for endless observation and conversation. When visiting, I feel like I am with my kind of people. Every meal counts.

Sometimes I'll go through extended periods—months—when all I want is different kinds of Asian food, or maybe I should say Asian-American food, because I spend most of my time in the United States. Yet it's not always easy. Even for the well-informed, Asian foods can be confusing, intimidating, too spicy, or just plain downright nasty (I defy anyone to tell me that they enjoy sea cucumber in any Chinese restaurant in the United States.) So what to do? How to proceed?

Dealing with Chinese food—especially in America—is really tricky. So, I'm going to save that for the end of this chapter. First let's set things straight with the Vietnamese.

Vietnamese Condiments

I'm a fan of Vietnamese food in the United States and also in Canada, where the Asian food is almost always above average. As a cuisine it travels relatively well and furthermore most Vietnamese restaurants in North America attract a majority of Vietnamese customers. That keeps standards relatively high.

The key point of Vietnamese dining is to use the sauces and condiments. You don't have to really understand them all from a distance; a lot of them are difficult to tell apart unless you are right in front of them. And they are almost always put right in front of you. Just use them. Asking for help is more important than learning any exact instructions about how to use which item. Gentlemen, you are going to have to ask for directions.

One important condiment is nước mắm pha, a mix of lime juice, fish sauce, sugar, and water; sometimes peppers or shredded carrot or garlic are added. It's the closest thing Vietnamese cuisine has to an all-purpose dipping sauce. I like to put this stuff on top of crushed rice, I dip spring rolls into it, and I put it on vermicelli and Vietnamese pancake with shrimp and bean sprouts. Nước lèo is used as a dipping sauce for a lot of beef dishes; it's made of tomato paste, peanut butter, sugar, sesame seeds, garlic, vegetable oil, and a bit of pork liver and pork, among other ingredients.

Using these resources is important for a tasty meal, but you needn't focus on remembering the details. Again, ask the staff, they will tell you what to do. If the waitstaff can't speak English well—admittedly a common occurrence in U.S. Vietnamese restaurants—they will show you.

Just pull out the table's sauces and condiments in front of you, point to them, pull off their covers if need be, and look puzzled. It is okay.

The rule of thumb here is simple: If you don't use sauces, sides, and condiments, as they were intended, your Vietnamese meal is almost certainly going to be far worse than it otherwise would be. The food will be either too dry or discordant.

The secondary rule is this: If your dishes don't require the use of sauces, sides, and condiments, your order from the menu is a mistake (unless you're at a Vietnamese sandwich shop, where the food is pre-seasoned in the proper way). You're probably getting some bland form of Asian food that is maybe not bad but more or less indistinguishable from so-so Chinese food with a Vietnamese twist. Most Vietnamese restaurants—even the relatively authentic ones—have plenty of Chinese dishes on their menus. That's authenticity, rather than inauthenticity, because there is a significant ethnic Chinese presence in Vietnam, but what do you care? Going the Chinese route will not give you an optimal experience at a Vietnamese restaurant.

Once you're using the sides and sauces, you're on the right track and you're also following the general principles about how to eat well in the United States. Look at some of the key ingredients in those sides and sauces, listed above, such as fermented fish sauce. Most of these travel and store pretty well and that is why your meal—if you like the cuisine in the first place—will be tasty. You'll get sensations of sweet, sour, tangy, tart, and sometimes a bit bitter.

Vietnamese food hasn't become extremely popular in the United States. There are large numbers of Vietnamese restaurants in this country but mostly patronized by Vietnamese. In my area, near Washington, D.C., if anything, I've noticed Vietnamese food retreating from mainstream status. The Vietnamese restaurants in Georgetown have lost importance or closed and many of the Vietnamese outposts in the suburbs have closed or scaled back their ambitions. The bánh mi sandwiches and Pho (*Phở*, or noodle soup) restaurants, mostly for lunchtime, have spread more successfully to non-Vietnamese areas than have "full-menu" Vietnamese restaurants. When it comes to the soups, the mixes of beef, noodles, greens, and herbs make for a good lunchtime snack—and don't forget to add some of the side condiments, most of all the bottled red stuff, which makes it spicy, and also squeeze in the lime.

The failure of most Vietnamese food to take off is an interesting outcome, because Vietnamese food rarely offends the American palate. Most of it just isn't that weird, or at least what turns up on the menus in America isn't that weird (the North Vietnamese are sometimes accused of favoring dog). The cuisine even has a notable French influence, which you can spot in the sandwiches and the combination of baguette with curry. You would think it could do better commercially, even if that might mean quality declines for everyday foodies. But nonetheless Vietnamese food is saved from the mass market, probably because most people never master the sides, sauces, and condiments. It's too much trouble and a lot of people don't like asking for help, especially if the interaction involves some linguistic awkwardness. If you take those sauces and condiments away, the glories of Vietnamese food just aren't that apparent. People are used to Chinese food and Chinese restaurants. Some of the other Vietnamese dishes, such as the curries, lean in the Indian direction; but, again, while those dishes are good, a lot of American customers don't see a compelling reason to switch away from Indian to the Vietnamese curries. To outsiders, Vietnamese restaurants can feel like exclusive clubs for Vietnamese, and that can be off-putting.

To everyday foodies I say eat more of Vietnamese food in North America. It's rarely too weird, never expensive, and it's also pretty healthy, for the most part, because it relies less on oils and deep frying than does a lot of Chinese food. Remember: sauces, sides, and condiments. Once you're comfortable with those, your love for the cuisine is likely to flourish.

Sweet Thai

Unlike Vietnamese, Thai food in the United States is becoming bad. It's getting sweeter—in the cloying, excess use of refined sugar sense—and the tastes are less strong and less reliable. There are in absolute terms, more excellent Thai restaurants than ever before, but I wouldn't want to vouch for the average quality of Thai food in America these days.

Thai restaurants are unreliable in part because it is so easy to make the food too sweet. Peanut sauces can be too sweet. The curries and the noodle-based pad thai can be too sweet, and often they dump in too much refined sugar (by the way, many people think of pad thai as the classic Thai dish, but it is a relatively recent invention, dating from the Second World War and not all Thai people embrace it). The best sweet Thai dishes mix sweet with tart, using pineapple or sweet and sour, but overall there's still too much abuse on the sweet side and not enough fish sauce or fermented shrimp paste or ground white peppercorns.

A second problem with Thai food is that the Thai people have such a wonderful service ethic. I don't think I have ever once been treated rudely or poorly by a Thai server or hostess in a Thai restaurant, whether in Thailand or in other countries. In this context the Thai people are unfailingly polite and wonderful. (In contrast, language-poor Vietnamese servers are often confused or they come across as indifferent.) That's made it relatively easy for Thai restaurants to become popular and to court wide audiences.

Thai food also looks healthy. It's easy enough to pile some noodles on a plate, or present some tofu, or have some bean sprouts on top of a dish. Thai food lends itself well to broccoli and other green vegetables. Thai food also does well with seafood—order a whole fish any way they offer it—and many vegetarians will be tempted by the vegetable curries. A vegetarian pad thai is usually as good as the same dish with meat or seafood. While it's true that coconut milk might be bad for you (high in saturated fat), lots of eaters are willing to overlook this, or they are underinformed, because the notion of a vegetable curry sounds healthy, whether or not it is.

Thai food also has beautiful colors, such as all those greens, reds, yellows, and oranges. It looks sharp on colored plates, including black plates.

In sum, what happened is that Thai food became cool. This trend started first in California, in the 1980s, when young people in black started turning up in larger numbers at Thai restaurants in Hollywood. It spread. Americans eating in a Thai restaurant are likely more hip than those eating in a Chinese restaurant. Yet, the truth is: Hip people do not always have superb taste in food.

The two worst signs for Thai restaurants are Thai restaurants with large bars and lots of drinks and also Thai restaurants that serve sushi. Those are both signs that the restaurant isn't that serious about food. Stay away.

It is not, by the way, a bad sign if a Thai restaurant advertises itself as Thai-Chinese in some manner. You see this a lot in parts of Hollywood, especially East Hollywood, and that is one of America's best neighborhoods for Thai food. It might sound like pandering to the crowd, but usually this term performs a different function. It recognizes that within Thailand there is a distinction between foods that are linked to the Chinese minority and foods that are not. For instance, a dish of fried rice noodles would be considered an especially Chinese dish in Thailand and it is usually delicious. The restaurant is advertising that it has some connection to Thai-Chinese culture and this is mostly a message for a Thai audience. The place (at least in most cases) is not trying to attract the untutored Americans who expect to feast on a gloppy, overfried, over-sweetened plate of General Tso's Chicken.

One good way to understand Thai food, and Thai restaurants, is to study what is commonly considered the best Thai cookbook, namely David Thompson's *Thai Food*. You don't have to buy it, just check it out of your local library. In fact, you don't really need to study it exactly; ten minutes with this book ought to make matters clear. Open up to any random page and try to make one of the recipes. Try to even think about making one of the recipes. You'll notice two things. First, each recipe has a large number of distinct steps and ingredients, often up to thirty. Second, most of the recipes refer you to other recipes, such as for the curry pastes. The recipes you are referred to are themselves often complex and involve many steps by hand and often involve obscure ingredients, even by the standards of a well-stocked Asian supermarket.

I opened up to a random page and came across the recipe for Curried Fish Innards (p. 305). The opening sentence has characteristic irony: "It may come as some relief to know that fish innards can be bought ready to go in bottles from Chinese food stores." Not a relief to everyone, perhaps, but getting fish innards isn't the hard part anyway. The recipe has a manageable ten ingredients, the most obscure being white turmeric, although this seems to be optional. The accompanying curry paste involves twelve ingredients, few of which are available outside a good Asian or even Thai supermarket. But wait—one of those ingredients is shrimp paste, presented on page 177. If you're going to make the real thing, it involves pounding, layers of cheesecloth, and fermentation for up to six months. You're also supposed to add half a cup of boiled, salted fish, which brings you to page 176. You vigorously massage salt into the fish, leave it overnight, and then dry the fish in the sun for two days. The recipe warns, "The best-quality salt must be used."

Get the idea? Proper Thai cooking is a serious matter.

Sometimes I think of Thompson's cookbook as "the book that is too good for me." (I find his wonderful *Thai Street Food* easier to cook from.) I'm a more serious cook than most people, and there's a local Thai supermarket near my house, but I'm simply not up to the demands of this book or should I say I am not up to the proper execution of this cuisine? I have no trouble following the detailed instructions in the best English-language cookbooks for Sichuan, Vietnamese, or Indian foods. I also can make a superficially good green chicken curry but Thompson makes you realize that that dish is a sideshow, compared to the more complex-tasting options.

For years my favorite Thai place in the United States was a restaurant called Thai X-ing, which I hope is still running by the time you read this. The proprietor's name is Taw Vigsittaboot, from the south of Thailand, and the restaurant is an offshoot of the guy's home. For much of the life of this restaurant, it has had only one table. In 2009 I showed up and suddenly they had two and then three tables to handle the crowds. Usually there was the cook—Taw—and a staff of one, to take your order and handle the bill. They're open for dinner and not for lunch. They're also in a somewhat rundown and relatively inexpensive part of town, namely the Shaw district (near Florida, U Street, and Sixth; 515 Florida Avenue NW, more exactly).

If you showed up to Thai X-ing unannounced, you may not get in. Even if one of the tables is free, you may have to wait two or more hours for your food. For one thing, the chef makes many of the dishes from scratch. He's a walking version of the Thompson book, and then some. That's why you need to order a day or more in advance, otherwise you probably shouldn't go at all because you will sit there for hours, assuming you can get a table in the first place.

That's what Thai food should be about but of course that's not what we usually get, especially when the cooking is for a larger audience. And that's why a lot of Thai food resorts to excess sweetness. The proper complex tastes are hard to summon up.

In 2010 Taw told me that something called The Food Network had contacted him about being on the air, but he wasn't sure he wanted to do it, as he was too busy cooking and already had enough customers. "Give it a try," I said dutifully trying to increase supply where I saw demand. He repeated that he was extremely busy and didn't seem very interested. Unfortunately, as I was submitting the final text of this book I visited the restaurant and saw it had expanded to a few more tables, with notable signs of decline; only half of the dishes were splendid. I still hope that Taw will manage to somehow make the new formula work, but I wonder.

If you're looking for good Thai food, try to find the original Thai X-ing model as closely as possible. Look for an eccentric chef who is cooking on a relatively small scale. Or look for a kitchen that will take special requests, which means the food is being cooked from scratch (more or less), the right way (more or less). A lot of Thai places will do this if you ask them to, though you may need persistence to get through to the right person to understand and implement your request. The phrases "Thai style" and "Thai spicy" come in handy; the term "very spicy" is not perfect and it brands you as a wannabe rather than a person in the know. You may end up getting very spicy versions of the regular dishes, which is okay, but it won't prompt them to make the tastes richer and subtler.

I also find that other people's recommendations of Thai restaurants aren't that reliable. A lot of those recommendations, even from relatively wise eaters, are geared toward identifying the best of the relatively sweet places. You need to reject that informational loop and identify one or two Thai places willing to cook and act outside the box. Once you've done that, I don't think it matters so much which dish you order—just about everything will be good, and you can go back to that same place again and again and again. I don't need that many good Thai places in my life, but I do need some that get the point; and in most major metropolitan areas in the United States you can find those, at least with some effort.

On a three-week visit to Thailand, I found quite a bewildering food universe. The median Thai meal there is probably *worse* than your median Thai meal in the United States, if only because the quality of the ingredients is so variable. Scruffy and chewy meats are a problem. But the peaks are astonishing and some time spent speaking with Thai people, and following their advice, will pay huge dividends. It's a country where a large number of people think seriously about what makes the food good or not at a particular restaurant or food stall.

Before moving on, I'll offer a speculative hypothesis about Thai food in North America. I can't prove it, but so far it's never led me wrong. Here goes:

Eat at a Thai restaurant that is attached to a motel.

That sounds odd, because most people don't think of Thai restaurants as coming attached to motels. But you'll find them, in locales as scattered as Santa Rosa, California, and Edmonton, Alberta. There are two reasons why I think this principle makes sense. First, if the restaurant is attached to the motel, they are not paying extra rent for the space. A Thai family already owns the motel and they are opening this business on the side. They don't have to cover high rents by appealing to large numbers of customers or by hurrying service and cutting corners. The odds are you'll get fairly authentic Thai food and at low prices.

Second, the restaurant is probably a family operation. By most normal standards, it doesn't actually make a lot of sense to combine a Thai restaurant and a motel. That's the whole point. It's not like combining a gas station and a car wash, which makes sense because people bring their cars to both. Or it's not like combining a coffee bar and a bookstore, which also makes sense. People who stay in motels, as far as I know, are not especially likely to eat Thai food. The common element between the Thai-owned motel and the Thai restaurant is most likely a hard-working, ambitious Thai family, with one or two wonderful cooks. And that's exactly what you want for a good Thai restaurant.

Spending on Japanese

There's sushi and then there's everything else, but let's start with some general principles.

Japanese food differs from most of the cuisines on this list in two interrelated ways. First, Japan is a high-wage country rather than a low-wage country, so Japanese don't migrate in large numbers to the United States to escape poverty. Many of the Japanese who come here to open up restaurants prefer high-expense places. They're not trying to get by on low prices and lots of family labor. Second, most Japanese live in cities and have known only urban life. They are especially likely to seek out major cities in the United States, or somewhere close to those cities (such as Fort Lee, New Jersey), whereas most other Asian immigrants are clustered in the outlying suburbs.

These facts have some implications for Japanese restaurants, which set them apart from a lot of the other Asian cuisines. First, the really good stuff usually isn't cheap. Second, the best Japanese restaurants are almost always in major cities, not the suburbs. Major cities mean higher rents, and that's another reason why the really good stuff isn't cheap. On top of all that, a lot of quality Japanese food requires quality ingredients, especially quality seafood, whether it's sushi or not. Did I mention that when it comes to Japanese food the really good stuff isn't going to be cheap?

As a result, we end up with a pretty simple equilibrium in Japanese restaurants in the United States. Cities such as New York, Los Angeles, Chicago, and San Francisco have first-rate but very expensive Japanese food. With or without sushi, these meals can run you two hundred dollars and up. You'll find slightly lesser versions of these meals—not the very best but still excellent—for a hundred dollars or maybe a bit less.

There are, then, thousands of lesser restaurants. If I were a strict foodie, I might feel that none of the lesser places are worth patronizing. Eat some sardines at home and save up your cash for an occasional big splurge on better Japanese food. Or if you live near Detroit, Columbus, Ohio, or a few other outposts with Japanese workers, you might find some decent mid-priced and fairly authentic Japanese food. (Hawaii is another story altogether.)

However, I'm an everyday kind of foodie. I don't live near a sizable Japanese community and yet I go to so-so Japanese restaurants all the time. I go for a few reasons. I go to socialize, I go because mediocre sushi is still pretty good for my waistline, I go to remind myself of the real thing, I go because other people want to, I go because I like being reminded of Japan, and I go because white tuna sushi at lower quality levels is still pretty yummy. Those reasons are good enough for me to show up, but I know that in terms of food I'm not getting a perfect outcome.

When it comes to Japanese restaurants, there are few gems hidden in the rough. It's simply a question of how much you are willing to pay and how often you can afford to go. Price really does come pretty close to measuring quality. If you want to eat better Japanese food, don't waste your time memorizing anybody's "tips." Just get your butt out there and earn some more $$$.

End of story.

Indian Partition

The first principle is that, on average, Pakistani food in the United States is better than Indian food in the United States. Often it's much better and yet a lot of the core dishes do not greatly differ. So much of the Indian food in the United States comes from northwestern Indian dishes that you can find substantial overlap on most Indian and Pakistani menus. You can't go to a Pakistani restaurant and find a masala dosa, or the mustard curries of Bengal, but you can get tikka, chickpeas, spinach, excellent bread, and a variety of curries. Pakistani restaurants cover a lot of the main dishes of U.S. Indian restaurants, although they are less likely to have hybridized Western dishes, such as butter chicken. They are more likely to have treats such as haleem, which is a slow-cooked mix of meat, lentils, and spices, with the consistency of a smooth paste. Haleem is also common in parts of India, but Indian restaurants in the United States shy away from carrying the dish, as it is gooey, spicy, and brings some risk of indigestion. More generally, Pakistani restaurants are more likely to use fresh rather than ready-made spice blends, and so the Pakistani food has a stronger and, to this customer, better taste.

So why does Pakistani food turn out better? I think it has to do with cultural associations. When a lot of Americans hear "Pakistan" they think of Bin Laden, drone attacks, terrorism, Daniel Pearl, and the sale of nuclear secrets. Maybe if they know some detail about the country they think of car bombs going off in Karachi or generals pondering civil war. When Americans hear "India" there is a greater chance that they think of Gandhi, "the world's largest democracy," and Ravi Shankar playing sitar with the Beatles. They might know some brightly colored Bollywood movies with vivid colors and happy dancing. Whether or not these portraits are fair or representative or balanced doesn't matter. Common images of Pakistan nudge away uncommitted customers. That means you should go more to Pakistani restaurants than to Indian restaurants. As I've noted, often for restaurants the quality of the customers matters more than the quality of the chef. I doubt if the Indian chefs are less talented than their Pakistani counterparts but they are more constrained in what they can produce, unless they are cooking for a predominantly Indian clientele, as you might find in one of the Indian restaurants near Edison, New Jersey.

You'll also find that Pakistani restaurants are more likely to have religious imagery or reminders of Islam on the walls, such as a photograph of Mecca. That's another plus. The more aggressively religious the decor, the better it will be for the food. A lot of Pakistani restaurants also hesitate to serve alcohol, which limits their American audiences and make them turn more to Pakistani customers, again to the benefit of their quality.

Pakistani restaurants are more likely to make you wait twenty minutes for completely fresh bread. U.S. Indian restaurants are more likely to bring you some naan that has been sitting around. The Pakistani customers have higher standards for bread, whereas more of the customers in the Indian restaurant are applying the American standard of wanting to have the bread right away, even if it isn't fully fresh. If you are ordering bread in an Indian restaurant, your best chance at freshness is to order the bread least likely to be ordered by others, because it will require special preparation. Be pleased if you end up waiting.

I love Indian food and my travels in India brought me some of the best meals I have eaten, ever, anywhere. The vegetables in India are especially fine and you can eat all-vegetarian there with no sacrifice of quality or diversity. Every region offers numerous special dishes that cannot be found anywhere else and certainly not in the United States. It's one of the world's food paradises for anyone earning a Western-level income; visit as soon as you can. That said, these days I hardly ever go to an Indian restaurant in the United States, at least not if Pakistani restaurants are around.

The blandness of Indian restaurants, like Thai restaurants, is a direct result of their popularity and the resulting ability to market the food to a mass audience. Yet this trend, while unfortunate, brings some good results too. The larger the market for Indian restaurants, the more we see entrepreneurs offering more than just the standard Indian dishes. Fifteen years ago, in my area, I had to drive to a single restaurant in Dupont Circle to eat a dosa and then wait about forty minutes for the woman to cook it. Now I can find dozens of restaurants serving dosas. The general rule is this: when you see an Indian restaurant, either wholly or partially, serving Indian regional cuisine, it is probably worth a visit. South

Indian food, Kashmiri food, Bengali food, Parsee food, and all the numerous other regional dishes are signs that you should give the place a try and of course the Pakistani restaurants won't be competing with those dishes either. Or if you're in a standard Indian restaurant, get the regional dish rather than the butter chicken. Again, the reasoning is simple. If it seems like fewer people have heard of something, or fewer people are likely to have a positive image of the cuisine or dish, the more likely it is there to appeal to the relatively informed and the relatively sophisticated diners.

What about Bangladeshi restaurants? Most of the restaurants run by Bangladeshis—and there are many—call themselves Indian restaurants, again to appeal to a greater number of customers. For all practical purposes, those *are* Indian restaurants, except that they are more likely to have some beef curry dishes. They don't try to replicate the wide variety of fish dishes you would find in Bangladesh itself. If you find a restaurant that deliberately advertises itself as Bangladeshi, there's a good reason to give it a try. Or if you see a Bangladeshi dish (such as beef curry) on the menu of an "Indian" restaurant, try it. The recurring advice here is that you should do anything to get away from the increasingly standardized formulas for cooking Indian food in the United States.

Korean Vegetables

This is a tough one because *most people don't like Korean food.* They like some Korean food, such as the sugary meats of a bul-gogi with rice or the dumplings, which could come from any number of Asian countries. But they don't like the stronger Korean tastes. A lot of Korean food hits you in the gut with garlic, red chilies, cabbage, more red chilies, sesame, more garlic, offal, and bizarre seafood stews with stringy octopus, dripping with red chili broth. A lot of the vegetables are pickled and fermented. It's not smoothed over the way you find with a lot of Chinese, Indian, and Thai food. I think of Korean food as a cuisine unto itself, perhaps more than any other. To add injury to insult, it's not unusual to visit an under-decorated Korean restaurant and see them charging thirty dollars or more for dishes you have never heard of and don't feel attracted to. How can they get away with that? Isn't food supposed to taste good? Isn't ethnic food supposed to be affordable?

I also love Korean food and the older I get the more interesting I find it. I find new revelations in Korean food more often than in just about any other cuisine. Is there any chance you will love it too?

I don't know. I'm reluctant to send you down the road of trying because in my heart of hearts I suspect most readers of this book will never really like it. But, if you dare:

First, you will find Korean dishes you'll like, like the bul-gogi, as I've already mentioned. I like bul-gogi too, but I don't love it. It's not enough to get me out of the house. If you want further tips, try the seafood pancake, dipped in the proper sauce, and the different forms of bibim bap, namely stone-cooked rice, vegetables, and maybe meat, mixed in a bowl with tangy and sweet hot pepper paste.

I think the way into Korean food is through the vegetables. If you can like the pickled, fermented, and doused in red chilies Korean kimchee cabbage, you can like a lot of the rest of the cuisine too. Also try buying some of their pickled spinach and bean sprouts and whatever else you can find in your local Korean supermarket, like at an H Mart or a Lotte Plaza, both excellent supermarkets for browsing and discovery.

Just keep on eating those Korean vegetables. Sooner or later you'll either give up or get addicted. If you're addicted, head to those Korean restaurants. You'll survive and with some trial and error you'll feel like you are in heaven.

Don't worry too much about finding the right Korean restaurant. Most of them are good if you like the cuisine at all. Do look for regional or unusual dishes, such as goat, Korean porridge, pumpkin, and anything else you don't see on all the other Korean menus. Don't order any single dish that costs more than twenty dollars per person. There is no need to because if you like the cuisine at all, you'll like the cheaper dishes plenty.

If you give up on the vegetables quest, well, you've given up.

At Home with Filipino

There are hardly any Filipino restaurants in the United States, at least relative to the number of Filipinos living here—somewhere between 2 to 4 million. Filipinos are probably the second most numerous Asian ethnic minority in the country, after Chinese. Yet, according to one source, there are only 481 Filipino restaurants in the country; that's about 1 percent as compared to the number of Chinese restaurants, even though there are barely more ethnic Chinese living in the United States and under some counts there are more Filipinos than Chinese in this country.

The Filipino home-cooked food I've eaten has been excellent. And I've heard reliable reports of some good food courts in Filipino shopping malls. Still, Filipinos don't have an especially strong culinary scene compared to many other Asian nations; perhaps this is because they emphasize dining at home or perhaps it is just one of those mysteries of culture. Manila has plenty of restaurants but it is famed for having a lot of non-Filipino fast food. It also seems that Filipino-Americans make the transition to non-Filipino foods quite easily; this may be because of the strong Chinese and Spanish influences on Filipino food provides them with ready gateways to non-Filipino cuisines.

Many of the best Filipino restaurants in the United States are in Los Angeles and San Francisco. The milkfish and braised oxtail—the richer the better—make for good dishes to try. Adobe dishes involve a nice use of soy and vinegar, though they are too sour for some eaters (not me). Restaurant lumpia (the Filipino version of spring rolls) usually aren't fresh enough, so I don't recommend them in most public dining establishments. My favorite Filipino place in northern Virginia is a drugstore counter that surreptitiously serves some Filipino comfort food; I lived next door to it for years before learning their secret.

The bottom line is that Filipino food has many unexplored wonders, so you're best off befriending a Filipino family or traveling in the back parts of the Philippines. The Filipino restaurant scene in the United

States is underdeveloped and I don't see that changing in the next twenty years' time.

There Is No Such Thing as Chinese

According to *Chinese Restaurant News*, a trade journal, there are currently over 43,000 Chinese restaurants in the United States. That makes over three Chinese restaurants for each McDonald's. Beware!

The Chinese will be the first to tell you that there is no such thing as "Chinese food" but rather there are many regional cuisines. Furthermore, there is a different version of "Chinese food" in each country around the world.

Here are some countries that do Chinese food relatively well:

Tanzania
India
Canada
Malaysia

A pretty diverse selection, no? In fact there's a common thread. First, the restaurants are run by Chinese with relatively strong connections to "real" Chinese food, whether it be from China, Taiwan, Hong Kong, or Singapore. Second, those restaurants are either trying to appeal to Chinese customers or at least they are selling to sophisticated customers with a good understanding of Chinese food. It's not about getting the right ingredients; it's about quality checks (customers) and what the restaurant is trying to do in the first place.

The good Chinese restaurants in Dar es Salaam, by the way, are patronized by foreigners, Asians, and aid workers. They're genuinely spicy and they're often fairly authentic. A lot of the best dining out in that city is either Chinese or Indian food, run by Chinese or Indians; Tanzanian food is tasty but you need to find someone to cook it for you. (I had to bribe the maid at my hotel to procure some for me and I loved it.)

Here are some countries that usually do Chinese food poorly:

Italy
Germany
Costa Rica
Argentina
Chile

These countries have a lot of good food of their own, but they fail to meet the two standards listed above. German-Chinese food is bland and starchy and it offers up a lot of meats in uninteresting sauces (what national cuisine does *that* remind you of?). A lot of it is aimed at conservative German eaters. You can find good Chinese restaurants in some of the major German cities—serving the German elite—but most of the Chinese food in Germany is a failure.

Italian Chinese restaurants are likely to treat Chinese noodles as a form of pasta with some soy sauce on it. In the Chinatown in San Jose, Costa Rica, the Chinese immigrants there date mostly from the late nineteenth century. Many seem to have lost all collective memory of Chinese food, though they can do a cross between fried rice and the classic Costa Rican dishes.

Sad to say the United States must be added to the list of countries where the Chinese food is, on the whole, not very good. Latin America is also a weak spot, Panama excluded because Panama City is a crossroads city and it has had significant infusions of Chinese traders and merchants. In this hemisphere, Canada is your best bet, or the suburbs of the major cities in California.

Chinatowns were long ideal for creating low-rent locations for good Chinese food, but the suburban strip mall has become more important over time. Most Chinatowns are now pretty pricey, arranged for tourists to eat Chinese food (San Francisco most of all), or they are simply depopulated because so many Chinese are seeking out the better school systems in the suburbs. And so it is to the suburbs, or peripheral urban concentrations, such as Flushing, Queens, that you must go for good

Chinese food. It is common to see the best ethnic restaurants grouped with mid-level or junky retail. My favorite Chinese restaurant in Virginia—Uncle Liu's Hot Pot—is next to a giant and chaotic thrift store (called Unique), with loudspeaker announcements in Spanish only (it's also next to the Great Wall supermarket). I infer from this that they are paying low rent.

Most Chinese food in the United States is classified into the major categories of Cantonese, Hunan, Sichuan, plus you will see lots of dishes in Imperial, Beijing, and Shanghai styles. For the most part those names are misleading. They do contain real information, but don't assume that a "Hunan" restaurant is serving the actual food of Hunan province. Let's get more specific.

Hunan: Hunan food is some of the most delicious Chinese food and Hunan dishes, such as Chairman Mao's Braised Pork Belly (sometimes called Red Braised Pork on a menu), are some of my favorite culinary creations. Hunan food is itself a complex notion, comprised of regional variants, but overall it can be described as spicy, somewhat oily, and purer and simpler in taste than a lot of Sichuan dishes. By the way, the pork belly dish has that name because it was a reputed favorite of the Chairman and it should be one of the staples of a Chinese cooking repertoire.

That said, over 99 percent of the restaurants labeled "Hunan" in the United States don't serve Chairman Mao's Braised Pork Belly and they don't serve many other Hunan dishes either. "Hunan" usually means the restaurant serves sweet, gloppy dishes with a lot of sauce and little connection to real Chinese food. Once "Cantonese" Chinese restaurants became widespread in the United States, the label "Hunan" was seen as an exotic means of differentiation. Beware.

If you want to try some approximation of real Hunan food, your best bet is either to cook it yourself or go to a legitimate Sichuan restaurant, many of which have some Hunan dishes on the menu.

Sichuan: There are two types of Sichuan restaurants in the United States. The first are just like the Hunan places mentioned above. In fact many of them will be labeled both "Hunan" and "Szechuan," using the earlier spelling of what is now "Sichuan." Again, stay away. The joint label is a bad sign and at best you are getting American Chinese food circa 1986.

The second group of Sichuan restaurants is genuinely Sichuan (more or less) and they are some of the best Chinese restaurants in the United States. They will offer Chinese food cooked for Chinese people and the quality is usually high. I've been to dozens of these places and all have been worth the visit. They can be recognized by their special menus in Chinese (not always present), specials on the blackboard written in Chinese, dan dan noodles, the use of the mala sauce "numbing" flavor in many dishes, use of pork belly, the presentation of black vinegar on the table, the paucity of sauce on the Kung Pao dishes, hot and sour flavors, cold noodles, and their predominantly Chinese clienteles, to name just a few of the differences.

Beyond some of the obvious factors of good chefs and owner dedication, there's an important reason why the Sichuan restaurants can be so good. In part they have Chinese customers but it goes beyond that: a lot of the core ingredients of real Sichuan food travel well. Much of Sichuan food is defined by its spices, including chili peppers but more uniquely Sichuan peppercorns, which are renowned for producing that numbing flavor of some Sichuan dishes. Despite a regulatory scare from a few years back, which threatened to ban the peppercorns from the United States, these little nuggets are readily available here and you can find them in some of the better Chinese groceries. I have a big pile of them in my kitchen and they store perfectly for months or indeed years. I can make a good Sichuan dish any time I want by frying some up, grinding them, and mixing them with some freshly ground black pepper, Chinese wine, and soy sauce, applied to the vegetable of my choice (usually asparagus or green beans), all cooked in peanut oil. You can do a lot more with these peppercorns, but the point is they are delicious outside of Sichuan province and they are also easy to work with. For similar reasons, it is possible to replicate reasonable versions of some key Sichuan dishes in your own kitchen with only a minimum of expertise.

Some of the other best Sichuan dishes involve fresh noodles (such as dan dan noodles), and the noodles can be made fresh and then combined with the spices. Pork belly is important and you can get a properly fatty version of the meat at most Asian supermarkets. Commercially designated bacon will work if you buy one of the better brands. Again, the key ingredients are durable and can survive transportation and freezing.

Sichuan restaurants in the United States aren't perfect and they're missing some key dishes, including lots of fresh Chinese vegetables. Still, they are one of the most reliable food choices in all of the United States. Right now you'll find them mainly in the major Chinese-connected suburban areas or in cities such as New York, Chicago, Los Angeles, and San Francisco; and they represent the most likely future of real Chinese food in the United States. Sichuan food may someday come to Cleveland, if it hasn't already by the time you are reading this.

If you're wondering—not everything in Sichuan restaurants is super spicy. If you just want good (nonspicy) dumplings, your best bet in the United States is to try one of the Sichuan restaurants. The same is true for good Chinese greens or simple tofu dishes, whether or not those dishes are properly Sichuan in nature. This works again because customer selection is such a powerful force. The spicy Sichuan dishes serve as a screen to keep out the less informed customers and the remaining dishes are usually better, whether or not they are spicy or properly Sichuan. One of my local Sichuan restaurants—China Star, in Fairfax, Virginia—does an excellent Lion Head in Hot Pot. It's not Sichuan at all. It's fatty beef and pork in meatball form, cooked in an anise-flavored broth. The spiciness quotient is basically zero and it reminds me a little of what they serve in Sweden (in fact I once brought some Swedes there for the dish and they loved it). The Sichuan restaurant is the place to get it, if only because they're used to cooking for demanding Chinese patrons and of course not all of those patrons want all Sichuan food all of the time.

Knowing what to order in these Sichuan restaurants is tricky. Most of all, often the Sichuan dishes are on an alternative menu for Chinese customers, mostly in English—make sure you demand that menu or all is lost. Many other dishes are written in Chinese on a separate board; ask for a translation or if you are brave just order from it willy-nilly. Tell them you want the food "home style." If you can handle spicy, copy the

Chinese customers around you. If you can't handle spicy, don't show any sign of weakness to the waitstaff or again all will be lost. They won't be willing to bring you any of the good stuff, whether it is spicy or not. This is a case where the Internet is especially useful. Unless you know your way around the menu, or are content to copy the other diners, the best strategy is to come armed in advance with online reports, from yelp.com, chowhound.chow.com, or other online outlets, and follow their advice more or less blindly. The food is different enough that trying to apply what you think you like ("I like chicken better than fish, etc.") probably won't get you far.

I've seen a lot of Sichuan restaurants open up in the last five years and commercially most of them are flourishing. They stay in business and they're often full.

Cantonese: Many Chinese consider Cantonese food to be their most refined cuisine and the one capable of hitting the highest peaks consistently. It arguably does the most to draw upon the wealth of seafood off the Chinese coast and it employs a wide diversity of fresh Chinese vegetables. It's fresh and subtle (or should be) and it requires a care with ingredients and handling comparable to that found in French haute cuisine. Unfortunately, most of that is bad news if you are sitting here in the United States.

As with Sichuan, there are two kinds of Cantonese restaurants in the United States, but neither is especially promising. The first kind of Cantonese restaurant stems from the original invasion of Chinese-American food in the 1960s and afterward. The food in these restaurants is not at all spicy and the proprietors serve up mongrel dishes such as Egg Foo Yung, Chicken Fried Rice, and mediocre Moo Goo Gai Pan. It's not worth rehashing the usual debates about how authentic these places are or whether it matters. It's easier just to call them Sino-American cuisine and declare it a matter of taste. I'll assume you've already made up your mind on these restaurants, one way or the other. They're certainly plentiful in number.

The second kind of Cantonese restaurant tries to replicate some semi-genuine version of real Cantonese food. But usually these establishments succeed to only a limited extent. Cantonese food, from the southern part of China, is so rich in seafood and vegetables that the American version of the product cannot compare. Seafood and vegetables are exactly what the American food supply chain is bad at. So when you combine fine tastes with impeccable raw ingredients, the American version of that idea is going to fall flat. The American food scene simply isn't good for reproducing the wonders of Cantonese food. If I want good Cantonese food, without leaving the country, my best bet is to seek out one of the expensive places in a major U.S. city, such as New York or Los Angeles. If I pay enough for the fresh seafood, I can get it, but it doesn't feel like much of a bargain. So I tend to leave Cantonese food be, while craving it often and feeling frustrated as a result.

Dim sum is one form of Cantonese food that is usually affordable and at least possibly good. Most dim sum relies neither on fresh vegetables nor perfect quality seafood. As a result, it can be pretty good in North America. For my taste dim sum reaches some of its highest peaks in Canada and in Vancouver in particular. In any case, dim sum is one good way to sample the delights of Cantonese cuisine while avoiding some of the pitfalls of the U.S. food supply chain.

When you do go to the semi-genuine Cantonese restaurants, your best bet is to order the casseroles, which you sometimes can find at non-Cantonese Chinese restaurants as well. A typical Chinese casserole might blend turnip and beef, or cook oysters, or mix tofu and seafood. The flavors meld together and at their best these casseroles offer the same kind of deep, hearty satisfaction that you'll find in some of the food from southwestern France. For the casseroles, freshness matters a bit less and the blending of the flavors, and the textures, matter more. Cantonese casseroles in the United States aren't an ideal choice, but a lot of them are pretty good. It's one way to overcome some of the limitations of Cantonese food in this country.

You and Your Chinese Takeout

Of course those are hardly the only Chinese regional cuisines, but they are the main ones you will find promoted in the United States. You'll find a fair number of Taiwanese restaurants and on the whole they are above average, even if they don't serve up Taiwanese food per se. They're cooking a mix of Chinese dishes, from various regions, for a partially Taiwanese clientele. Your best bet for Imperial dishes is to go to a somewhat older, fancy, and expensive Chinese restaurant, like Shun Lee Palace in Manhattan. As for the delicious Muslim food of the Chinese west, every now and then these restaurants pop up, most likely in California or New York, so catch them while you can. You'll see a different vision for Chinese food (if you can even still call it that), organized around bread rather than rice and rich with scallions, cumin, and lamb. Overall, if you encounter any other form of Chinese food you haven't heard about or seen around, give it a try. Odds are that it is aimed at a specialized audience and that augurs well for the quality of the food.

No matter which regional Chinese cuisine you are faced with, one of the biggest no-no's is Chinese buffet. Indian buffet works relatively well because many of the foods are in any case cooked for long periods of time at low temperatures; you can think of the heated buffet as continuing this longer-running cooking process. Furthermore some central Indian ingredients, such as ground lamb, respond quite well to long periods of simmering. But a lot of the best Chinese dishes are flash-cooked rapidly over high heat. They should be served and eaten immediately once they are ready (for this same reason it makes sense to eat Chinese food more rapidly than say Indian food, although most dining guides won't tell you this, for fear of making you feel lacking in manners). Chinese food that has been sitting is often Chinese food that has become soggy. I have known exceptions, but as a general rule of thumb a Chinese place that offers a buffet is probably not worth eating at. It's a sign they don't care about their food or their reputation.

Sometimes, even when it seems you have no good choices, and all the circumstances are operating against you, there is a way forward because you are convinced, as I am, that every meal counts.

When all else fails, I have one important tip: *With some effort, you stand a chance of turning just about any Chinese restaurant into a good one.* That's right, I said *any.* You can't turn it into a good, all-purpose

Chinese restaurant, but you might manage to get a good dish or two from them. Here's how.

Overall, Chinese restaurants are some of the least "safe" dining establishments. That is, if you stumble upon a bad Chinese restaurant—which is frighteningly easy to do—it can be really, really bad. It can mean your worst nightmare of deep fried whatever, if you can even tell, dipped in a sweet orange sauce with the color of liquid Cheetos and the consistency of goop.

The funny thing about these bad Chinese restaurants is you can find them virtually anywhere. You can find them in small towns and you can find them where there's nowhere else to eat. You can find them in the inner city and in midtown Manhattan.

But, when you are stuck somewhere and looking for good food, you're conflicted. I suspect you've already had some of these run-ins with the orange and with the goop. But still, you need a meal and you see a "Chinese" restaurant in front of your eyes. You see an ethnic restaurant and you know that you're otherwise marooned. You're tempted. You think: "Isn't there some chance that it's *real* Chinese food?" Okay, maybe not real Chinese food like they eat in Chengdu or Guangzhou but still something a bit authentic and also tasty?" You peer inside and you see Chinese waitstaff, feel a connection to China, and wonder how the culinary heritage of the home country could be so totally violated and denied. I know people who try this strategy and usually they end up burned.

For such cases I suggest this rule of thumb: *Every Chinese restaurant can be a good one.* That restaurant need only have a Chinese cook on staff and that describes virtually every Chinese restaurant in the United States (and just about any country). But how can you get that Chinese cook to make actual Chinese food for you?

I once faced this dilemma in a town called Bridgewater, Virginia. I was driving back home, from North Carolina, I believe, and I was hungry. I stopped in Bridgewater mainly because I couldn't find anywhere else. A former Ph.D. student of mine ended up in Bridgewater for a few years; he called it a "backwater" and complained about the food. It is a town of about five thousand people and there is no major city nearby. I was a little curious to see what the place was like.

As I pulled into the center of town I saw a Chinese restaurant—or should I say a "Chinese" restaurant? Or should I say Chinese "restaurant"? It was more like a place to sit down with a counter than a true restaurant for dining. Like many small-town Chinese food places, most of their business is food takeout. I didn't do a comprehensive scan of the area, but it was the only ethnic place I noticed. Sadly, I didn't see any barbecue around. So I went in and glanced at the menu—unsurprisingly unimpressive. Still, I thought . . .

The rule here is simple: You need to communicate with the Chinese cook and impress him. The restaurant wasn't busy and I asked to speak to the cook; the waiter produced a guy from the back who was plausibly the cook. I repeated to him a simple incantation, at least ten times: "Ma Po Tofu, like you eat it." Every now and then I would toss in, perhaps fruitlessly, "real Chinese food" or "family style" or "Sichuan" or "spicy." Of those phrases, I believe "family style" is the best to use.

Those words were not randomly chosen. First, I knew that while they had tofu on the menu, the phrase "Ma Po Tofu" is not uttered often in Bridgewater by non-Chinese. I even tried to say it the tonal way the Chinese do and while I failed badly perhaps he noticed the effort. Basically I was signaling that I was familiar with some version of real Chinese food. The very fact that I asked to speak with the chef also let on that I cared about the meal. I was guessing that not many residents of Bridgewater pursued this approach.

Second, I figured the restaurant probably used bad ingredients. How many people in Bridgewater were demanding high-quality Niman Ranch free-range pork? I didn't want to go near their shrimp. Maybe their chicken was okay. The beef was unlikely to impress. But—what actually can they do to tofu? It's a block of stuff and you can refrigerate it for weeks. Probably they can't ruin it. The dish also comes with ground pork and ground pork stands up to abuse or low quality better than does sliced pork. It doesn't have to be soft and a lot of its flavor is drowned out in the sauce and the spice. I can make an okay Ma Po Tofu using the ground pork from the Safeway and I figured their ground pork was no worse (or better) than that.

And so I ordered. The chef seemed happy to receive a personal request. And when my Ma Po Tofu came out, it was really quite good. It wasn't "awesome" but it was better than the median Chinese meal in the far more cosmopolitan northern Virginia, or for that matter Manhattan. It was yummy. And so Bridgewater, Virginia, has—if you play your cards right—at least one good Chinese restaurant.

7

Another Agricultural
Revolution, Now

J uan Camilo Ayala, a Mexican farmer living in the village of San
Agustin Oapan, has been a corn farmer for his entire life. He gets
up in the morning, walks out to his cornfields, and works those
fields with an ox and plow, sometimes a burro. He doesn't own any other
agricultural machines, and in his early sixties he still worries about the
harvest and spending the day in the fields.

He has highly informed opinions about when it is going to rain. Most
of his village's fiestas, one way or another, have something to do with the
rain. A bad rain means not enough food and Juan Camilo has plenty of
memories of when people in the village used to starve.

That is a tough life. Still, without corn, Juan Camilo's family, and
indeed his entire civilization, would not exist in the first place. Juan
Camilo's family eats the farmed corn every day of the year, or at least
every day they are at home. The corn is not sold but rather it is brought
into the home, where it can be stored in dried form for months or even
years in a domestic granary. It is ground in a machine, mixed with lime
(the mineral, not the fruit) and water, and fried on a griddle to make
delicious blue corn tortillas. Before the 1920s, a pounder and stone base

(*metate*) were used instead of the machine, but the machine freed up a lot of the women's time. A mother, grandmother, or daughter still tends the live fire.

At least two civilizations were built on corn. The first is what we now call the Aztecs, but more generally covered a large part of Latin, Central, and North America. When Cortés and the Spaniards visited the New World, they were awed by the cities and the canals. They also encountered some of the world's most advanced agriculture. The inhabitants of Mexico didn't have so many large domestic animals to eat, because for instance they lacked cows and pigs. Nonetheless, they had tomatoes, corn, chilies, beans, squash, and potatoes, all of which were raised, bred, and cultivated scientifically. Mixed with small amounts of meat, this was a sufficient diet.

The second civilization based on corn is our own. Without corn (not to mention the potato), the Industrial Revolution in England might not have happened. A slower agricultural revolution preceded the industrial breakthroughs of the nineteenth century and formed their foundation. Because we could first grow more food, it was possible for a lot of workers to leave farming and try commerce, science, and engineering, all of which led to invention. Following the discovery of the New World and its crops, corn helped European economies move from subsistence to slow rates of economic progress.

Even today, numerous food products are based on corn, one way or another, for better or worse. Americans pioneered the use of corn syrup as an ingredient and preservative in Coca-Cola, candy, ketchup, and commercial ice cream. Corn syrup provides a feeling of body in foods, soups, and liquids; it helps foods hold their shape, it prevents discoloring, it binds ingredients together, and it keeps moisture content stable. Corn in various forms also goes into our mayonnaise, soap, baby food, chewing gum, canned and frozen vegetables, beer and wine, crackers and breads, processed meats, cough drops, toothpaste, lipstick, shaving cream, shoe polish, detergents, tobacco, rayon, tanned leather, rubber tires, urethane foam, and embalming fluid, among other substances.

Yet corn did not originally appear in nature, without human intervention. The closest "natural" plant to corn is *teosinte*, a hardy Central American grass with small coblike seed heads; it doesn't look or taste much like corn. Over the generations, Nahua farmers in what we now call Mexico bred corn to be hardier, tastier, and easier to grow. Corn as we know it is a product of genetic engineering, inasmuch as farmers intentionally altered the genetic composition of *teosinte* to produce a cultivated crop that is substantially different and which would not have arisen in nature. Thus corn is a product of human ingenuity, as is the domesticated dog (some say dogs deserve more credit than that—perhaps they improved themselves as much as we improved them). The original breeding of corn took place right in Juan Camilo's home region, near the Río Balsas, between Mexico City and Acapulco.

The breeding of corn occurred over generations and from genetic tests it is identified as coming between 8,990 and 8,610 years before the birth of Christ. Juan Camilo is a corn farmer who is the descendant of the farmers and scientific breeders who created corn.

The history of corn is one of the most significant stories in human history—and the Nahua farmers who invented corn through selective breeding, over the generations, were some of the most valuable human scientists, ever. In terms of world-historic importance, they put Einstein to shame.

The Great Green Revolutions

You can think of Juan Camilo as still living in the midst of one of the world's earliest green revolutions. The final word in the name of his village, San Agustin Oapan, means in Nahuatl, the language of the Aztecs, "where the green maize stalk abounds." I'll call that the first Green Revolution.

The second Green Revolution came in the middle of the nineteenth century (discussed in chapter 2). During that breakthrough, the food supply network grew longer and suddenly was knit together by an extensive collection of steam- and electricity-driven machines. Circa 1929, W. P. Hedden wrote the triumphant book *How Great Cities Are Fed*, recounting how large-scale cities were being fed and by an ever smaller number of farmers. Suddenly transportation and machinery were paramount. Hedden traced the movement from foodstuffs from the American countryside to New York City, and his account shows how far the new world of food had moved away from local production and sale. To most of us this tale sounds a bit old, but for a lot of the world it is quite new or still has not yet arrived.

The North American food revolution worked like this. In the case of oranges, a carload would be shipped from California to Chicago and then turned over to the Erie Railroad at the Harbor Belt Line in Hammond, Indiana. In the classification yard at Hammond, the Erie Company segregated railroad cars according to their contents and organized the appropriate ongoing trains. The length of trains was determined by destination and the grades they will encounter passing through the Appalachian Mountains. En route, the railroad cars would be kept cold by periodic stops at re-icing platforms; at each stop a telegraph would update a New York City handling agent. The train would arrive in Croxton, New Jersey, about three miles west of the Hudson River. Since the trains would not average more than twenty-five miles per hour, the trip would take days. Upon arrival, the cars would again be classified into different categories and further icing might occur. The items for immediate delivery would be dispatched to the waterfront.

When the train arrived, the consignees in Manhattan decided whether they wish to sell their commodities, receive delivery, or hold them temporarily in the rail yard. The appropriate information was again exchanged by telegraph, at which point a switch engine brought some cars to the Hudson River waterfront. The relevant train cars were then pushed onto a pontoon bridge and onto floating car ferries. Tugboats pulled these car ferries across the Hudson, typically to prespecified piers. Usually the first floats arrived at about seven in the evening. Groups of workmen met the cars and unloaded them with hand trucks, leaving the train cars on the float. All of the unloading would be completed by seven A.M., at which point the fruits were auctioned. Buyers carted away their hauls by both horse trucks and motor trucks to the city's food markets.

Except for the use of the horse trucks at the end, no step of this process would have been possible in the first half of the nineteenth century. It's also very different from the supply chain that Juan Camilo grew up with—simply, bring the corn by burro to his home, which is less than a mile from the fields.

This later and second Green Revolution reached Juan Camilo only in the last ten years. Today, if you visit Juan Camilo, and you're hungry, and you can't wait for them to make more blue corn tortillas, they'll pull out a packet of noodles from the refrigerator and heat it on the stove with some water. The noodles come from a store in Iguala, the nearest city to Juan's village. Those noodles don't taste as good as the blue corn tortillas, but it reflects a new world where the family will never starve, not even when the skies are dry and the harvest is bad. As recently as the 1970s, extreme hunger was a common occurrence in the village. Today, the young people are getting taller rapidly but the older people are still very short. The women have a lot more free time, in part because they are not making blue corn tortillas all day long, yet still the tortillas are available.

Another Green Revolution, the one associated with the formal name, originated from Norman Borlaug, and it too arrived first in central Mexico. I call this the third Green Revolution.

Borlaug was an American scientist of Norwegian background who became fascinated with maximizing the yield from agricultural crops. He found himself working in Central Mexico, as part of a Rockefeller Foundation program to improve agricultural yields. Starting in the mid-1940s, Borlaug developed several major breakthroughs, including rust-resistant wheat crops, "shuttle breeding" programs that accelerate crop engineering, and stronger and higher-yielding wheat plants. Rather than hoarding this knowledge, Borlaug tried to spread it to as many Mexican farmers as possible. And unlike some of the Mexican farm managers, Borlaug gladly went into the fields to work and "got his hands dirty," rather than drawing up plans from his office.

Borlaug's Green Revolution started in the 1940s, but it wasn't the work of a sole genius, toiling away in the fields without external support. Borlaug was indeed a genius but his efforts were embedded in an era that saw repeated improvements in crop yields over many decades, based on the idea of breeding stronger and hardier plants. While U.S. agricultural productivity had been rising for a long time, the productivity acceleration in agriculture took a big leap upward in the 1940s. Between 1880 and 1940, agricultural productivity in this country rose at the rather modest rate of about 1 percent a year. After World War II, the trend rate of growth jumps to 2.8 percent annually and this can be traced back to advances starting in the mid-1930s. This progress was part of a broader trend toward more and better fertilizer, greater use for mechanized vehicles, better crops and hybrids, larger farms, and the application of large-scale businesslike practices to growing food. Borlaug's Green Revolution made some specific advances in manipulating genetic material through cross-breeding but more generally it was the culmination of a longer process of American technological refinement, adapted for use in some of the world's poorer countries.

In the early 1960s, Borlaug started collaborating with agricultural scientists in other countries, most notably India and Pakistan. During 1969–1970, 55 percent of the wheat hectares sown in Pakistan used Mexican or Mexican-derived varieties of wheat; in India it was 35 percent. Domestic farmers rapidly became advocates of the new and more productive crops, and political leaders in India and Pakistan allowed the changes to proceed. By 1970, the countries showing significant increases in cereal production were Afghanistan, Ceylon (now Sri Lanka), Indonesia, Iran, Kenya, Morocco, Malaysia, Thailand, Tunisia, and Turkey. Later in the 1970s, Borlaug encouraged the Chinese to move to a more productive variety of hybrid rice, which rapidly increased agricultural productivity.

The result of these innovations was millions of lives saved and millions of children saved from the unpleasant pains of hunger. Since 1950, global population has increased by more than 150 percent, and over the same period of time the real price of foodstuffs has declined about 75 percent. As late as the 1970s, before Borlaug's Green Revolution was commonly understood, it was a standard prediction that the world was facing a future of mass starvation. While hungry people remain, the world is feeding many more people than ever before.

In China, the 1959–1961 famine led to more than thirty million unnecessary deaths, or more than forty-five million deaths, by the count of Frank Dikötter, a historian of the period. Today almost everyone in China is well fed. This isn't just because of technology. The Chinese also moved away from a murderous dictatorship and instituted a better system of property rights in agriculture. Unlike during Chairman Mao's tenure, you can make a lot of money by running a better farm in today's China.

This progress represents much less of a burden on the land than it might seem, and probably it has relieved pressure on the land. In the United States, the percentage of the land that is harvested remained roughly constant during the twentieth century and even declined by a few percent. If not for technological progress, to meet growing food demands, we would have needed to harvest an additional area equal to the United States east of the Mississippi River, but that turned out not to be necessary. At the global scale, this progress was less intense; but starting from 1950, global affluence increased by a factor of 6.99 while global cropland increased by a factor of only 1.32. Globally, cropland used per capita peaked in 1930, which means we are feeding more people and using less land for each person to do so.

The mechanism here is simple: agribusiness wants—ever so desperately and greedily—to economize on costs. Think of there being two kinds of costs: costs borne by the company and costs borne by broader society, such as pollution. Sometimes the corporate drive for profit backfires, and that causes agricultural companies to impose large costs on society, such as when they emit too much pollution. But very often when the companies economize on private costs it also means that they will economize on social costs too. This coincidence is easiest to see when it comes to land use. Land costs a lot of money, and so agribusiness tries to use as little land as possible. The net result is an environmental boon:

A lot of America has been reforested and this footprint of agribusiness is shrinking rather than rising.

To put all this in broader context, there are plenty of contemporary critiques of commercialized agriculture, big business, and new technologies such as genetically modified organisms. In all these heated debates, the balanced perspective is too often lost. The broader history shows that technological progress and agricultural commercialization have brought major and lasting improvements to the lives of billions. For all of its problems, the agribusiness *platform,* as I have called the food infrastructure of the modern world, is one to build upon and improve rather than throw away.

Food Production and Obesity

We're not going to solve obesity problems by going back to the food world of 1890. It may sound simplistic, but we need more self-control. That is a sort of innovation on the part of the consumer. The segments of American society that have the least problems with obesity are the upper-income classes, and they are the individuals who are the most firmly embedded in our new world of diverse, plentiful food. They are the most likely to travel, to try new foods, to read books on food, and to try to eat better food. Both Asians and Asian-Americans are groups especially likely to take strong or even obsessive interests in dining out, cooking, and food quests. Again, even though their weights rise over the generations if they move to the United States, they are not the group most prone to obesity, if anything the contrary.

The obesity problem has come about because imperfect self-control has met up with the modern food world, and some marketing and taste improvements get a lot of us to eat more than we ought to and to eat the wrong things. A lot of features of our daily food environment, in the United States, encourage overeating. Yet workable anti-obesity practices exist. Are they, circa 2011, compatible with an extreme love of food? Absolutely.

The question is how we will get ourselves to show some restraint—it probably won't be coercion or taxes. A study by three economists looked at the notion of placing a 100 percent tax on all foods considered to be unhealthy. The expected result would be "BMI [Body Mass Index] is reduced by less than 0.2 points, which is less than 1 percent of average BMI and just 13 percent of the increase in BMI that occurred from 1982 to 1996 alone." In other words, the tax isn't going to make a big difference for weight loss, not even cutting off 1 percent of average BMI. Intuitively, that is because food, including bad food, is already pretty cheap and it doesn't take up a big part of our budgets. A big tax on bad food wouldn't force us to cut back so much. You have to eat something, and Frito's corn chips will be there or, if not, something else pretty cheap—and bad for you—in its stead. In other words, the change will have to come from us and it will more likely come from a stronger interest in good food than the contrary.

I do understand that addressing the obesity problem won't be easy and we should resist the temptation to give glib answers. Still, we should be looking forward toward an age of stronger and better consumer innovation, rather than looking backward to an age of more expensive food.

My shopping experiment at Great Wall also has caused me to rethink the obesity problem. A few Latinos and foodies aside, hardly anyone non-Chinese shops there, yet I believe that exclusive shopping at Great Wall, for years, would cause most non-Chinese to lose considerable weight, or at least give them a good chance of losing weight (remember my indifference toward the salty shrimp chips?). Yet no one is trying that method. It's not that would-be dieters are trying Great Wall, but through weakness of will relapsing into the trips to Safeway and attacks on chocolate chip cookies. No one is trying at all, even though Great Wall customers could be considered walking advertisements for the store as a useful diet.

And so I wonder if a lot of American weight gains stem from people simply deciding that they are willing to weigh more, if they get to eat more of certain foods. Being overweight in a particular way, and through a particular process, is an option that did not always exist in times past.

And when it did, we often saw evidence—obvious from a lot of seventeenth and eighteenth century portraits—that the wealthy took pride in their ability to carry extra pounds. Today we have a culture where well-educated rich people criticize the poor for not sharing their preferences or for not being aesthetic enough, by the standards of rich people of course. I do think a lot of obesity is a real social and health care problem, but also a lot of the fuss may well be a kind of social and food snobbery. You and I don't have to agree with the decision of another person to tolerate a greater number of pounds, but if it really is a decision—and in many cases I believe it is—we're not going to fight and win a war against it.

Obesity aside, what are the main food problems in the world today and how do they fit into the idea that modern agribusiness is a pretty useful and effective structure?

Our Biggest Food Problem

Sadly, malnutrition (not obesity) remains the biggest global food problem by far. If it's not starvation, severe hunger remains common in some parts of the world. It is suggested that there are more than one billion malnourished people in the world and almost one billion undernourished people. While I take these numbers to be approximate, and possibly an exaggeration, the problem would be a very real one at half that size.

What are the causes of these maladies? Usually it boils down to lack of wealth, lack of infrastructure, some bad government policies, and also lack of democracy. The countries where there are famines are always countries that do not build their food institutions on top of a well-functioning agribusiness platform.

Overpopulation is overrated as a cause of starvation. Usually the worst problems occur in rural areas, not in cities. Africa, the poorest region of the world, is also not very densely populated by global standards. Population concentrations make it easier for the very poor to find some kind of job, it is easier to beg, it is easier for charity to operate, and more densely populated areas are easier to reach and politically more difficult to ignore, due to the greater presence of media and the greater number of onlookers.

A lot of hunger comes in hard-to-reach areas. It comes during wartime or other catastrophes. Well-functioning roads, combined with freedom of movement for goods and people, helps bring people together with food supplies. It is easier for both the food to come in or for the people to leave in search of food. A lot of times the infrastructure barriers are political rather than economic. For instance the transportation of food may require payments to local warlords, as has been the case during conflict periods in Afghanistan and Somalia.

Most of the world's hunger-related migration in the eighteenth century was from crowded cities to the free land in the New World, or later in Australia and New Zealand. Free land was very important then in part because many cities had become cesspools of infectious diseases. Today, the diseases are mostly gone (in the wealthy countries), the economic infrastructure of cities works better, and so most hunger-related migration is to more densely populated areas, including the mass migration from Western China to the Chinese cities in the east of the country. Migration has been directed at cities since at least the late nineteenth century. For instance, given how much land there is in Australia, it is remarkable that it is one of the most urbanized nations in the world with cities full of first- or second-generation immigrants.

Democracy helps avoid outright famine, as democratic governments are more likely to rush aid to stricken regions; Nobel economist Amartya Sen is famous for making this point. Dying babies make for bad press releases and lost elections. That is a good reason to favor democracy, if we needed another reason. Still, when it comes to hunger rather than outright famine, democracy per se isn't as effective as one might think. India has perhaps more hungry people than any country in the world today, and it has been a democracy since the late 1940s. Democracy works best at fixing hunger when it is allied with a lot of capitalism, a lot of wealth, and a lot of infrastructure and technological progress in agriculture. India is growing in these areas but still has a long way to go. Democracy alone will not get the job done.

After all, democratic governments make bad policy decisions all the time. When a famine arrives, it's pretty common for governments to institute price controls, crack down on food speculators, and in general penalize rather than reward food distribution networks. It may seem that high food prices are unfair in light of a famine, and indeed they are. Nonetheless, legally controlled food prices are far worse, and the result of that policy is to take food off the market altogether. Curing famines through price controls has never been a successful strategy in human history. In the case of the Chinese famines of the early 1960s, or the recent North Korean famines, tyrannical communist regimes simply refused to allow food markets to function at all.

Finally, a longer-term source of food problems is relatively low productivity gains in agriculture. The supply of food grew much faster than the world's population from the years 1970 to 1990, in part because of Norman Borlaug's Green Revolution. But since that time, agricultural gains have come at a slower rate. In particular agricultural productivity has not spread to Africa at the same rate as it spread during the Green Revolution. Since 1990, food production has grown at a slower rate than has population growth. In India, food productivity gains have slowed dramatically.

But it's not just India and Africa where the problem lies. Even American agriculture is growing in productivity at much slower rates than it used to. The skyrocketing increases in crop yields that were common in the second half of the twentieth century just aren't there anymore. And it's not clear when they are coming back.

For instance, during the period 1949–1990, new technological innovations (as distinct from simply sending more machines or more laborers to work the land) boosted agricultural productivity by an average of 2.02 percent a year. From 1990 to 2002, this same rate of improvement fell to 0.97 percent, less than half of the previous rate of gain. Investments in agricultural R&D have been falling since the 1980s, and a closer look shows that falling R&D numbers are more problematic than you might think; estimates suggest that 35 to 70 percent of agricultural R&D is directed at "breaking even"—protecting crops from various disasters—rather than moving forward and achieving new gains. Erratic weather, ranging from storms to droughts to heat and cold waves, has compounded these underlying problems.

Jonathan A. Foley, a food and environmental researcher at the University of Minnesota, put it well: "We've doubled the world's food production several times before in history, and now we have to do it one more time. The last doubling is the hardest. It is possible, but it's not going to be easy."

This productivity slowdown is by far the most important food problem in the world today and yet you hardly ever hear foodies talk about it. We, as foodies, are too often overly concerned about our own consumption patterns and we lose sight of the bigger picture. For all of its altruistic cloaking, maybe that's a kind of narcissism. We focus on possible mistakes of commission—eating asparagus that was flown in—and don't spend enough time worrying about unseen omissions, in other words what doesn't happen, which in this case means slower technological progress. It hardly sounds sexy, or refined, or even interesting to talk about "declining gains in agricultural productivity," but that topic should be on the mind of the everyday foodie because it is an everyday problem in today's world. It's the missing concept in today's discourse on food.

The result of these slowdowns is that food markets are experiencing some special problems. In particular, headlines declare food prices reaching new highs and suggesting that food prices are contributing to political unrest, for instance in Egypt. The political unrest is not always bad (Egypt needed a new government), but of course the high food prices are bad.

Economist Robert J. Samuelson has labeled this "the great food crunch." The first great food crunch of modern times came in 2007–2008 and the second came in 2010–2011. To give an example, a lot of countries, such as in the Middle East, import more than half of their wheat. Over the course of eight months during 2010–2011, grain prices more than doubled. A typical poor household spends most of its money on food and in many countries such a household uses bread as a staple of consumption, so that's a significant burden. The years 2007–2008 saw big rice price spikes too, and as I am writing this in the summer of 2011, there is a chance that the pattern will be repeated in the second great food crunch.

There are some special reasons why these recent food crises erupted, even though the overall level of starvation has fallen.

Think of the supply and demand for food as a race between two quantities. On one side of the scale is how effectively human beings produce food with advanced technology. That capacity is growing all the time, albeit at varying rates; and, as mentioned above, with a recent slowdown. On the other side of the scale is how many people are demanding food and with how much income. Poor people eat more rice, lentils, and bread. Richer people eat more meat and, indirectly, consume more grain, as the cows must be fed.

When the first side of the scale is progressing rapidly—the new technologies—food prices fall. It is easier to grow lots more, which increases supply in the marketplace and lowers prices. When the second side of the scale—demand—is progressing rapidly, food prices tend to rise because demands are going up. If food prices are going up, one possibility is that the trend of rising demand is outpacing supply. And that is exactly what is happening in today's world: the demand for wheat, rice, corn, and soybeans—and meat—is rising faster than their supply.

Looking back at American history, the growth of the United States meant a lot more people were buying a lot more food. But still food prices fell. America brought path-breaking food technologies to the market, including hybrid corn and effective mechanized tractors. International Harvester was an American company.

Today a lot of countries are engaged in what is called "catch-up growth." A Chinese peasant who used to grow rice now works in a factory in Shanghai, earns a lot more money, and eats a lot more meat. He is catching up to the living standards of the wealthier countries. Yet while China is getting richer at about 10 percent a year, the average for its last thirty years, it is not growing 10 percent more food every year. Their manufacturing productivity has grown more rapidly than has their agricultural productivity. In other words, Chinese demands push up the price of food, yet without bringing a new Green Revolution comparable to what Norman Borlaug did. The odds are that some Chinese will eventually make such an agricultural breakthrough, but in the meantime global food prices will be higher than usual. It's not just that China is making no major new agriculture technologies, but fundamentally new agricultural productivity improvements have slowed down since at least the 1990s, another kind of "great stagnation."

The problem is worse because the United States is increasing its demands for foodstuffs through the use of biofuels, most of all corn-based ethanol. To put ethanol in gasoline, the government has to mandate that the private sector buys up a lot of corn and turns it into gasoline. This is a popular program in Iowa, and thus it is popular with many politicians, but it is reviled by both economists and environmentalists. It costs a lot more money than does traditional gasoline, once the cost of the subsidy is included. Sadly, it doesn't even make the environment a cleaner place. The energy expended in growing and processing the corn is an environmental cost too, just as traditional gasoline would be; for instance the nitrogen-based fertilizers used for the corn are major polluters. Ethanol subsidies are a lose-lose policy on almost every front, except for the corn farmers and some politicians, especially those who care about the Iowa political caucuses.

The biggest losers of course are the people in poor countries who now face higher prices for food. For millions of them, it is literally a matter of life and death and yet we proceed with ethanol for no good reason. It is a sign of our political dysfunctionality. During the second half of 2010, the price of corn in the United States rose 73 percent and much of that increase is attributed to biofuels; about 40 percent of the U.S. corn crop now goes into biofuels. It has thrown millions of people around the world back into food poverty. China had the good sense to ban grain-based biofuels in 2007, although now the Chinese are turning to cassava.

Food supply problems are worse in the stagnant and poorer regions.

Let's say you live in Egypt, where the population has risen from just under twenty-six million in 1960 to over eighty million today. Yet unlike China, Egypt is not so much richer than it was a few decades ago. There are higher global prices for foodstuffs, and the richer Chinese and certainly the Americans have the means to afford it. Most of the Egyptians have a harder time of it. Some countries today are caught in the middle: They have not grown rapidly enough to keep up with the higher prices caused by the demands from the rapidly growing nations, such as China.

It will seem to some countries—again citing Egypt—that food is a more pressing problem than before, and indeed it is. But it's wrong to conclude that food problems are worse overall in the world, because they're not. The problems of Egypt arise precisely because overall the food situation is getting better. The tightness in Egypt is the mirror side of the prosperity of China and the higher global demands for meat, combined with relatively stagnant technologies for production.

One solution is that Egypt undertakes reforms and starts growing its economy more rapidly. Possibly they've already started along this path, although as I write the end result of the democratizing reforms in Egypt remains an open question. But if Egypt does succeed in improving its economy, the country could better afford higher grain prices. The next step would be reforming the remaining nations that lag in terms of economic growth.

What else can be done? The second "great food crunch" may be over by the time you are reading this chapter, but it is likely to recur. In part, the United States and Europe have not come up with a big new agricultural breakthrough. And in part, many countries, such as large parts of Africa, India, and the Middle East, are failing to make much headway with their agricultural productivity and so we remain in a vulnerable position.

A lot of agricultural markets in the poorer countries have too much politics, and too much politics of the wrong kind. There is often an unholy mix of subsidies to domestic foodstuffs, subsidies to water, and subsidies to energy, creating a vicious cycle of broken food markets, which also damages the local environment. Arguably government policies toward agriculture are the worst and most ill-conceived set of government policies in the entire world.

Why do they grow water-hungry crops like bananas in Egypt and qat in Yemen when water is in short supply? In part the Egyptians grow the bananas at home to protect the native farmers, and in part because they don't trust other countries to deliver foodstuffs in time of a war or crisis. But how can you grow all those bananas in a desert? How can Yemen grow so much qat—an intoxicating leaf chewed by most Yemenis—that it consumes 10 percent of their GDP? Governments subsidize irrigation to keep these crops going. Water is overused and water tables are being depleted, especially in Yemen, where it is estimated that Yemen will run out of economically viable water in less than ten years, right around when its supplies of oil give out. Pumping all that water requires a lot of energy and so Yemen subsidizes energy too, as a means of subsidizing water. Domestic agriculture, water use, and energy use are oversubsidized in many developing countries and the result is an economic and environmental mess.

From 1980 to 1992, Saudi Arabia boosted its wheat production by a factor of 29, which made the country the world's sixth-largest wheat exporter in the world. When all the water and other subsidies are taken into account, this wheat was produced at a cost of about $500 a ton. During that same time, the international market price for wheat averaged about $120 a ton. The total cost was at least $85 billion. Toward this foolish end, the Saudi government wasted 300 billion cubic meters of water, which is equal to about six years' flow of the Nile River into Egypt. Most of this water usage was nonrenewable.

The best reform is to have fewer subsidies and more trade across borders. Ideally the relatively water-rich countries of the Middle East—Syria, Lebanon, and Turkey—should be selling water to the rest of the region but for political reasons that remains a distant prospect. In the meantime, note that you don't have to sell water by putting it on a truck or ship and sending it across the Mediterranean. *Sometimes the easiest way to trade water is inside a tomato.* A market in food is, in reality, also a market in water.

That's one reason (we'll see more reasons in the next chapter) why locavores have such a misguided philosophy. It overlooks that some parts of the world are running out of water and that trade of food—often long-distance trade—is the best or indeed the only real answer to that problem. Very often, trading across a distance solves more environmental problems than it creates.

Another recommendation is to spread modern agribusiness to more parts of the world. For all the talk about India as a great economic power on the rise, most Indian farming is still done by hand on a small scale. Indian agricultural productivity is low, as agriculture employs more than half of the Indian population, but it makes up only 15 percent of India's output of goods and services. The Indian economy is growing at a rate of 8 or 9 percent a year, but agriculture in India is growing at about 3 percent a year. That's a problem. It also means that the Indian economy is a lot more of a mess than many people realize.

In India, very little modern, large-scale agribusiness is allowed, mostly because of the Indian government and its labyrinthine system of laws and regulations. There are restrictions on transporting, storing, and marketing agricultural commodities, there are limits on the size of agri-business firms, there have been limits on foreign domestic investment, there are legal limits on efficient foreign retailers, and there are high taxes on processed products such as foods. You won't find a lot of mechanized corporate farms operating on a large scale to produce the cheapest food possible. Indian law makes it very difficult for large corporations to farm the land directly; other laws make it very difficult to assemble and maintain large holdings of land; usually a farm is capped at 15 to 20 hectares. The result of all these restrictions is that agriculture remains the most backward major sector of India's economy, and the rate of investment in Indian agriculture is barely increasing.

This underdevelopment shows up in the poverty figures: nearly half of the children in India, age five or lower, suffer from malnutrition. It's not just about the suffering of these children. Over the longer term, from the malnutrition, they will grow up less healthy, less intelligent, and less able. In other words, even if the food were to come tomorrow, the fallout from these problems would be with India for decades. This hunger is the number one food tragedy today, and to fix it we need more and better agribusiness. Circa 2011, food prices are rising more rapidly in India than just about anywhere else in the world.

Solving the Problem of Hunger

The closer one looks at India, the more one appreciates agribusiness. Let's take foreign direct investment, or in other words when foreigners try to put money into businesses in India. Before 1991, this was hardly allowed at all, but even after the 1991 reforms hardly any foreign investment flowed into agriculture. There is no doubt that foreign companies have superior and more productive techniques, but it's simply not worth entering the Indian market. Until very recently, foreign direct investment still was prohibited for retail trading of agricultural products and most forms of agricultural production. As of April 1, 2011, India allows 100 percent foreign direct investment in seeds, plantation, horticulture, and cultivation of vegetables. Furthermore in 2009 Wal-Mart outposts started opening in India. But still, don't expect a massive flow of foreign interest. These Wal-Marts, for instance, are allowed to sell to wholesalers only, not to customers, to protect India's domestic retail establishment, although as of 2011 there are some signs that India will relent and allow the company to expand to retail. But don't expect too much. When it comes to the overall ease of doing business, the World Bank ranks India 134 out of 183 countries; when it comes to ease of enforcing contracts, India ranks at 182, below Angola at the very bottom.

Land rental is another mess. Many Indian states (Bihar, Gujarat, Karnataka, Kerala, Manipur, Orissa, Rajasthan, Jammu & Kashmir, and Uttar Pradesh) ban land rental altogether, often there are no legally clear ownership records, and often the law places landowners at risk when rental is allowed. Once land has been rented to a tenant for a few years, the landowner loses some ownership rights to the tenant.

India also has some of the worst roads and worst infrastructure in the world, as anyone who has been a passenger or driver on them can attest. Even the best roads are slow going, full of animals and nonmotorized vehicles, and extremely dangerous, especially in light of the blind passing that is induced by the slow speeds. It's the scariest part of any trip to India, so take the train if you can.

These bad roads are one reason why a lot of the food crop in India rots on the way to market; according to an estimate from *The Economist* magazine a quarter or more of the produce goes to waste. According to an estimate from Kaushik Basu, India's chief economic advisor, two-thirds of the wheat crop rots on the way to market. Another reason so much produce rots is that there is little or no cooling along the way from the farm to the point of ultimate sale; you will recall in the 1929 W. P. Hedden book *How Great Cities Are Fed* that cooling is a big part of the story, and yet India still has not caught up with this earlier Green Revolution.

If you sum up all these problems, the bottom line is this: Allowing more agribusiness to develop in India would save lives and fill bellies and over the longer haul improve lives too. As it stands right now, the best Indian food is very tasty. But relative to what most people earn, it is extremely expensive and it is often out of reach for millions of poor families. It's time for India's next Green Revolution and this one will have to start with the laws and the courts, and it will involve a green carpet for lots of big business, including sometimes foreign big business.

In closing this chapter, I would like to bring up one topic that has become a real political bugaboo, but which is probably a part of any future Green Revolution. For all of the attacks that have been directed toward it, it has the potential to save millions of lives.

One of the next Green Revolutions may come from the direction of what are called Genetically Modified Organisms (GMOs). I dislike that name, because it implies that other foodstuffs are not genetically modified (remember Juan Camilo's corn?), but it seems to have stuck. All three of those key words—Genetic, Modified, and Organisms—sound a little creepy and they sound especially creepy together, as if you cloned an extra head onto your newborn baby. But agriculture always has progressed by allying itself with artificial interventions into nature. It is nature that is cruel and harsh, not commercial engineers and gene splicers and Monsanto.

For purposes of definition, Genetically Modified Organisms are organisms in which genetic material has been changed using modern biotechnology—typically, directed DNA recombination—to create new genes.

GMOs already have had a big impact. In 1995, GMOs (in the modern sense of that term) were brought to market, and by 2010 over fifteen million farmers in twenty-nine countries were using them, though the vast majority of these crops are grown in the United States, Brazil, and Argentina. They currently account for about 94 percent of the soy crops and 88 percent of the corn crops in the United States. That's mostly because they are easier to grow, more robust, and capable of producing more food more cheaply. The truth is that 300 million Americans, and millions of visitors to this country, have been eating these crops since the mid-1990s, without serious evidence of any ill effects or serious negative effects on the environment.

Around the broader world, GMOs haven't spread nearly as much. They have faced significant legal restrictions in Europe and that has limited their use in nations that export crops to Europe, such as most of Africa and parts of Asia. Those European restrictions are holding back agricultural progress in countries that really need it.

GMOs can make crops more nutritious, such as when provitamin A is put into golden rice in the Philippines, a technology that could remedy vitamin deficiencies for millions but still is caught up in government-run trials. There are breeds of sorghum and potatoes designed to produce greater micronutrients and it is easy to imagine this trend spreading. Over time, genetic engineering promises to expand beyond corn, soybeans, cotton, and rice. Sugar beets, canola, and papaya already have been improved by GMO techniques. The next steps might be drought-tolerant cassava, insect-resistant cowpeas, fungus-resistant bananas, virus-resistant sweet potatoes, and high-yielding pearl millet, yet such developments still face bureaucratic obstacles.

While the derogatory term Frankenfoods continues to grow in currency, the underreported story that GMOs have considerable environmental benefits is overlooked. In the United States, the genetic engineering of corn, cotton, and soybeans has increased yields, removed pressure on the land, and reduced the necessity for agricultural chemicals and pesticides. For instance cotton is prone to pests and it usually required high doses of pesticide, but genetically modified cotton has made it possible to reduce this pesticide use, at least where GMOs have become common. Scientists are working on new breeds of corn that do not need as much nitrogen and would limit the use of fertilizer, sending less runoff into the water and less carbon into the air (natural gas is used to produce nitrogen fertilizer).

GMOs may help limit global warming through other advances. Grass-fed cows emit (i.e., fart) methane into the environment, which worsens climate change problems. The grass they eat contains lignin, which is what triggers the methane-producing enzyme in the cow's digestive system. Recently, an Australian biotech company, Gramina, has developed a new, genetically modified grass with less lignin. Syngenta and other companies are producing GMO crops that absorb more nitrogen and limit the negative environmental results of nitrogen fertilization. In Canada they are working on genetically modified pigs (inelegantly, "enviropigs") with less phosphorous in their manure, to limit the environmental costs of runoff.

The National Research Council of the National Academies of Science commissioned a recent book-length study of GMOs, published as *The Impact of Genetically Engineered Crops on Farm Sustainability in the United States*. The report concluded that GMOs were likely to help feed humanity and also to ease the burden of agriculture on the natural environment.

If GMOs are so great, why don't we have more of them? There's a pretty clear answer and it has to do with the public, most of all the European public. Prior to 1998, Europeans did not seem especially opposed to the GMO idea, but after the "mad cow disease" scare, public opinion switched. Europeans view GMOs as a strange technology that they cannot understand or control. It's similar to when, after the Japanese earthquake, deaths from radiation assumed a much greater prominence in the public mind than the more numerous deaths from the tsunami; or when many people are more afraid of dying in a plane crash than in the far more likely outcome of a car crash. Across much of Europe, GMOs have become a symbolic bugaboo and that has held back agricultural progress in poorer parts of the world.

In most of Europe there are significant bans and regulation on GMOs, both at the European Union level and often at the national level as well. Attitudes have softened in the last few years, but for the most part it's not a friendly commercial atmosphere. There's also a cultural problem: In Europe, GMOs are met with protests and sometimes even eco-terrorism, such as when a GMO crop trial was sabotaged in Spain.

Rich countries do not need GMOs, but poor countries do. The biggest losers from these restrictions have been African farmers, the group in the greatest need of a new green revolution. According to one index of production, African farmers produced more per capita in 1970 than in 2005—obviously a move in the wrong direction—and yet agriculture employs about 70 percent of Africans. Agricultural productivity is perhaps the major economic issue in most African economies. Africans, however, are afraid of losing access to European markets and so often GMO crops do not get grown. Angola, Sudan, Malawi, Mozambique, Namibia, Nigeria, and Zimbabwe all have refused food aid with genetically modified (GM) ingredients, for fear of "contaminating" their crops and thus losing European market access. Ghana, Benin, and Zambia banned GM foods and crops, and in Africa only South Africa has embraced the technology wholeheartedly, along with GM cotton in Burkina Faso.

Most African nations simply cannot afford the requirements for safety, labeling, and control that European-style regulation imposes on them. In effect, Europe is taking a continent where death or sickness by E.coli, hepatitis, cholera, and salmonella—through the food—is common, and is requiring that food adopt extreme GMO safety standards that are (at best) suitable for wealthy nations only. It's as if we made every African buy an SUV rather than allowing the purchase of smaller and less safe cars; it's a recipe for disaster, and it is the very opposite of thoughtful consumerism. What Africa needs now is more and cheaper food, followed by better food sanitation. Worrying about GMOs should be among the least of their problems.

One group that doesn't seem to mind GMOs is the Amish. Contrary to common impressions, the Amish are not antitechnology per se, they simply do not wish to allow those modern technologies that would threaten their way of life. The Amish took a look at GMOs and many Amish farmers have adopted them with enthusiasm and also with commercial success; they appreciate the ability of some GMOs to economize on pesticides.

There are problems with GMOs, just as most other crops grown on a large scale will bring some issues, environmental, economic, and otherwise. For instance GMOs can give rise to herbicide-resistant weeds, but the most likely way forward is to improve GMOs, not to shut them out (furthermore similar problems arise with non-GM crops). Extreme patent protection is another problem. Maybe a corporation should not have the right to patent the genes from an Amazonian plant, grown for centuries by indigenous peoples, and to charge farmers in the region for using those genes. Whether it is about GMOs or not, we have overly restrictive intellectual property policies. We should change those, but in the meantime let's lay the blame on the right culprits. The patent protection for Amazon.com's one-click shopping technology is also foolish, it seems to me, but we don't condemn the idea of buying books online.

Given all this, you might wonder how the critics of GMOs rationalize their opposition. I found this exchange from Laura and Robin Ticciati, who wrote a book criticizing GMOs, instructive:

CLAIMS VERSUS FACTS

CLAIM: Genetic engineering will feed the world.
FACT: The world can already grow enough food to feed everybody . . . most hunger is not due to lack of food, but is caused by an inability to buy it.

The Ticciatis don't understand economics, and they don't understand that a lack of technical progress will doom some people to hunger or starvation. It's true that giving poor people more money would help them buy food—but, whether we like it or not, the rest of the world isn't that charitable and won't be anytime soon. In the meantime, lower food prices help poor people get more to eat. GMOs increase the supply of food, thereby lowering food prices and feeding the poor, just as the Green Revolution did. It's a sad kind of economic illiteracy—all too common in GMO critiques—that does not grasp this simple mechanism.

The biggest problem with GMOs is simply that they may underperform their initial promise. It's not always easy to come up with a new technological breakthrough, and so the degree of future importance for GMO growth remains an open question, especially since progress in agricultural productivity has been slowing down. Let's hope at least that we have a chance to find out whether further investments in GMOs can save millions of lives.

The world would need another agricultural revolution if we were only facing Africa's plight. But the problem is far more general. There will be nine or so billion of us soon and we need new ways to feed people. We need to look forward, not backward, and the relevant alternatives of starvation, strife, and violence are indeed part of our past. Let's do better. In order not to thwart a new Green Revolution, we need to remember that technology and business are a big part of what makes the world gentle and fun.

8

Eating Your Way to a
Greener Planet

Who is the greenest man or woman alive?

Is it Ed Begley, the well-known actor and environmental activist? Ed tries not to fly at all, but when he must he purchases a $5.95 carbon offset to reverse the carbon impact of his trip. Since 1990 Ed has hooked up his bicycle exercise machine to a battery, which he uses for toasting bread. He also claims he has reduced his weekly waste to a physical size that would fit inside a glove compartment, mostly by eliminating paper from his life. He has a wind turbine attached to his home and he hosts a TV show on living green, called *Living with Ed* and shown on Planet Green.

There is a Greenest Person on the Planet award, and in 2008 it was won by the German Matthias Gelber. Working out of Malaysia, Matthias promotes the idea of green cement. He claims that traditional forms of cement are responsible for 6 to 7 percent of CO_2 emissions and for more than 10 percent of the emissions coming out of China. Since the technology of cement has barely changed in centuries, perhaps it is time for an environmentally friendly upgrade.

Some sources claim the greenest man in the world is Mike Duke, CEO for Wal-Mart. Starting in 2005, Wal-Mart found comprehensive energy savings in their trucking, refrigeration, energy, lighting, and other store operations. From one year to another, they used 4.8 billion fewer plastic bags and its trucks delivered 77 million more cases of goods, yet while driving 100 million fewer miles. Wal-Mart also insisted that its suppliers try to find comparable energy savings and sent them a detailed questionnaire, toward the end of measuring the energy sustainability of each of its products. All of this was done in the name of corporate profit.

I'd like to nominate a Pygmy living in Central Africa. There is no good figure for Pygmy per capita income but many Pygmies still live as hunters and gatherers. Most Pygmies, at least the ones who have stayed in Pygmy communities, do not own anything beyond what they can carry on their backs. Prowess in hunting elephants is important. With an average height of less than five feet, Pygmies put a minimum of strain on their natural environments and they are not the main reason why elephant populations are dwindling. Pygmy life expectancy is somewhere between 16 and 24 years of age and it seems that many branches of the Pygmies are dying out.

Of these people, who is on the right track? That's the question I've been asking myself since I started thinking about food and the environment.

Advice on how to "eat green" or "live green" is plentiful, but too often the comments are marred by broader political agendas, misunderstandings of how food markets operate, or a search for "feel good" answers that aren't actually effective. If you watch the recent bestselling movies on food, such as *Super Size Me*, *Food, Inc.*, and *The Future of Food*, they share a common feature: a snarky and somewhat self-righteous approach to the choices that other human beings make in markets, most of all with their food. However, for all the virtues of our food markets, they do sometimes require correction.

Choosing Friends and Enemies

There are plenty of policies or choices that make us feel good about ourselves, and we are too likely to choose those policies, even when they are not going to prove effective.

Human beings feel an instinctive need to ally with the wise, the generous, the benevolent, and the righteous. Caring people wish to stand against the brutal, the unfeeling, and the rapacious. We *feel* better by constructing alliances with moral individuals or by linking ourselves with apparently moral qualities, but that's not always the same as being effective in achieving our desired practical ends.

If we move beyond the bromides and look to formal laboratory studies, there are some startling (but perhaps not surprising) results. For instance, given a choice, a lot of people prefer to actually *be* wasteful than to do something that *feels* wasteful. In experimental settings, people hate the feeling of "I could have gotten this for less" and they will engage in wasteful behavior, such as inefficient methods of search, to keep that feeling at bay. This is part of our general tendency to incur costs to avoid a feeling of regret or inadequacy—and this is a testament to our powers of rationalization.

A consumer psychology study conducted by Nina Mazar and Chen-Bo Zhong found that consuming "green products" does not make us better people. If anything, buying green products seems to encourage individuals to be less moral. In a series of experiments, the groups of individuals who were licensed to buy products in a "green store" had higher rates of cheating and lying during subsequent game-playing in the course of the experiment. That is, once they had assuaged their consciences with some green behavior, they became more rapacious and more self-seeking in other contexts. Finding this result in an experiment doesn't prove it's always true in the real world, but we're all familiar with the underlying mechanism: Once we've done something good, we too often relax our standards and perhaps do something not so good. If nothing else, you can take this study as a sign of how little we really know about do-good behavior, its motivations, and its final effects.

Other times people bathe in guilt and self-doubt, to alleviate their consciences, and then proceed to act in very environmentally unfriendly ways. The guilt helps them feel better. There is a Swiss inventor and computer artist named Annina Rüst, now teaching at Syracuse University, and she has a keen eye for satire and for this kind of human failing. In 2008 she invented a new device. It consists of a translucent leg band that monitors the electricity consumption of the wearer. If the band detects that the user is consuming too much electricity, a wireless device slowly pushes six stainless-steel thorns into the flesh of the user's leg. Rüst referred to it as therapy for our environmental guilt and her Web site serves up the phrase "Exercising Environmental Devotion One Thorn at a Time!" The lesson is that we often choose the equivalent of these thorns rather than making better lives for other human beings.

A lot of people don't like the idea of buying plastic or affiliating with plastic. It's artificial and it's usually not "local." Its manufacture requires petroleum products and it is a symbol of excess consumerism and the artificiality of modern life. We use "plastic" as an adjective to criticize somebody's looks or personality or manner.

Yet plastic is often more environmentally friendly than paper or cardboard. It doesn't rot or break down in compost heaps, which are a significant source of gas emissions. Paper and cardboard require a lot of energy to make. Glass, for your bottles, consumes a lot of energy in its production and transportation. Plastic just sits there and reminds you of the excesses of modern commercial society. That doesn't sound great, but overall a lot of environmentalists should be more willing to use plastic, compared to the relevant alternatives. The mistake is to focus too much on the affiliation with the notion of plastic, and to judge plastic use as some people might judge joining a club ("who or what am I affiliating with?").

Under some plausible estimates it takes four times as much energy to manufacture a paper bag than a plastic bag, and it takes 98 percent less energy to recycle a pound of plastic than a pound of paper. I don't want you to obsess over those particular numbers, which depend on context. Still, plastic seems to have a less harmful environmental impact—much less harmful—than does paper. Plastic bags are usually better than paper bags. If you really can't stand plastic, the way to make an improvement is to copy the Germans and carry your own cloth bags to the store, don't switch to paper. But you'd better do it pretty consistently. I've seen one study that suggests the cotton bag has to be reused 171 times before it "breaks even" with the environmental impact of the plastic.

Where else does this idea of affiliation lead us astray?

Locavores—those who eat local foods, either mostly or exclusively—are also pursuing a feel-good attitude rather than effectiveness. In a lot of cases you shouldn't worry much about where your food comes from. The shipping of food is only a small part of its total energy cost, no more than 14 percent by one U.S. government estimate. According to Rich Pirog, who developed food-miles analysis, transportation is only 11 percent of the total energy cost of food. Ocean transport is especially cheap in terms of its energy consumption because floating things are just easier to move. The most comprehensive study comes out of Carnegie Mellon University and was done by Christopher L. Weber and H. Scott Matthews, and it was published in 2008. The results are clear: The environmental impact of food comes from its production, not its transportation.

The real culprit here is food that is flown in, as flying is an especially environmentally unfriendly activity. But the problem is the flying, not when food travels a great distance by water.

In other words, eat turnips rather than asparagus, which is often flown in by plane. Go *hardy* because the hardy items can be farmed in a lot of different climates and probably they are not flown in. Good root vegetables are kale, carrots, parsnips, and leeks. Once I bought a good cookbook for using root vegetables, such as Andrea Chesman's *Recipes from the Root Cellar: 270 Fresh Ways to Enjoy Winter Vegetables*, my desire to eat the hardy product went up.

Flowers are also flown a lot, usually from Africa or South America, often via the Netherlands, so that is another way to cut back on supporting commercial aviation, if you don't want to forgo your favorite food.

Another solution is to cut back on the meat you eat. The Weber and Matthews Carnegie Mellon study, mentioned above, found that shifting your eating away from red meat, one day a week, does more for the environment than eating all locally sourced foods for all of your meals.

Buying from a local farmer can mean that he makes a two-hour extra truck drive, which can damage the environment more than a bunch of bananas on a boat. The local farmer is also shipping a smaller number of units, and so the per unit energy cost of his supply can be relatively high and there is also a better chance that a small purchase from him can tip him into making extra trips. When it comes to protecting the environment, local isn't always better and very often it is worse. Sometimes it's not possible. What would it mean to live in the American Southwest and eat all of your food locally, given that you are surrounded by a large desert? Even if there is a way to manage local food for millions, it would put an immense strain on already overburdened and heavily subsidized water systems. The environment is better off if the residents of Albuquerque import most of their food from far away.

It feels greener to buy from the local farmer than to patronize a large, multinational banana company, perhaps with a dubious political history at that. But there's nothing especially virtuous about the local farmer, even if it feels good to affiliate with him.

Sometimes the local apple is put into refrigerated cold storage for several months, which of course consumes energy. It would be better to buy a fresher apple, sent by boat from further abroad.

A lot of green advocates adopt the strategy of the boycott. April Dávila, a youthful writer from southern California, saw the movie *Food, Inc.* and decided she would boycott the Monsanto Corporation for an entire month; after all, the movie portrayed the company as a major source of agribusiness evil and she wanted to remove genetically modified organisms from her life. She read an academic paper showing that GMOs cause some toxic effects in rats; I read the same paper and saw that the researchers thought the pesticides accompanying GMOs were the most likely culprit, not the GMOs themselves. To be sure, that's a reason to be careful, but is it a reason to boycott GMO crops as a general idea?

Was that a noble crusade? In any case, April found that executing her plan wasn't easy. Monsanto grows 55 percent of the nation's lettuce, a lot of its sugar, and even some organic crops. She also realized that her clothing couldn't come from plants grown with Monsanto seeds or that her food couldn't come from animals fed Monsanto corn. She could wash her hands only at home.

She drank a lot of organic green tea, bought some Girl Scout cookies, and drank whiskey. Coconut milk was important. Once the month was up she went on a Monsanto binge and even after the binge was over it wasn't so easy. Here is one of her calculations:

"Monsanto count: Breakfast was clean, but my entire lunch is questionable. The avocado and cucumber were organic, but that doesn't mean not Monsanto, the tortilla and hummus are big question marks. The rice was Lundberg, so I know that's some Nonsanto [*sic*] goodness and the chard was organic, but again, not sure of its seed source, so could be Monsanto."

At this point Monsanto sounds less than villainous. Maybe Monsanto is so hard to avoid because most of its products don't have any history of doing the world harm. Even April admits that Monsanto products may feed millions of starving people, require fewer herbicides, and may be more robust under conditions of climate change. She calls that a "****ing excellent argument" for GMOs. So why the boycott?

I'm skeptical of most boycotts. Boycotts are a morally popular stance, but often they are not effective and thus I view many boycotts as a way of feeling good about ourselves. Counterintuitively, boycotts are often most effective when we are less likely to do them.

Analytically, boycotts usually work best when the boycotted producer isn't very profitable. Boycotts work least well when the producer is making a lot of money on each unit of the good or service that is being sold. Look at it this way: Unless the boycott mobilizes most or all of the relevant consumers in the world, which is very hard to do, the profitable producer will keep on selling, even in light of the boycott.

Imagine that a group of consumers boycotts New Zealand lamb, on the grounds that it costs a lot of energy to ship that lamb around the world. The United States and the Arab world are two of the major export markets for New Zealand lamb. If enough consumers in the United States stop eating this lamb, under some assumptions about the structure of the market, and how the market works, the price of the lamb will fall. And what will then happen to lamb purchases in the Arab world? They will go up. The American boycott of New Zealand lamb might not do a lot of good. It doesn't necessarily put a big dent in either lamb consumption or the production of lamb in New Zealand or the shipping of lamb across long distances.

The boycott will be weakest when the supplier is committed to selling the product no matter what, or in other words when product sales are profitable no matter what. In that case if one group of buyers leaves the market, the seller will either cut price or expand promotion until other buyers pick up the slack. More technically, boycotts are least likely to work when the supplier faces what economists would call high marginal returns to seeking out new buyers.

Studies of successful boycotts bear out this prediction. Brayden King of Northwestern University, who has studied the issue, finds that boycotts are most likely to succeed when they are directed against declining companies with good reputations. Those companies fear a further loss of business and thus they respond, to some degree, to address the concerns of the boycotters. The notion of finding a declining company corresponds to how I am pinpointing the importance of an unprofitable or not very profitable company. Furthermore, when the boycott is directed against a company with a bad reputation, very often the company is not responsive, as the company has a bad reputation anyway.

This analysis—in particular the recommendation to focus a boycott on the more marginally profitable corporations—runs counter to our moral intuitions. Many people, out of a feeling of self-righteousness, are most inclined to boycott corporations that make a lot of money and have bad reputations. It feels just—after all, aren't they the villains? Aren't those corporations ripping off the rest of the world, and selfishly enriching themselves, all the while doing something environmentally unfriendly? Maybe so. Certainly, a lot of people don't want to be affiliated with the profitable, rapacious corporation. Nonetheless, a hard truth remains. If the corporation is truly profitable, it will probably end up selling the product no matter what—boycott or not—unless the entire world joins the boycott, which hardly ever happens. And the bad reputation of the company implies yet another reason why the boycott won't succeed.

If protestors are boycotting a very profitable corporation, there's a good chance they're making themselves feel better, by ceasing to affiliate with the said corporation. There's a lower chance they're being effective or making the world a better place.

The strangest story of affiliation I have heard comes from the United States government itself. I don't mean to be taking the overall side of either political party here, and I am not a member of either, but this story represents some key themes pretty clearly.

When the Democrats held the House of Representatives, prior to the election of 2010 and over the course of 2007–2008, they made a big change: they introduced into the dining halls new cutlery made from corn, in part because the forks and knives could be easily turned into compost. Yet the idea was not well thought through. The new utensils cost more, estimated at $475,000 a year, and they didn't stand up well when exposed to hot foods such as soup. It wasn't clear that anyone was reaping a big environmental gain and in fact a House internal report suggested that, due to the need to truck away the disposable waste, there was probably a net environmental cost. Still, maybe it felt better to have the compostable cutlery.

When the Republicans took over, they too made a change. The most cost-effective option for the new utensils turned out to be polystyrene, which is a plastic made from petroleum and natural gas. Styrofoam is back, but in the cafeterias for the Democratic Senate the forks are still compostable.

Why not use metal knives and forks you might be wondering? The sorry truth is that this option was studied, but rejected on the grounds that too many Congressional staff—the people working so hard to improve America—would take these utensils away and, quite simply, never bring them back.

Actually Helping the Environment

There is a broader point here, and I am reminded of a *Financial Times* interview with Tyler Brûlé, a very well dressed man with flair, a member of the jet set, an expert on travel and high-end consumer goods, and editor-in-chief of a fancy international periodical called *Monocle,* as well as a regular columnist for the *Financial Times.* Here is a snippet of his views on "being green":

> **REPORTER:** Do you feel bad about your carbon footprint?
> **BRÛLÉ:** On balance, I don't think my carbon footprint is particularly large. I do fly an enormous amount, but I don't own a car, I walk most places in London and opt for trains over aircraft where possible (in Europe and Japan).

I believe that to a lot of readers, especially those familiar with Brûlé's public profile, this answer was less than convincing. How could this famous rich guy not have a large carbon footprint?

Maybe Brûlé is right or maybe not (I should note, by the way, that once I was paid a small amount to write a piece for *Monocle*). The broader point is that we can't trust our intuitions. It is very hard for individual consumers, or for that matter outside observers of individual consumers, to know which of their actions have the biggest adverse environmental impacts. It's hard for consumers to "see" the real environmental costs of a lot of their decisions. Memorizing facts about bunches of bananas, boats, and boycotts will not do it. Even if a person knew all the relevant environmental facts, about all of his activities, that knowledge would become obsolete as the years passed and the costs and benefits of different choices changed. Most people, even well-informed people, don't have a good sense of how much an afternoon drive in a Mercedes contributes to the climate change problem, relative to buying a batch of flown-in asparagus or subbing in a steak for a chicken breast.

You might think that carbon labeling of products is the way to go, and while that is not an idea to be opposed, it is hardly a satisfactory answer. Consumers ignore such labels and suppliers will try to make them sound as good as possible. The more fundamental problem is that labels do not encompass the same economy-wide information that is communicated by the price system in its assessment of competing uses for resources. Here's a simple example: A foodstuff grown close to the city might receive a favorable label, because of its low transport costs. But putting the food close to the city pushes commuters further out and the net effect will not be so good for the environment.

What's striking about the act of consuming is the odd mix of how much we know about some sides of what we are doing—the quality of the product—and how little we know about other sides, most of all the costs to the producers. Other than looking at the price, consumers really don't have a good sense of the *non*-environmental costs of their decisions, much less the environmental costs. That is why they patronize businesses—businesses can figure out the least-cost way to produce a valuable good or service. Through a competitive market process, businesses offer prices, and consumers rely on those prices to judge what is too costly or not. I never try to figure out the cheapest way for someone to make a suit for me, rather I compare the price of the good with its final quality and decide accordingly. I have no idea how much the buttons or the transportation add to the final product cost.

When it comes to tailoring, the model that works is the one that has the business worry about how to make the thing in the cheapest way possible—I just look at the final price. That's one manifestation of the division of labor. Businesses too rely on prices for most of their information and they don't look back and try to solve the calculation problems of all prior stages of production. A tailor doesn't generally know the best or cheapest ways of making the cloth, but rather he compares the quality of a cloth offering to its price and decides accordingly, just as consumers choose by looking at the prices of the suits. The neat thing is that when everyone behaves in this manner, markets tend to minimize the privately borne costs of production.

This is all economic common sense and it reflects business and consumer practices that have survived, and done us well, for centuries and indeed millennia. Prices are important, in large part, because most of us cannot see very far behind the price to estimate the real costs of production or to figure out the cheapest combinations of inputs. We economize on resource use and costs by dealing with the prices alone.

Now let's get back to the environment. When it comes to relieving climate change problems, there are two approaches. The first, to put it squarely, is to have everyone memorize facts about boats and bananas, and update that analysis as often as is necessary. The second approach is to rely on the price system, specifically to modify prices so that they reflect *more information* about the value of the environment. That's the economically smart way to address climate change. The first method is like wielding a pea shooter and the second is more like a bazooka; only the second method has a chance of succeeding. The second method is working through the price system, which is the miracle that brought us modern civilization, and also brought us plentiful food.

We do, however, need to tweak the price system. When it comes to assessing environmental damage, the price system as it is currently used is in some ways broken. There are social and environmental costs to a Mercedes that are not reflected in its competitive market price, most importantly the pollution and its long-run impact on climate change. The market economy economizes on the costs borne directly by Daimler-Benz, but it does not economize on the broader social costs of production, which in this case includes the climate change.

In this context, relying on prices means taxing fossil fuels and it also means higher taxes on meat, which through methane emissions (e.g., cow farts) contribute to climate change problems.

This tax makes the "green living" problem easier for consumers. If the production and transportation of a foodstuff uses more fossil fuels, the tax will increase the price of that foodstuff automatically. Consumers will buy less, whether or not they are good calculators as to what best helps the environment. That's pricing at work: Prices are far more powerful than lists of instructions to green-minded consumers. The tax also eases the motivational burden on consumers. Once the tax is in place, consumers don't have to care very much about the environment or at all. The higher price on the taxed goods induces consumers to economize and to behave as if they care about the environment, whether or not they do.

The tax does involve an informational burden on the government, which must levy the tax and determine its rates on different types of carbon emissions. For instance the government has to decide that dirty coal requires a higher carbon tax than does an oil well. That is a problem, because governments don't always get those decisions right. Still, it is a more manageable problem—in terms of both information and motivation—than relying on 310 million American consumers to know which inputs are being used to produce which goods and services. The former problem can be solved to a partial and imperfect degree, but making progress on the latter is unlikely.

Ideally a carbon tax should be done in conjunction with other major polluters, most of all China, the world's number one carbon polluter at the moment. Still, even a unilateral carbon tax is better than no change at all. It's not just that we might shame China into following suit. Look at it this way: America is aging rapidly, and so there will be a stunning overall rise in Medicare and also Medicaid expenditures; it's already under way. Even if we limit per person Medicare expenditures, the rise in the number of elderly and rising life expectancy will still make the Medicare program much more expensive.

The likely result is that taxes will need to go up, even if you think, as I do, that we also need some significant cuts in government spending. In any politically feasible scenario, we will need some spending cuts and some tax increases, though of course people will disagree about the appropriate relative proportions.

Given this budget outlook, what should we tax? It's pretty simple: We should tax those items with some negative consequences for the environment. Even if those taxes do not always prove effective (perhaps China will continue polluting at a very high level), this tax is painful and the tax offers at least some chance of improving the world. And a carbon tax doesn't have to be anti-business. If we wish, we could offset a higher carbon tax with a lower corporate income tax, thus helping out business in general, while encouraging business to pollute less.

Even though the prospects for a carbon tax right now are slim to none, the aging of the American population will put more pressure on government finances. In less than twenty years, probably in less than ten, the debate will be some higher taxes vs. Medicare cuts. What will come out of that conflict, I am not sure, but the elderly vote and are politically active at above-average rates. That limits the feasible cuts to Medicare, whether we like it or not, and then we are back to raising some taxes. Keep in mind that the number of elderly voters rises every year; and during the last few years the Republican Party—which in the 1990s tried to cut Medicare benefits—has at times played the role of Medicare defender. (Remember the famous town hall proclamation: "Tell the government to keep its hands off my Medicare!")

A carbon tax will have a chance only when the Medicare crunch comes, but it will have some chance, no matter how slim the prospects may appear today. As I write in 2011, the United States is still in denial about the need for long-run budget balance and also in denial, at least on the electoral stage, when it comes to climate change. The country needs two wake-up calls at once, and in fact they can, rather propitiously, both come together in the form of a carbon tax.

The people who are preaching fiscal austerity—and mean it—are some of the best friends of the environment, whether they know it or not. They are the ones paving the way for a carbon tax. The whole idea of a carbon tax is less painful, once people realize that some taxes will have to go up in any case.

The biggest problem is that even a new green energy source wouldn't, taken alone, solve the problem of climate change. If China and America go the green route, a lot of oil and dirty coal will then be very cheap because the world's two largest economies will be demanding much less of the stuff. That's good news, but those fossil fuels might get sold and used anyway, if only in Vietnam, Indonesia, Africa, Latin America, or other parts of the world. The odds are that somebody is going to use all the remaining oil, which is indeed valuable. (This resembles the problem with boycotts, discussed above; for this reason bombing and destroying some of the stuff would be more effective than a tax, but that's not going to happen.) And indeed, since higher energy prices mean higher food prices, we don't want the poorer nations of the world to be the ones doing the most cutbacks on energy consumption. In a poor country, the marginal usage of energy is more likely a matter of life and death than it is in a rich country. The poor countries aren't going to have stiff carbon taxes anyway, nor should they. That means when it comes to carbon adjustments, a major burden should be on the United States.

The hope is that good enough and cheap enough green energy can spread rapidly enough to limit the demand of other countries to use up all the dirty energy anyway. A second hope is that even if all the oil is used up, we can make dirty coal—the biggest offender—an uneconomical and therefore unpopular energy source, perhaps through an international convention led by America and someday China. We're far away from that, but it's another bazooka in this game.

The good news, if I can call it that, is that carbon taxes are likely to prove more effective over time at limiting carbon production. For instance, as the global economy pumps and uses more fossil fuels, the most profitable supply sources—which get used first—tend to dry up. In other words, we used readily available, "suck it up with a straw" Texas oil and Saudi oil quite early on, and we will use oil from tar sands—a far more expensive technology—later in time, and indeed we are already making that switch to the tougher processes. That means we have a world of only marginally profitable fossil fuel producers, and it is easier to induce everyone to switch to new technologies. In contrast, we're not going to get the Saudis out of their oil-pumping game until they run out of the easy stuff, no matter what kind of tax we enact.

Finally, to the extent that animal welfare is a concern, taxing meat production cuts down on the number of animals being raised inhumanely. Not all animals are raised under unacceptable conditions, so we should consider making this a more selective tax. Not every tax has to raise revenue for the U.S. Treasury. One way to "tax" meat is to require the animals to be raised and slaughtered under more humane conditions. As a first order approximation, imagine applying the current animal cruelty laws, as we might apply them to household pets, to agribusiness. The end result?—a higher price of meat, fewer methane emissions, and better treatment of billions of farm animals. The cost is fewer meals with meat but overall that's a good trade-off; and if we replace that meat with vegetables, rather than junk food, it might even help our waistlines too.

Toward the end of green energy and greener food, here are some other policy changes that green-conscious economists and environmentalists are working on:

- Greater efforts to support green forests abroad and other carbon sinks.

- Cut back on requirements for minimum parking to accompany suburban developments; minimum parking requirements encourage car use and sprawl.

- Ease zoning restrictions on high-density construction in urban areas. City dwellers are less likely to have cars or to travel long distances and thus they are "greener."

- Eliminate all subsidies to large agribusiness. I am pro-capitalist but I think agribusiness should stand on its own. On top of everything else, subsidies to corn and soybean meal are major subsidies to the cattle farmers who use them as feed. We are subsidizing cow farts when we should be taxing them.

- Phase out water subsidies, which encourage inefficient agriculture and overuse of water supplies.

These changes all allow for automatic marketplace adjustments, they don't require consumers to understand the energy costs of different goods and services, and once passed they are enforced by selfish behavior rather than requiring ongoing altruism and extreme levels of environmental consciousness.

The bottom line is this: I would rather propagandize for these changes than spend my time adding up the energy miles in my asparagus. (If it makes you feel better, I do now also eat less asparagus.)

In the meantime, there is no carbon tax in the United States, so there's still some environmental value in cooking that rutabaga, however much it means we are attacking the problem with a fly swatter. I have some additional proposals at the personal level:

1. Make virtuous behavior more fun

I have succeeded in cultivating a taste for sardines. Unlike a lot of other fish, sardines are in no danger of running out and they are at the bottom of the food chain, not the top. They also taste good out of a can, so they are always handy for a meal. The cans last for a long time, and they are small, so I don't end up throwing out much food to rot. Sardines also offer a lot of protein and they are a good substitute for meat. You can add to this list other fish low on the food chain, including mackerel, smelts, anchovies, and herring. Most small fish fit the bill, as do mussels and oysters.

2. Cultivate expensive tastes for environmentally dangerous items

In addition to making virtuous foods easier and cheaper to enjoy, I have tried to make a lot of environmentally dangerous foods more difficult to enjoy and more expensive. If I enjoy some foodstuff that is bad for the environment, and yet I am too selfish to give it up, often I go out of my way to cultivate a taste for an expensive version of that item. The end result is that I will buy less of it. I've made my taste more particular and so it's hard for me to be happy with the lesser quality product. At the same time, the very best items are either too expensive or too hard to come by for me to eat them all the time.

When I visited southern Brazil in the mid-1990s, I made a point of eating what I thought, at the time, was the world's best steak (I later realized Kobe, Japan, was another contender for that honor). The result is that I hardly ever eat steak now. Last year I went to Peter Luger Steak House, in Brooklyn, a place that is sometimes considered the finest steak house in New York and possibly in the entire United States. Critics rave about this restaurant. It was good, and I can see why some people like it, but overall I was disappointed, especially for the price. I don't intend any criticism of the restaurant, which did its job as promised. The waiter was chatty in that New York sort of way and the steak was tasty. I just don't find the promise of the restaurant so valuable anymore. It wasn't the very best steak in the world and it also wasn't a bargain, at about $70 for lunch, with the vegetable sides and fries. Why did I go? It all felt so ordinary. "$70 for the best steak in the country" sounds maybe worthwhile, but I had a new framing, something more like "$70 for the sixth best steak I've had." Eh. But I got the experience out of my system and now it will be some time before I eat a large steak again. I think of myself as liberated and in that regard the $70 was a good investment.

If you are looking to cultivate expensive tastes, there are plenty of expensive restaurants and food books to help you do this. Along these lines, many people believe that foie gras is unfair to the animals that suffer in its making. If you agree with this assessment, but can't give up the product altogether, try some especially fine foie gras, and most of the offerings in the marketplace will suffer by comparison. Ordinary "good" foie gras, with the right framing, can feel to you as the Peter Luger steak now feels to me—something expensive that I can take or leave. Of course this recommendation may not work for people who are extremely wealthy, and who can then purchase the very best foie gras, as much as they want, for the indefinite future. For most people, however, this remains a path toward overcoming some of our own selfishness.

3. Give up refined sugar as much as you can

Processed junk food is a major consumer of energy, compared to the total energy cost of the fish or eggs consumed in the United States. Sugar refining and processing is another culprit. One way to lower environmental costs is to cut back or eliminate junk food altogether. You'll save money, help the environment, have a healthier life, and you still will be able to eat tasty food. Every time you substitute some canned sardines for junk food, just about everyone is better off—most of all you—and you're again showing that every meal counts.

4. Wash more dishes by hand

Run the dishwasher fewer times. Use plastic cutlery and paper plates. Wash an individual dish or glass by hand, once you are done with it, each time. Let your large pots soak.

But isn't this inconvenient? Well, to use the dishwasher less, sometimes I use my own weakness against myself: I don't like unloading the previous wash. That's laziness, but it can be mobilized on the side of virtue. When I am reluctant to unload what's in my dishwasher, I have to wash what's in the sink with soap and hot water. I cultivate this "weakness," and try to explain its virtues to my wife, with varying degrees of success.

A study by the U.S. Department of Agriculture suggests that home preparation and storage is the single biggest category of energy flows in the food sector, accounting for about 29 percent of the total. It's not just about what we eat, it's also about how we eat it, prepare it, and wash up after it.

5. Limit food waste

There are lots of foods that we tend not to finish, most prominently bread. Often bread is sold in fairly large loaves, and, furthermore, to a lot of foodies bread stops tasting good within a day or sometimes even within a few hours of its baking or its purchase. And so we throw it out. A lot of people don't finish strawberries, which also don't stay fresh for very long. When many foods rot on compost heaps, they give off methane gas and contribute significantly to climate change problems.

My current food project is to figure out what it is that I am wasting, and to buy less of it. I don't ever waste frozen dumplings or lentils in a bag, so those I should buy more of.

6. Minimize the number of car trips

I am buying a bigger haul of foodstuffs when I go to the store, and thus lowering the number of my car trips. Often that means doing the food shopping on the way home from work, or attached to some other trip I will make anyway.

When it comes to energy and pollution, the U.S. Department of Agriculture estimates suggest that car trips are more important than food consumption. The total energy flow created by the food service sector (including both restaurants and supermarkets) is in per capita terms about sixteen gallons of gasoline a year. So if a person can manage to spend $50 to $70 less on gasoline each year, that's a gain roughly equivalent to eliminating the energy impact of the food purchased by a typical American. If you're an everyday foodie, and determined to keep on eating your favorite meals, even in some environmentally unfriendly versions, this is one area where big savings remain on the table. We can outdo the locavores with some simple changes to our driving behavior, namely fewer trips.

Food consumption is always not the easiest or most effective area for helping the environment. Our food consumption matters less than our gasoline consumption, and when it comes to energy and pollution, cars themselves matter less than does, say, the use of dirty coal. We can't have zero environmental impact, or even an impact as small as that of the Pygmy, so we need to choose battles wisely. Food is neither the major environmental culprit nor the biggest source of energy consumption. *We* are.

9

Why *Does* Mexican Food Taste Different in Mexico?

I t might now seem that eating our way to a greener planet is your burdensome duty. But wait. Everyday foodies delight in new flavors, new experiences. Travel is one of the great ways to nudge yourself out of your boring bad habits, and I'm not just talking about taking that other freeway exit to get to the Asian supermarket. The next couple of chapters are about eating in places that have different approaches to food, often both legal and cultural. Everyday foodies who travel can see how a country's prosperity and style of government affects the food. I'm particularly fascinated in how an ethnic food can taste so different in its home country.

Food snobs often claim that Mexican food is unambiguously better in Mexico than in the United States. It sounds right? But is it? And if so, what are the real reasons?

One of my strongest food obsessions has been with Mexico. I've been to the country more times than I can remember (over fifteen), and it's a place where I've taken a lot of risks with food. And not just with foodborne parasites. As I hope I've made clear by this point, much of what I think about food stems from a desire for adventure and discovery, and that usually feels risky. Venturing into the unknown has so many surprising advantages. And Mexican food is a great way to better understand food in the United States. It is a bit like the insight one gets into grammar when studying one's first foreign language.

If you are careless, or just spend a lot of time in Mexico, you will have some mediocre meals, as you would in any country. You can find Mexican fast food, Mexican chain food of indifferent quality, stringy Mexican chicken, okay Mexican food smothered in sauce, or home-cooked Mexican meals that are no better than ordinary. These meals can consist of anything from simple boiled noodles to generic casseroles to chicken in molé sauce out of a can. An American Taco Bell outlet—whatever its vices—is better than many places you will find in Mexico. And if you really hate Taco Bell, well, they have that in Mexico too, except they seem to view it as a strange and humorous American oddity.

Mexican food in Mexico, rather than being better across the board than Mexican food in the United States is sometimes *much* better—and sometimes much worse.

But guess what I really care about? Some of the best meals of my life I've had in Mexico for less than five dollars, sometimes for less than two dollars. My experiences there are one of the main reasons I was so hopeful about my food tour in Nicaragua that I recounted at the opening of this book.

So, how do Mexican and American-Mexican foods differ? (I'll use that term "American-Mexican" to cover the broad array of semi-Mexican choices you find in the United States.) And why do they differ *so much*? Even El Paso, which is 70 percent ethnically Hispanic, produces very different Mexican-style foods than does Cíudad Juárez right across the border.

And finally, why do Mexican and American-Mexican foods vary within each country so much? Why have gourmet Mexican restaurants in Manhattan chosen different paths than Houston taquerías or suburban Tex-Mex? The Mexican neighborhoods of Chicago or Los Angeles differ from the foods of El Paso. In Mexico, the open-air *comedores* offer different styles than the fine restaurants of Mexico City. The southern city of Oaxaca differs from the newer and more industrially based cities of northern Mexico.

For all this regional diversity, Mexican society doesn't quite have the

U.S. notion of catering to minority customer groups. This may be one of the first things an everyday foodie from the United States notices when visiting Mexico. Most Mexicans find vegetarians odd or maybe even absurd. I have heard American visitors announce that they are vegetarians, only to be asked whether they ate chicken, or perhaps pork or fish? Mexicans ask whether there is some kind of medical problem. In short, outside of some hip circles, vegetarians are laughable, that is if the concept is understood in the first place. Mexico also has fewer Jews and Muslims than does the United States. Dietary restrictions may arise at Lent, but the notion is not otherwise significant in Mexican society.

On the other hand, suppliers and demanders are always significant.

A Tale of Two Cities' Supplies

I conducted an experiment, which I think of as a "tale of two cities." I thought I could get a better understanding of Mexican vs. American-Mexican food by going right to the border. I wanted to find the point where America and Mexico are closest to coming together, closest in geographic and ethnic terms. That meant going to Texas.

El Paso and Cíudad Juárez are sister cities, each lying right on a common border. These two cities share a climate, a location, an early history, and they are developing an increasingly common ethnic mix. About 70 percent of El Paso is counted as "Hispanic"; one survey counted 40 percent of El Paso residents as claiming birth in Mexico. If we consider illegal migrants and underreporting, the strength of Mexican heritage in El Paso is probably even higher than the published numbers indicate.

The cities split only after the Mexican-American War in 1848. The settlement to the north kept the name of El Paso and the southern part took the new name of Cíudad Juárez. Up through 1917 there were few restrictions on migration from Mexico. The Border Patrol started only in 1924 and even then casual crossing continued at high levels for decades. To this day, many people live in Juárez but work in El Paso, crossing daily with special work passes.

The locales nonetheless differ in two significant ways. First, they operate under differing laws and regulations, including food regulations. Second, El Paso is much wealthier than Cíudad Juárez. We thus have a (rough) field experiment for how *law* and *wealth* matter for food.

El Paso surprised me when I visited in 2006. The "Mexican food" there just wasn't very Mexican to my nose or taste buds, despite the presence of plenty of Mexican and Mexican-American customers in the city. Most of all, I was surprised how few Mexican raw materials I could find in El Paso. If you eat American-Mexican food in the United States, it is possible that only the chilies, or perhaps the winter tomatoes, come from Mexico. Almost everything else will taste different. El Paso was no exception.

Chopped Meat

We looked in depth at how barbecue differs from one side of the border to the other, but skirted one issue: the strong flavor of the meats is the most obvious difference between Mexican and American-Mexican foods. Ours taste bland in comparison.

Mexican cattle munch on grass and thus their meat develops a stronger and gamier taste. It's also well known that grass-fed whole steaks tend to be chewy rather than tender. But given how the meat is sliced, chopped, cut, or roped into smaller and more manageable pieces, toughness isn't a big problem. So a Mexican beef taco or fajitas, if done properly, is going to be better than what you get in the United States. Mexico is a land of chopped meat.

For a large, whole steak the American product has significant advantages, and you'll see that many Mexican steak houses advertise their use of U.S. beef. The commercially produced feed given to American cattle leads to blander tastes but also softer meats. Texas steaks are easier to cut and chew, especially when large pieces are on your plate. The bland taste can be covered with salsa, or spicy Argentinean chimichanga, both of which are prominent in Mexican steak houses.

The difference in cattle feeds in turn springs from some basic economic considerations. U.S. farms are larger and they can raise any individual cow more cheaply. Cows often graze outside when young, but then
they are moved indoors to regulated pens. On one hand the American
system raises more animals on a given piece of land, but the animals
must receive commercial, corn-based feeds because they are not always
outside to chew grass. Plus the U.S. government subsidizes corn heavily,
thus encouraging the use of corn feed. Poorer Mexican farmers, many of
whom run family farms, rely on the local grass to feed their cows. The
lower value of land in Mexico means there is less pressure to consolidate
farms to economize on space. Furthermore, many Mexican farmers do
not have access to the vitamins, antibiotics, and waste disposal techniques that make U.S. factory farms profitable.

Apart from barbecue, Mexicans use dry aging and open-air techniques to treat their beef. In fact, they sometimes age the beef to such a
point that the meat turns a near shade of green. Refrigeration is less
affordable in Mexico and until recent times many parts of the country
had little refrigeration at all, and so they stuck with earlier methods. The
dry-air aging technique relies on constant vigilance and cheap human
labor. The meat hangs on hooks or otherwise sits out in the open air.
When part of the meat turns a sufficiently unholy color, someone must
shave it off with a knife and discard it. Inevitably some of the meat will
go bad, attract too many flies, or meet other open-air hazards. Dry aging
also causes the beef to lose more volume, or in other words dehydrate
and shrink.

I guess you already know by now that, for a lot of foodies, dry-aged
beef tastes a lot stronger and richer.

In contrast, U.S. beef suppliers rely on refrigeration. They use "wet"
aging, in vacuum-sealed packets. This guarantees a predictable outcome
and meets health and safety standards with greater ease. It is easier to do
en masse. That said, some of America's top beef restaurants use safe and
thus expensive versions of dry-aging techniques. Wegmans offers some
dry-aged beef, albeit at a much higher price, and sometimes you'll find it
in Whole Foods too or in specialty butchers. It's not in your typical Giant

or Safeway. Mexican methods of beef aging are cheap only in Mexico. A U.S. steak house ordering dry-aged beef might have to pay a premium of an extra four dollars a pound.

Mexican meats of all kinds are produced under looser health and safety standards. The number of suppliers is too large; the Mexican bureaucracy is too inept and corrupt. Most family farms in Mexico are not subject to serious inspection. The problem with importing Mexican beef into the U.S. is not tariffs (remember NAFTA?) but rather a bewildering variety of regulations from the FDA, USDA, and state and local governments. Furthermore, liability laws discourage food suppliers from carrying products that might be risky to consume.

Mexicans also prefer fattier cuts of meat, just as they prefer or tolerate higher levels of fat in their food consumption more generally. It tastes good and it's an easy way to get protein. Fajitas, in their classic form, use the relatively fatty "skirt steak" part of the cow. The notion of fajitas has since broadened. Fajitas started as ranch food in Texas as one means of eating the entire slaughter. Mexican fajitas typically stick with skirt steak but American fajitas now use top round, chuck, flank steak, or for that matter chicken, shrimp, and fish. In the United States the notion of fajitas has come to mean the more general use of trimmings. Google brings up over a million mentions for "tofu fajitas." Americans have moved away from the fattier skirt steak cut, even though those meats have more flavor.

Restaurants in Mexico don't feel the same pressure to offer less fatty options. Health-consciousness is only starting to enter the Mexican culinary scene and Mexico is a far less healthy country, with one of the highest rates of diabetes in the world. Given that health maladies are so common in poorer countries, individuals do not expect that a good diet will save them or much prolong their lives. So why not eat the fattier meat?

Pork is not the staple in northern Mexico, but it is the most commonly consumed meat in the country as a whole. Once again, we see big differences on each side of the border.

Mexican pigs are more likely to be free-roaming corn-feeders, again on family farms or simply attached to a rural home. In contrast,

American "factory pigs" eat ground-up viscera and fish meal, mostly because that is the cheapest way to do mass pig farming. Mexican pork has a more natural taste and offers greater variation in flavor, although it is not always as soft or as tender as the U.S. cuts. Peter Kaminsky writes: "Pigs are not ruminants: They don't process the fat they eat in a second stomach. For this reason, pork fat has more of the subtle flavors of the acorns, soybeans, peanuts, and corn that the animal consumes. If the fat tastes good, so will the meat."

Poorer countries generally eat more pork than beef. Pigs are easier to raise on a small-scale basis. They are better foragers and can live off garbage, whereas cows require feed or larger tracts of grass. It is common in rural Mexico to see pigs sleeping in the shadow of the owner's house, and that is one reason why Mexicans have found it so easy to produce so many tasty pork dishes.

A lot of countries make a transition from pork to beef as they become wealthier and this is true for the United States as well. In the nineteenth century, Americans ate more pork than beef. Pork was easier to salt, preserve, and store. Salted and preserved hams remain prominent in the South, but most customers prefer their meat fresh, which favors beef more than many forms of pork. U.S. beef gained significant ground only with the advent of refrigerated train cars, as discussed in chapter 2, which allowed entrepreneurs to ship Midwest beef around the country without much risk of spoilage. In the United States beef consumption equaled pork consumption by the time of World War I. By the 1950s, beef had become decisively more important.

Parts of northern Mexico, including near Juárez, are an exception. There, unlike in most of Mexico, beef is a more important meat than pork. In the north, land is open and cows can digest the cellulose in grass but pigs cannot. That is one reason why American-Mexican food continues to draw heavily from northern Mexico food rather than from the more vegetable-based, pork-based food from Oaxaca.

As with beef, Mexicans are less concerned with the health implications of the kind of pork they prefer. American pork holds increasingly less fat; according to one estimate the average pork tenderloin in the

United States has 42 percent less fat than in the early 1980s. This is a victory for fat-conscious American consumers, but it drains the meat of much of its taste and texture.

Mexicans are more likely to fry their meats, including pork. A walk around the food market in Juárez shows a wide variety of delicious *chicharrónes,* which are a version of fried pork skin, similar to pork cracklings. *Chicharrón* in the Juárez market, however, is not limited to pork. One can find *chicharrón de pavo* [turkey], *de botanero, de pellita, de res* [beef], *prensado de puerco, de tira, de pella*—and who knows what they all are? This variety of fried products is lacking in El Paso and in this country more generally, even though basic *chicharrónes* are in Latin food markets around the United States.

The preference for frying foods has historical roots. In rural Mexico, gas and electric stoves have been common only in the last several decades. Many villages still have many families without stoves. This eliminates baking and broiling as food options. Soups and stews and molés can be cooked in pots over fires. But otherwise frying food on top of a fire remains an easy option for a hot meal. Mexicans even will fry their pasta for a richer taste. Similarly, Mexicans often fry their enchiladas rather than baking them, as would be done in the United States.

Stringy Chicken, Non-Local Seafood

Mexican chickens are likely free range, and they do not receive the additives, hormones, and genetic engineering used on U.S. chickens. That being said, Mexican chicken is not up to the standards of Mexican pork. Chicken has less fat in the first place, so free-range treatment adds less to the taste. When it comes to Mexican chicken, often the flesh is tough and stringy and the meat is somewhat skimpy. Growth hormones do put more tender meat on the breast and other critical chicken parts. Furthermore rural Mexican farmers do not kill their chickens by surprise, so the chemical reactions of the chicken's body—in response to the act of killing—can toughen up the meat.

Mexico has produced many delicious chicken dishes, most of all from Oaxaca, where chicken is the default household meat. But much of the credit goes to the spices and blends, rather than to the chicken meat itself. The small, fresh chickens of this region can be delicious. But if we are comparing northern Mexico to Texas, I would pick the United States as the winner when it comes to chicken, even if the very tastiest chicken dishes are in Mexico.

When it comes to Mexican seafood, its quantity and quality depends greatly on locale, even more than in the United States. Cíudad Juárez, which is just south of Texas, is not representative of the country as a whole, and it has an inferior selection of seafood.

The best Mexican seafood is pulled right out of the ocean or a freshwater lake. It is consumed almost immediately. Variety can be hard to come by, but it depends on how much a given area has to offer. The coasts will have remarkable seafood. Many rural Mexicans have sampled only one kind of fish in their lives, perhaps the local variety of *mojarra*, which is a bit like trout. The quality nonetheless is high, as it is eaten within hours of having been caught.

A Mexican coastal community will enjoy much better seafood—per piece—than a comparable American coastal community. Tijuana has much better seafood than does the adjacent San Diego, except perhaps at the expensive uppermost tiers of the market. The reasons are simple: the varying length of the supply chain, and rents. A Tijuana stand will sell (or cook) fish tacos at the waterfront for about two dollars. The fish is delivered from a boat in the waters right to the store and it is usually sold and consumed quickly. The person who runs the outlet—or a family member—cooks. Décor is minimal and the facilities are little more than a few stools and tables. Needless to say, the places might not satisfy U.S. health code inspectors.

A comparable arrangement would not be possible in San Diego. Higher rents mean that the waterfront is dominated by higher-volume, higher-expenditure activities. Restaurants near the water require high turnover. This usually necessitates a bar, a heavy investment in décor, and a polished atmosphere. Volume must be correspondingly higher, which means that they will order their fish from larger-scale and better-organized suppliers. The fish will be processed, stored, and maybe frozen or refrozen to a much greater degree than is the case in Tijuana. The cooking and preparation will be done by a group of (imperfectly) trained workers, operating at high volume in a hurry. They might be the same Mexicans who used to eat fish tacos at the beach in Tijuana. While the San Diego restaurant may be good, it will lack the immediacy and sheer deliciousness of the fish taco in Tijuana.

That being said, longer supply chains will give San Diego a much more varied supply of seafood. San Diego can sell seafood from around the world, whereas Tijuana, and Mexico more generally, is better at handling the purely local product.

Both the United States and Mexico also offer frozen fish products through supermarkets and big box stores like Wal-Mart. In this category the United States is usually superior, again because of American specialization at handling long supply chains. Our average fish will be better in America than in Mexico, even though fresh fish of a particular kind will be much better and much cheaper in any part of Mexico that has access to that fish in a fresh form.

Fatty Cheeses and Mennonites

Just as the meats may make Mexican food richer and tastier than American-Mexican food, the cheeses cement this basic difference. Mexican cheeses are gooier, yummier, and heavier than the cheeses used in the United States.

American-Mexican food uses Monterey Jack, bland cheddar, or even American cheese, instead of the richer and tastier *asadero* and Oaxaca cheeses of Mexico. Chihuahua cheeses—often made by Mexican Mennonites—are especially popular in the north of Mexico. These cheeses are a big reason why the best Mexican main courses taste so good.

The weaker American cheeses and meats influence the subsequent presentation of the meal. A restaurant is more likely to resort to thick sauces to cover up the blander taste of the food and the weakness of the cheese.

In the streets of Cíudad Juárez, artisanal nonpasteurized cheeses are widely available. These same cheeses cannot be found in El Paso, except in the form of occasional illegal contraband, typically in small food markets in the Latin part of town. Yet nonpasteurized cheeses are richer, better tasting, and subtler in flavor. They're more beloved by most foodies—but most American everyday foodies are cut off from them. In France, however, nonpasteurized cheeses are the highlights of the local production.

The United States federal government bans nonpasteurized cheeses unless they have been aged for sixty days or more. In practice, this ends up banning most nonpasteurized cheeses and it bans the main nonpasteurized cheeses from Mexico, including the renowned cheeses of northern Mexico. To put it simply, Mexican cheeses, in their best forms, are not allowed in the United States.

Even if these regulations were repealed, U.S. tort law still would effectively block importation and widespread sale of many of the best Mexican cheeses. Nonpasteurized cheeses do make some people sick and can cause listeria or tuberculosis. Whether this is more or less frightening than, say, driving on a Saturday night, most deep-pocket, mainstream food retailers would be reluctant to market such cheeses for fear of lawsuits.

Pasteurization, however, is not the major issue. The best nonpasteurized Mexican cheeses also exist in pasteurized forms, including in Mexico. Today most Mexicans are likely to consume these cheeses in their pasteurized forms. Nonetheless the American product still does not measure up.

Critically, the artisanal nature of Mexican cheese production boosts quality. At the same time, it is difficult to supply these cheeses in large numbers and in regular, predictable quality. Many artisanal cheeses must be brought to market quickly and consumed within days. This meshes better with local networks of production and distribution than with national brands and long-distance transportation. U.S. cheeses are more highly processed and more likely to be injected with chemicals and preservatives. They will last in a supermarket or refrigerator for a much longer time, but the preservatives make the taste flat. They are designed not to be sold and consumed in totally fresh form.

Mexican cheese production methods are rooted in earlier times. To give one example, around the turn of the twentieth century, thousands of Mennonites moved into northern Mexico, mostly from Western Canada but tracing a longer path from the Netherlands, Prussia, and Russia. The Mennonites had been looking for freedom, isolation, and the ability to avoid public schools. Most of the Mexican Mennonites settled in a 650,000-acre area near Cuauhtémoc, about 250 miles south of El Paso. The Mennonites brought both farming and cheese-making skills from their European background. In their new Mexican homes, they developed the white cheese known as Chihuahua, which has become a staple of northern Mexican food. It is indicative that such a technologically backward community could dominate cheese-making in the region, to this day. By no means are all Mexican cheeses from the Mennonites (this is a peculiarly northern Mexican phenomenon), but artisanal cheese-making was never displaced by mass production. In America artisanal cheeses have made a big comeback in specialty shops and gourmet restaurants, but they are hardly the staple in our supermarkets or our dining.

Even when artisanal cheese is not an option, Mexican cheeses tend to have stronger tastes and to be fattier. The Juárez Wal-Mart has a large cheese case, filled primarily with manufactured, non-artisanal versions of the famous Mexican cheeses. *Asadero,* Chihuahua, Cotija, and Oaxaca cheeses are prominent. They are sold in the form of bars, circles, or roped knots. U.S. cheeses are available but they are not the main focus of attention. The El Paso Wal-Mart, even though it caters to a largely Hispanic clientele, does not offer cheeses made in Mexico. The cheese section there focuses on cheddar and Monterey Jack (European cheeses are not in vogue in El Paso). Unlike in Mexico, the cheeses are usually stringed or shredded; they are added to food as bits rather than as gobs. The Mexican cheeses of *asadero* and *queso quesadilla* can be found, but only in shredded form and mixed with cheddar and Monterey Jack in a Kraft plastic package. A Texas version of Cotija can be found in the deli section but otherwise the Mexican cheeses from the Juárez Wal-Mart cannot be found in the El Paso Wal-Mart.

American producers have never had much success with marketing Mexican cheeses on a large scale. Kraft experimented with a line of Mexican cheeses but abandoned them, due to the costs of specialized production and the difficulty of turning a profit. Some smaller specialty companies have made progress with the idea, but without changing the broader practices of cheese eating in the United States. Most Americans prefer blander flavors, in part an outcome of being less willing to consume fatty cheese products in large quantities.

Lard Glorious Lard

When it comes to beans, the best-tasting beans are found in Mexico, but not because of the beans themselves. Beans can be shipped without great loss of value. Instead the differences come from cooking fats. The peaks of Mexican cooking involve the use of fresh lard. Mexicans do not take lard from a can but rather they make it from high-quality pork fat. Lard adds taste and richness to refried beans, lightness to tamales, and flavor to many baked goods. In parts of northern Mexico, beef suet is used in place of pork lard, but with broadly similar results. The beef is added to flour tortillas.

American-Mexican food uses the blander media of vegetable oil or vegetable shortening. We do produce lard, but it is processed and thus less fresh. It is not used by many quality cooks. It will make your food seem greasy, and it also brings a milder and nuttier taste. Mexican lard makes almost anything taste good, which allows Mexican beans and tamales to reach higher peaks. The most prestigious English-language Mexican food cookbooks (e.g., Diana Kennedy, Rick Bayless, Patricia Quintana) recommend the use of fresh lard or sometimes they mention bacon drippings as an imperfect substitute.

Nonfresh American lard does last longer. Since it is loaded with preservatives, it does not break down or go rancid. The Mexican product is made by hand and then applied to cooking in a discretionary and unregulated basis. U.S. lard is ideally suited for mass production, national distribution, and health and safety regulations. Again, Mexican cooks prefer flavor at the expense of scale.

The top Mexican restaurants in the United States usually cook with fresh lard. As in Mexico, the lard is made from pig fat and a large batch can be refrigerated for months. Arguably lard from U.S. pigs does not taste as good, given that Mexico has better pork. But this lard still offers a richer and more authentic flavor than does vegetable oil, and so these top restaurants come a bit closer to real Mexican food. The more general problem is that cooking with Mexican-style lard is not well-suited for mass production.

Some more specific problems limit the use of fresh lard in U.S. restaurants. As a form of pig fat, lard is unacceptable to vegetarians, Jews who keep kosher, and Muslims. A restaurant that cooks with lard must forgo the patronage of these individuals. Even if these groups are small in number in a geographic area, their existence exerts a commercial influence. For legal and public relations reasons, a restaurant that cooks with lard must publicize this fact. (Recall that McDonald's used to cook its above-average French fries in horse fat; objections from vegetarians ended this practice, much to the dismay of many everyday foodies.) Many American consumers dislike the idea of knowingly eating lots of lard and indeed American-Mexican restaurants sometimes advertise that they use no lard.

The prominence of lard in Mexican cooking has historical roots. The Spanish attempted to grow olive trees in Mexico, but found it difficult (they had more success in the climate of Peru, where olive oil became important in the national cuisine). Colonial cooks therefore had to fry their dishes in some other medium and lard was a natural candidate. Lard became so important that in 1562 the pope issued a special dispensation saying that lard consumption did not violate fasting requirements from meat. Originally the Mexican indigenous peoples reacted to lard with disgust, but they learned quickly that it made tamales and other dishes tastier and more nutritious.

Cookbooks show the evolution of American-Mexican cooking with regard to lard. *The El Paso Cookbook* (1898) is believed to be the first cookbook ever published in El Paso, or at least it's the first I can find any sign of. Many of the recipes are Anglo-American or European in origin, but a section of the cookbook—covering 59 recipes—is devoted to Mexican dishes. It is common for the recipe to suggest that these dishes be cooked in lots of lard.

Vegetable oil displaces lard and other animal fats in the United States in the early part of the twentieth century. By 1910 Proctor & Gamble had turned vegetable oil into a patentable commodity. Within a few years, a national advertising blitz was under way. If we look in the first English-language Mexican cookbook, dating from 1929, some lard uses remain, but vegetable oil has become more common. After that, the momentum is on the side of vegetable oil.

The later concern with health in the United States, starting in the 1970s or so, cemented this change. There have been some interesting studies on how the diets of Mexicans change as successive generations assimilate into U.S. culture. By the second generation, most Mexican-Americans are aware of cholesterol issues and they recognize a negative connection between lard consumption and health, or at least they believe that such a correlation exists. The consumption of lard, cream, and chorizo meat and sausage (and other high-fat meats) falls significantly and consistently as Mexican-Americans have spent more time in the United States. On the negative side, complex carbohydrates such as corn tortillas are replaced by greater sugar consumption in the forms of packaged foods, snacks, and desserts.

So much for lard barrier—what about the rest of the meal?

Tortilla Diversity

U.S. tortillas are more commonly from flour, whereas Mexican tortillas are more commonly from corn. About 60 percent of tortilla sales in the United States are of the flour variety.

Mexicans are more likely to combine their corn with hand labor. They grind corn and pat it by hand into fresh tortillas. In rural Mexico fresh handmade tortillas accompany most meals.

Flour tortillas can be found in the north of Mexico (such as in the states of Sonora, Chihuahua, Coahuila, and Nuevo León), but otherwise traditional Mexican recipes are likely to use corn tortillas. Flour tortillas were an early example of fusion cuisine in Mexico; the inventors of the flour tortilla blended the indigenous idea of the tortilla with the European crop of wheat. But flour tortillas caught on only in the remote northern areas (including Juárez), where indigenous traditions were weak and the Spanish influence was relatively strong. For the remainder of Mexico, wheat was used for bread and for the *"torta"* sandwich, which has become a national dish in the cities.

Wheat (flour) tortillas failed to spread through Mexico. Growing wheat requires a higher upfront investment than docs growing corn. For instance a wheat crop must be accompanied by a greater number of expensive plow animals. Irrigation is needed for both a December planting and a March maturation. The particular wheat crops tried in Mexico often brought low yield and were susceptible to disease. Once the wheat is harvested, grinding the crop into flour required a European-style mill. Most rural Mexicans rejected the flour tortilla and stuck with their beloved corn, for reasons of taste, culture, and also economics—namely, price or the ease of making them at home.

The corn tortilla remains a symbol of national or regional pride. Before the Conquest, maize may have accounted for as much as 80 percent of the caloric intake of indigenous Mexicans. Throughout the nineteenth century, Mexican elites promoted the ideas that corn, and tortillas, were inferior to wheat and bread on the grounds of diet, sophistication, economic development, and even morality. This debate was part of the general struggle in Mexico between European and indigenous notions of national identity. By the 1940s, however, this opposition faded and the corn tortilla (and corn more generally) was accepted as the staple of Mexican cuisine.

Recently flour tortillas have been spreading through Mexico and gaining in popularity. In part, serving U.S. tourists has influenced Mexican food. Many Mexicans are trying flour tortillas and liking them. As more Mexicans move into cities, they identify with Mexico as a nation, rather than with their rural communities; they can take pride in "tortillas" rather than "corn tortillas." The blander flour tortillas are also easier to combine with the blander tastes of Americanized Mexican food, which has a growing presence in Mexico, partly through chain restaurants. The growing mechanization of agriculture, combined with NAFTA, has shifted the relative profitability of wheat and corn. Most fundamentally, once it is easy to ship in the flour—and most tortillas are made by factory machines, in any case—flour tortillas enjoy a cost advantage over their corn counterparts. For instance Texans switched to flour tortillas in the 1930s, shortly after tortilla factories became widely available.

Americans consume corn tortillas—if they still can be called that—most commonly in fried chip form. The Spanish word *fritos* has become the trademarked American brand name Fritos. In 1932 Elmer Doolin ate some corn chips in San Antonio and decided he had found a viable commercial product. He bought the recipe and some equipment from a Mexican cook for a hundred dollars. Over time, increasing amounts of chemicals have been added to the basic product.

That said, the United States is now consuming more corn tortillas of the traditional kind. Many recent immigrants, such as El Salvadorans, Hondurans, and Guatemalans, come mostly from traditional corn tortilla areas. Mexican immigration over the last fifteen years has come increasingly from the rural parts of the country, which also favors corn tortillas. So habits of tortilla consumption in the United States and Mexico are to some extent converging.

Putting aside the question of corn versus flour, tortillas still differ on the two sides of the border. U.S. flour tortillas are made with bleached flour and have a paler, whiter look. Mexican flour tortillas are grainier and less pure. The greater mechanization of agriculture in the United States makes for a more regular product.

When it comes to corn tortillas, the U.S. corn crop has fewer varieties of corn and fewer flavors. The tastes are blander. This difference dates from the 1920s, when commercially available corn hybrids were bred for ease of handling by machine, yield, time of maturation, uniformity of grain, and resistance to disease, among other qualities. Mexico has a far greater diversity of corn breeds, so corn tortillas taste differently in each part of the country or sometimes in each village. Furthermore, a single village has numerous varieties of corn for its tortillas, although some of these corns are fed mostly to the pigs.

In rural Mexico corn tortillas are more likely made by hand than in a factory. If a mother or grandmother spends her day making tortillas, she is not giving up much outside income. If she were to spend that time working, she might earn less than it would cost to buy a comparable amount of food.

Nonetheless the tortilla-making process is arduous. First the corn must be stripped (the men perform this task) and the kernels soaked in mineral lime water, typically overnight; the mix fortifies the tortillas with calcium hydroxide, a substance otherwise lacking in the traditional diet. (The alkaline processing of corn, the scurvy-limiting benefits of which were understood by Western science only recently, was a major scientific contribution of early Mexican civilization.) In the morning the corn must be ground into *masa*. The flour was formerly done by hand, using stone pounders; today it is usually done by a machine in the home. The kernels are then fed into a running machine; without skill it is easy to lose a finger doing the work. The resulting *masa* is then patted into shape; one legend suggests that precisely thirty-three pats are needed. The patties are cooked on a flat surface over a smoldering fire. This fire must be maintained at the correct temperature, yet without mechanical assistance. Neither cooked tortillas nor shaped *masa* stay good for long (stale tortillas are often used as "scoopers" in spoonlike fashion), so tortillas must be made fresh at least once a day. Tortilla production is one of the central chores in the life of a rural Mexican woman, but the payoff in terms of flavor and freshness is significant. They're the best tortillas I've ever had.

We again see a trade-off in the world of food. It is possible to have regular fresh food, of very high quality, if you are willing to put in considerable amounts of time and energy. Most of us, even most foodies, do not find this worthwhile on a daily basis. We would rather have the quick and easy. In some poorer societies, institutions and technologies are such that many people do not have the option of quick and easy food. That is when we find especially delicious food in poor settings. Yet as soon as those regions become wealthier, they tend to prefer greater convenience. We thus see that the freshest and most delicious foods are eaten by two groups of people: the relatively poor, who have no choice, and the relatively rich, who spend lots of money trying to re-create the food supply networks that the relatively poor have been working with for centuries.

Tortilla factories do not follow the handmade techniques. Most importantly, the *masa* for the factory product is prepackaged and to some extent dehydrated, rather than freshly ground from corn. The dry *masa* was introduced to Mexico in 1949. A fresh corn tortilla should contain about 40 percent moisture; this cannot be maintained during freezing and shipping across any distance. Furthermore, the shaped *masa harina* is produced and moved by rollers and flippers, rather than by the human hand. It is believed that hand pats produce just the right thickness and texture, and adjust for any idiosyncratic qualities of the materials.

In Mexico, handmade tortillas tend to be thicker, less uniform, and stronger in flavor. By using machine-made tortillas almost exclusively, the United States forgoes these advantages, albeit with savings of time and aggravation. On the plus side, the drier and thinner tortillas of the United States are better suited for frying and thus they work better for tostadas and related dishes.

In another sign of tortilla convergence, Mexico has been moving toward tortilla factories since the early part of the twentieth century. The first automatic tortilla factories in Mexico date from the late nineteenth century, although they functioned poorly until design advances in the early twentieth century. This trend toward machine production accelerated when the Mexican government subsidized the price of tortillas, ending that only in 1999. The subsidies kept many neighborhood tortilla factories in business, as it enabled them to compete with the dehydrated tortilla flour of Maseca, a Mexican corporate giant. Just as handmade tortillas are better than machine-made tortillas, so are local machine-made tortillas better and fresher than nationally produced brands. Tortillas spoil easy and are vulnerable to mildew, so the national product is flatter in taste and drier. But more restaurants in Mexico are moving to factory-made tortillas, if only because of their greater convenience and lower cost.

U.S. tortilla production also has moved toward greater consolidation. The first small U.S. tortilla factories were operating in the 1920s in San Antonio. Larger factories entered the sector in the late 1960s, to make tortillas for the El Chico restaurant chain. Today there are still hundreds of tortilla producers in the United States—mostly small, family-owned factories in Texas or California.

Some small U.S. Latin markets are resurrecting handmade tortillas for their immigrant customers. These tortillas have a stronger taste, although the need for refrigeration dries them out quickly. Select restaurants offer gourmet handmade tortillas at high prices. For instance a handmade tortilla might be available in a gourmet "Southwestern" restaurant in Santa Fe or New York City. Tortilla makers in New Mexico are experimenting with flour tortillas flavored with chocolate, blueberry, and pesto, among other flavors.

In sum, the world of tortillas is becoming more diverse. Both the United States and Mexico are converging to a world where most tortillas are machine-made, although the supply of handmade tortillas is becoming more resilient as well.

The Big Red Ones

The tomato encapsulates the broad situation with fruits and vegetables across the border. The United States needs to use refrigeration in its supply chain and that ruins the taste of a lot of food, especially tomatoes.

Chilies are not all that different on either side of the border. Mexico has a wider range of chilies. Nonetheless, enough brands of chilies can be found in the United States to replicate many Mexican dishes. You can toast chilies at home and then hydrate and puree them and have something pretty close to the real Mexican product.

The importance of predictable supply helps explain why chili peppers from Mexico make it into the U.S. market. It is easy to store chili peppers for weeks, or longer, without loss of taste or value. Restauranteurs and food suppliers can buy those chilies in bulk on a periodic basis. If one day's shipment is delayed or somehow unsatisfactory, one can draw down one's inventory.

Tourists are often impressed by Mexican offerings of fruit. Visitors to Cancún are often amazed by the quality of the fresh pineapple. The better restaurants in Cíudad Juárez have more and better fruit juices than would be found in an American-Mexican restaurant. But many of these offerings are not affordable to most Mexicans. Many Mexicans consume only their locally grown fruits, such as watermelon, oranges, guava, peaches, papayas, mangoes, pineapples, as well as tunas, capulines, nanchis, mamey, jocote, nance, or quince, among other options, varying by region. These fruits will be high in quality and fresh but usually available only seasonally and in some parts of the country. Good supermarket fruits are expensive and hard to come by.

A summer visit to Wal-Marts in El Paso and Juárez, showed the Juárez Wal-Mart to be lacking in Rainier cherries, regular red cherries, watermelon, pears, grapefruit, apricots, peaches, sweet peaches, and nectarines, compared to the U.S. store. The U.S. Wal-Mart also had a much larger and better (less bruised and stale) selection of plums, even though the Mexican plums were advertised as from the United States. The Mexican Wal-Mart had a superior selection of papaya (the U.S. offerings were few in number and bruised), but otherwise El Paso won the fruit competition by a wide margin. The excellent regional fruits of Mexico are not well-suited for placement and sale in a large Wal-Mart.

Cíudad Juárez is not the best Mexican locale for fruit, so this comparison is biased. It is just like the seafood story. Fruits from outside an immediate local area usually require extensive transportation,

AN ECONOMIST GETS LUNCH

refrigeration, and storage. Since neither Juárez nor El Paso lie in tropical locales, they both rely on fruit shipments and the U.S. supply network works better. Some of the Mexican fruit is superb, better than anything obtainable through U.S. supermarkets, although not necessarily better than the fruit of a small U.S. farm. Overall Mexican food markets don't deliver a wide variety of fruits on a year-round basis.

A comparison of Mexican and American vegetables yields much the same picture. Mexico has some superb pumpkin, various squashes, and cactus nopalitos, but Americans enjoy a greater diversity of vegetables year-round. U.S. vegetables are also more uniform in quality, which is again what we would expect from a greater use of agricultural technology. The Mexican vegetables will grow in a more irregular manner, be more susceptible to bruising, and will more likely arrive in the home bad.

Even when Mexican fruits and vegetables are satisfactory, they vary in size, quality, and texture too much for the demands of the U.S. marketplace. Restaurants do not like the idea that one customer's plate has a larger side dish than another customer's plate. They also do not like having to do too much post-purchase sorting of the delivered product. The longer control networks for American food favor the durability, regularity, and reliability.

The Mexican supply chain is also less regular and less predictable. Fruits and vegetables must be transported through a variety of Mexican states. Transportation is often poor and the commodities face periodic inspection for infestation. The corruption of the inspectors raises costs and may delay or stop the shipment. It is often easier to buy produce from the better-governed Chile, despite the far greater distance of that country, than to rely on shipments running through many Mexican states.

But getting back to tomatoes.

The word "tomato" is of Nahuatl origin, from Mexico, taken from *tomatl*. Like some other Nahuatl-derived words (ocelot, chocolate), the "tl" sound disappeared and it entered Spanish and then English as "tomato." For a long time tomatoes were not widely eaten in the United States but tomato-growing became much more popular in the early nineteenth century and it has since become a food staple.

Widespread export of Mexican tomatoes dates from the 1880s, but the 1920s were a watershed era. At that time Mexican tomato producers began using standard shipping techniques, such as packing the tomatoes into crates for easy transport. Mexican tomato production moved out of the artisan realm and encountered modern capitalism. By the mid-1990s, tomatoes accounted for over 22 percent of the production of fruit and vegetables in Mexico. Unlike in the United States, Mexico can produce tomatoes all year-round, simply because it is a warmer climate. December through February, a tomato in America most likely comes from either Florida or Mexico.

Mexican tomato networks are designed to send the prime tomatoes to the United States, but in reality many of the best tomatoes—from a foodie point of view—remain in Mexico. Once the tomato crates are unpacked by distributors, the tomatoes are sorted into categories. Agricultural workers, often young Mexican women, pick out the best—largest, firmest—tomatoes by hand. These not only appeal to American consumers but can be packed and shipped with a minimum of damage. The tomato sorters also look for an absence of scrapes, blemishes, and scars. An ideal tomato for export should have a pleasing shape.

If a Mexican tomato is selected for export to the United States, it immediately triples in value. But that tomato will undergo more processing. Most importantly, it is refrigerated at a temperature of no higher than fifty degrees. In part this is to preserve the tomato for a long voyage, in part it is to satisfy the law. A random sample of truck-driven tomatoes will be inspected by the USDA on the Mexican side of the border. Any tomatoes carried at a higher temperature will be rejected, which throws suspicion on the entire cargo. Therefore the tomatoes are kept cold. Yet cold damages the flavor and freshness of a tomato. Furthermore, the largest tomatoes have the most water, which also makes them the blandest.

Approved tomatoes find their way into warehouses on the U.S. side of the border. It then can take several more days before the tomato ends up in the supermarket, all the while kept yet longer at a cold temperature. If you'd like to perform a simple experiment, take a good tomato and put it in the refrigerator for two days. Then see what it tastes like.

While the America-bound product has been sitting in the cold, the "inferior" and usually smaller Mexican tomatoes have long since been consumed. A domestic Mexican tomato will be sold on fruit markets, as one finds in Guadalajara or Mexico City. The tomato will arrive there quickly. Despite its blemishes it will be closer in taste to a home-grown tomato. The worst tomatoes are used for animal feed.

This is not the only network for tomatoes in either the United States or Mexico. Both countries have a supply of home-grown or farmers' market tomatoes. But when it comes to regular restaurant supply, tomatoes available to purchase in Mexico by the consumer will be uglier and tastier.

The real reason is that consumers have been allowed to take risks rather than being constrained by other people's ideas of what is good for them. But food snobs are right about one thing. The best cheap Mexican food is in Mexico, by an order of magnitude. Good Mexican food is hard to make, and you can see this if you try to find good Mexican food in Paris. It's virtually impossible.

What are the real reasons why Mexican food can be so much better in Mexico than in the United States? I think of Mexico as a country that straddles two food worlds in a very advantageous manner. They have enough technology and enough modernity to manage modern food supply networks, run good restaurants, and send a fair amount of diversity the way of the everyday foodie. At the same time, Mexico still is in close touch with more artisanal methods of food production. The country has agribusiness, but it doesn't *only* have agribusiness. At its best, it's a unique combination of the best of the new and old worlds of food. Take advantage of it while you can.

10

The Finding Great Food Anywhere Encyclopedia

Jodi Ettenberg is eating her way around the world, one country at a time, as she puts it. Her modus operandi: seek out undervisited locales, stay in a very cheap hotel, befriend the local street food merchants, and max out on beautiful photography and tasty food. Her best shots are either of the scenery or of the food, including the local markets, the food stands, the street stalls, and the roadside restaurants.

This life didn't come without preparation. She is a former lawyer from Montreal who worked for five years at two law firms in New York, but all the time she was thinking about how she could save up money and take off. She dates her obsession with travel to a PBS documentary on the Trans-Siberian Railroad, which she viewed in high school. Finally, in 2008, at twenty-eight years of age, she quit her job and hit the road with little more than a backpack—with tightly compressed clothes—and a bank account. Since then she's spent time in South Africa, Mongolia, China, Russia, the Dominican Republic, the Philippines, Malaysia, Indonesia, Thailand, Myanmar (Burma) and Laos, not to mention a rapid trip through South America. She radiates curiosity and her goal is to "soak it all up like a sponge." She refers to a "density of purposes" which keeps her moving. Sri Lanka, India, and Nepal are slated for the future but she is the first to admit she doesn't have a long-term plan. In the meantime, these are not vacations; this is her life. She believes fervently that travel helps us retain perspective on ourselves "as one person in a wider tapestry," as she wrote to me.

To chronicle her philosophy, Jodi writes a blog (www.legalnomads. com), which covers such topics as "My 5 Worst Bus Rides in Burma," "Military Crackdown in Bangkok," and "How Not to Kill a Poisonous Spider on the Perhentian Islands: A Lesson in 3 Parts," in addition to the photography.

She has become a master of eating cheaply. In part she wants her stash of money from law to last as long as possible. In part, on the road, Jodi has learned that the cheapest meals are very often the best, especially in Asia. And in part it is a focus—some might say a preposssession—based on the premise that learning and absorbing information makes us more culturally connected, more closely tied to other people, more structured in our daily enjoyments, and in some fundamental way more human. Jodi reports: "The more I travel in Asia, the more I realize how much of my days are planned around food." In fact, a lot of Asian society is organized around food, so there seems to be a good match.

My favorite of her blog posts is about food in Laos, hardly known as a gourmet country. Yet in her three weeks in the country (not nearly enough, in her view) she unearthed culinary treasures virtually every day. She describes the Laotian soups; for instance one has "a light fish-based broth with vermicelli noodles, shredded banana heart and sprouts and topped with mint and cilantro." Another is "a rich broth topped with piles of freshly cooked pork, fresh herbs, fried garlic and springy thick rice noodles." Yet another soup was coconut milk and shredded pork. "It's always soup o'clock in Burma," she wrote. They are all exquisitely photographed, as is the roasted eggplant dip—jaew mak khua—which turned out to be her favorite. The average price for these soups runs under fifty cents. It's all cooked by hand, from scratch, with fresh raw ingredients.

Laotian barbecued meats became another of her specialties, as did the French-style baguettes. Finally, Jodi wrote on her blog: "Lao cuisine is much more than what I've posted here—I didn't even get into the specialities such as laab or the complicated *pâtés*, tightly wound inside banana leaf wrappers, the myriad of stews on offer or the sweet fruit I had never seen prior."

Jodi has found superb, cheap food in just about every country she visited; if there is anyone who innovates as a food consumer, it is Jodi. Even in Russia, not renowned as an excellent food country, she enjoyed ground meat folded into rich pancakes, bright red tomatoes, and ham on bread, all of which she ordered during the stops of the Trans-Siberian Express. And elsewhere? Here is her advice: "Ultimately, I found the tastiest foods were served trainside at our brief stops, or at cafeterias where taxi drivers would eat in Moscow or Yekaterinburg. Communication was tough, but once I had someone translate for me it was inevitably the best food I had in town." Jodi insists, as I do, that no matter where you are, the best food recommendations come from local transport drivers and operators.

What Jodi understands is that eating out while traveling isn't just about the food, it's also a quest. It's a chance to create an adventure, a memory, a connection to the local culture; and it's also a chance to help define what your trip, and indeed your life, is about. Traveling can spur the realization that *eating is a creative art.*

Since she is slight of build, only five foot tall, and female, she also carries around a safety whistle, which she has used to scare off marauding monkeys in Burma and which waits in reserve for other possible dangers.

My travel routine hasn't been as extreme as Jodi's but any traveler or tourist has faced a lot of the same issues, namely how to find a great meal while on the road or in a strange place. I've carried online printouts, consulted information in my iPhone, and more or less known in advance where I was going to eat. But often when traveling for work or pleasure we suddenly need to improvise and find some good food on the spot. There's not always a simple answer online, or maybe I don't read the appropriate language, or I wish to supplement my online research with some on-the-ground observation. In any case, the non-Web-assisted experience is the most fun to have and the most likely to give you a wonderful memory of discovery. In the longer run, on-the-ground experience is also the best foundation for interpreting what is on the Internet, when it comes time to consult it.

I see Jodi's experience as reflecting some fundamental principles: that you can almost always find an excellent meal, there's value in innovating as a consumer, and that these meals can be relatively cheap. The underlying economic principles governing food in other countries are not different from the United States, but how to apply them varies because the laws, wages, and surrounding environments are never the same, just as we saw in Mexico. In this chapter I'd like to offer a personal encyclopedia: a tour around some parts of the world, demonstrating the application of those basic principles I mentioned in the first chapter: *Food is a product of economic supply and demand, so try to figure out where the supplies are fresh, the suppliers are creative, and the demanders are informed.*

Adventures in Asia

Tokyo

Tokyo is perhaps the most fascinating place I've visited, whether for food or otherwise. After returning home from each of my two trips there, I felt like I had come from a different planet. It has all the conveniences of an advanced capitalist society, and then some, yet hardly anything works the same way as back home. What should I make of a society in which strangers return your lost wallet; the toilets talk back to you; foreigners who speak Japanese are mistrusted; and the most impressive run of rapid economic growth in the history of mankind has been experienced, moving it into an extended period of near-zero growth? There are also a lot of food "codes" to decipher in Tokyo.

Population density shapes the commercial structure of the city, including the dining. Within a few hours of the city center there are tens of millions of potential customers and they support an unprecedented density and variety of commercial activity. Since public transportation is rapid and reliable, and Tokyo residents are often willing to commute and take long train or subway trips (over 3 million people a day pass through Shinjuku Station alone), most of these individuals are potential customers within the Tokyo greater metropolitan area. Apartments are usually small, so people go outside for their entertainments, including dining.

In terms of real purchasing power, the Tokyo area brings more people, more money, and more wisdom to bear on food markets than anywhere else in the world, ever.

The supply side of the Japanese economy, including cuisine, is rooted in specialization. If you are a major cook in an ethnic restaurant, you are responsible for mastering the cuisine you produce. You are expected to have studied it for years. You are expected to make trips to the home nation of that cuisine to learn how it is done properly. You are expected to know everything about that cuisine and judge it by the highest standards. To be sure, it makes for less career freedom; Japan is not a country where you go from "Mexican chef" to "automobile salesman" overnight or vice versa. From the point of view of a diner, this is ideal. I ate in a first-rate Singaporean restaurant in Roppongi and the chef proudly announced that he had been to Singapore more than thirty times to study the cooking.

The dining scene in Tokyo has a number of distinct *layers* and I'm not sure I've discovered them all.

Layer 1, Japanese food: Americans are used to the idea of an all-purpose Japanese restaurant with tempura, sushi, noodle dishes, tonkatsu, and so on. This horrifies the Japanese, who expect a restaurant to specialize in one of these genres. A good rule of thumb is to find a restaurant that serves from only one of these food areas and then eat there. I've found it's not necessary to try hard to judge how good the restaurant is. Most Japanese restaurants in Tokyo are very good, most of all because picky Japanese customers enforce high standards.

Contrary to reputation, Japan is not a country where good food costs very much. It's easy to find excellent meals in the $10 to $20 range. When it comes to noodles, you might get a first-rate dish for $5 or less. They do have the $100 melon in the gourmet supermarket, or the $1,000 sushi dinner, but for the most part Japan is a country with remarkably affordable food. It is a middle-class country and the prices of the cuisine reflect that. You can't feed a middle-class country of a hundred million people with $100 melons.

By the way . . . it's hard to find your way to a lot of Japanese restaurants. Even in Tokyo, not many people speak fluent English; Japanese is hard to learn; the street addresses are not in any coherent order; many restaurants are in shopping malls, towers, or underground; and, in general, when it comes to finding your way around, the city is a sprawling mess. Does your guidebook tell you to get off at "Shinjuku Metro"? Fair enough, but there are more than sixty different exits from the Shinjuku Station. They bring you to different parts of the aboveground world and not all of the exits are easy to find. Getting directions to your destination is simply the first step of your journey.

When it comes to finding Japanese restaurants, especially in Tokyo, I see a few options:

- Show up in an interesting neighborhood and walk around until you see something good.

- Get out of the correct Metro stop, using the correct exit, and ask strangers numerous times how to arrive at your destination. Most people will understand enough English to be of some help, especially if you have the address written out in Japanese characters. Even if your restaurant is only a few blocks away, it may take five or more "asks" to get there. Don't get discouraged and don't forget that a lot of places are underground or otherwise hidden to the naked eye.

- Have the exact address, printed on a card, and take a cab to where you are going. This is expensive, and often the cabbie gets lost too, but all you have to do is sit there and pay for the privilege of watching him struggle.

Any one of these is an acceptable option. The problems arise when you are unwilling to commit yourself to any one of these options and then perhaps you never get there.

Layer 2, Ethnic food: You can find just about every kind of ethnic food in Tokyo and also in other major Japanese cities. Of the seventy-five or so countries I have visited, Japan is by far the most likely to simply *copy*—obsessively—how a dish is made in the home country. In other words, you can find a perfect Mexican molé sauce in Tokyo.

Chinese food is one cuisine that the Japanese have their own version of. Because Japan has long had its own community of Chinese migrants, it's not just about copying the home country. Rather, something distinctly Japanese has emerged. In Japanese-Chinese food, there's a greater emphasis on noodles; dim sum is especially influenced by Japanese gyoza dumplings; many of the Chinese regional distinctions and innovations disappear; and tofu, Japanese eggplant, and hot pot dishes are found with special frequency. In any case, it has high-quality ingredients and it is usually made with care. Japanese-Chinese food is a cuisine of its own, and overall much better than American-Chinese food, mostly because it is lighter, more elegant, and pays greater attention to the quality of ingredients.

Layer 3, Fine dining: Absolute rankings are hard, but every now and then something so wows you that it stands out forever. I regard the best fine dining of my life as from Tokyo—at the Japanese branch of Pierre Gagnaire (a three-star Michelin restaurant in Paris) in the Omotesando shopping district (subsequently reopened elsewhere in town). In terms of taste, originality, and quality of service, I found this to be better than any expensive meal I've had in Europe. It wasn't cheap—$200—but in Paris a comparable meal might have cost $300. The funny thing is, it is not even considered the best restaurant in Tokyo and many people wouldn't put it in the top five. Michelin at the time gave it only two stars. I called less than twenty-four hours in advance to visit a half-empty restaurant for lunch the next day. They also assigned me my own server, who spoke reasonable English and who did everything possible to make me feel welcome. In other words, for the very best French food, consider a trip to Tokyo as a way to save money and aggravation.

You also can find a lot of Japanese restaurants that offer sushi, *kaiseki* multicourse menus, and other national specialties at very high prices. You can pay $1,000 for dinner or more for what I can only assume is a superb meal of sushi or other Japanese specialties. Many of the restaurants are used for business deals or building business connections. My inclination is to recommend against these outings, unless you are wealthy.

This may sound strange, but if you're going to spend big bucks on food in Tokyo, I don't think you should spend it on Japanese food. I think you should spend it on French, Italian, or maybe Chinese. Maybe I didn't spend enough, as I've tried only the $150 version of the wonderful sushi meal in Tokyo, for lunch. (I might have been more impressed by the $1,000 meal.) But was it *much* better than a random $35 meal at a good sushi restaurant at the Tsukiji fish market or at a neighborhood sushi joint? I'm not so sure. The problem with "really, really good Japanese food" is that it has to compete with "really good Japanese food." The latter is "really, really good" too. Japan is a wonderful place to splurge on food, but be careful about where you're spending those extra dollars because in fact you don't need to do it to eat very well. Economics is about choice at the margin, and in Tokyo you don't have to spend a lot to do very, very well.

Jodi Ettenberg, by the way, in an e-mail to me, offered her own recommendation for dining in Japan: an *izakaya* bar. The sake aside, she describes these as "a wondrous experience, with its incredible atmosphere and rowdiness and fun bar snacks like pork belly and cabbage dishes and mini udon hot pots and grilled yakitori options, even the grizzly ones. Prices are usually more reasonable than other restaurants too, and you can pick and choose your meal pretty much as you wish."

Layer 4, Western food at lower price levels: This is where it gets interesting. Standard Western food in Tokyo can be of remarkably high quality or strange and extreme.

Let's start with the upside. Once I was walking with my wife along near one of the major shopping districts of Tokyo, Omotesando. It was past 2:30 in the afternoon, and while we could see many restaurants, most of them in that area were closing for lunch and not taking additional patrons. We grew hungrier and increasingly eager to eat.

Finally, we decided to do something that appeared an egregious food mistake. On a main shopping street, we chose an Italian restaurant that did not close all day, was up a flight of stairs, and which was populated by what appeared to be shrieking eighteen-year-old Japanese schoolgirls. We were hungry, what can I say?

I ordered a simple spaghetti and it pleased me as much as a lot of what I've had in central-northern Italy, say in Parma or Bologna. I left paying about ten dollars for the meal.

I'm not saying that will happen every time, but sometimes it will happen. Other times you'll end up with ketchup on the noodles instead of tomato sauce. And that's what makes eating Western food in Tokyo so interesting. Of course the ketchup will be good ketchup, not bad ketchup, but does it matter? I most fear Japanese treatments of Western food when it comes to the condiments.

I recommend you visit any major Japanese department store and walk through their food court. You'll find remarkable sections devoted to French and Italian delicacies, most of all pastries and baked goods. Try them. When it comes to food, the Japanese have an obsession with Italian and above all French styles and it shows. There's a whole cooking school in Paris, run in Japanese, which trains prospective Japanese chefs in the French culinary arts. I think it's quite possible to argue, with a straight face, that the best French food in the world today is served in Japan.

The bottom line is that a trip to Japan is not a mistake. In the Japanese urban centers, economic activity—especially retail—has reached new heights in the history of humanity and that includes the food too.

Singapore

Singapore is one of my favorite places to eat, most of all because of their superb food stalls. The general wealth of the city allows people to eat out a lot, and land-use policies have ensured that stalls are not pushed out by higher rents. Tiong Bahru is the best I've been to, but buy one of the published guides to the stalls and their best dishes, available at city bookstores.

Collections of these "hawker centers" as the stall areas are called—can be found throughout the city, but as you might expect, those in the city center are not the best. Still, in most parts of town, the stalls will sell an excellent dish—enough for a moderate-size meal—for two or three dollars. Given that Singapore is about as wealthy per capita as France, this price is astonishing—and for my tastes it's some of the best food I've had.

A contemporary hawker's center is typically found outside the center of downtown, usually under a large metal roof. It might contain fifty or more food stalls, usually of Chinese, Malay, and Indian cuisines. The Chinese food in particular is quintessentially Singaporean, mixing in Indian and Malay ideas and emphasizing seafood and noodles. For instance, fish head curry, which is original to Singapore, draws its curry sauce from South India but the idea of the fish head is Chinese; Indians would use fish fillet. Singaporean chili crab, one of the country's classic dishes, combines Chinese (bean paste), Malay (chilies), Indian (sauce texture), and Western (tomato sauce) influences.

Most stalls specialize in a small number of dishes, and often the stall builds its reputation on a single dish, or a single dish with close variants. So there will be nasi goreng (fried rice with egg), rice porridge, roti john (a kind of meat loaf with chili sauce), grilled stingray, and many other choices, but usually at different stalls.

The stalls also showcase the benefits of cultural blends. Even the Chinese food in Singapore is a mix of quite different regional Chinese cuisines. Cantonese cuisine lends the idea of roast pork, dim sum, and noodle soups. The Hokkiens (Fujian province) are the most numerous ethnic Chinese group in Singapore. Their cuisine favors hearty braised dishes, especially with pork. Garlic and soy sauce are prominent and soups are popular. The widespread use of pork lard in Singaporean cooking is Hokkien in nature. The slow simmering soups and stews of that region are ideal for food-stall production and sale. Teochew food, another influence, emphasizes steaming, light soups, and seafood dishes. Fishball, fishcake, and porridge—three Singaporean staples—come from Teochew cuisine. The chilies in Singapore come from Sichuan and other "interior" Chinese cuisines, in addition to the Malay connection. Singaporean chili is not a single item, but rather an entire range of chili concoctions that cooks can prepare, be it spreads, dipping sauces, or condiments.

Seafood has remained a staple of Singaporean food stalls. The country is surrounded by water and has a convenient harbor and airport. The transportation of seafood into the country is easy. Seafood also avoids many of the dietary taboos of Muslims and Hindus, two large minority groups in the country. Muslims will not eat pork and Hindus will not eat beef, making seafood relatively safe ground. In terms of either climate or available land, Singapore is not well situated to grow many vegetables. Finally, meat or chicken of any kind was uncommon before the 1950s in Singapore. Many of the famous hawker dishes evolved to rely on seafood, not meats. At that time, seafood was two or three times cheaper than meat.

The best cooks spend years working on their own, perfecting their specialty dish before taking it public into a hawker center. The owner usually is on-site and is cooking or at least overseeing the food. Since many different kinds of stalls are right nearby, a single stall can specialize in two or three key dishes. Customers buy their fried oyster egg from one expert and their laksa (noodle soup in coconut milk) from another expert. This specialization, combined with tight monitoring of quality, is another reason why Singaporean food is so delicious. The Singaporean stalls bring together just about all the core features I look for in quality food. The Singaporean institutions differ from those of Tokyo, but both food networks mobilize the force of extreme specialization in their favor.

The main problem is the waiting time. The stalls cannot easily scale up the volume of food when demand is high, so get there early or wait in line for half an hour or more.

Fortunately, the technocratic Singaporean government reserves land for food stalls throughout the city and the stalls are seen as a kind of public right or public utility. Even though the value of land has risen dramatically in Singapore, for regulatory reasons it is not easy to buy out the stalls and set up a large shopping center on the same ground. The whole system is a massive subsidy to foodies, based on fixing cheap rent for a lot of food establishments. I've also heard it rumored that the government continues the system of stalls because they think that cheap, readily available meals will lead the citizenry to work longer hours, thus contributing to the economic growth of the country.

The hawker stalls are exceptionally clean. The Singaporean government sends around a food inspector who gives a letter grade to each stall. Everyone in Singapore knows it is safe to eat in the stalls; customers can see the kitchen and the cooking. Most of the stalls receive a B grade from the inspector. The standing joke is that the stalls with grades C or lower have the tastiest food, and that an A grade represents too much attention to cleanliness and not enough time spent on what really matters—namely, the food.

If you're wondering: I've never gotten sick from eating at food stalls, and I've done it many times in many countries. I've been really sick from food twice in my life, and I'll spare you the details but the lesson is instructive. The first time I got sick from food was the first time I visited Mexico, in the mid-1980s. I ate only in "established" restaurants but got sick anyway. The second time was a few years ago, staying in the Sheraton Hotel in Zurich, that's right, Zurich, *Switzerland*. I made the mistake of eating the (raw) smoked salmon on the breakfast buffet and the result was too awful to describe.

So, no, getting sick from street food isn't my main worry. Junk food, which I avoid, is a greater danger to the health of most of us than is street food. One thing about street food is that you can see what is going on, right out in the open. Street food also is aimed at locals, who know if a particular vendor serves up dangerous wares. It's the best built-in monitoring you're likely to find in food markets. I'm not saying you won't ever get sick from street food, just as sometimes people get sick from non-street food. I'm saying that if you want to try street food, the best place to do so is in the clean and orderly Singapore.

India

Outsourcing to India is now a global trend, yet it is less well known that the major production outlets have to create their own infrastructure. You can see these self-sufficient business "islands," with their own electric generators and water supplies, in the major Indian cities. It's not an ideal arrangement from a commercial point of view, but it works. It's necessary because the government-supplied infrastructure is not reliable enough for many major commercial players.

I look for good Indian food with this basic model in mind. It's an often amazing food culture, especially for someone with money, but it has lots of patches, unreliabilities, and danger spots in terms of your health. For most visitors, including dedicated foodies, the best Indian food, all things considered, is in—don't laugh—Indian hotels.

India has many of the most luxurious and extravagant hotels in the world and these lavishly decorated buildings create an entire world for their guests, including their own electric, water, and food infrastructures. The hotels have a lot at stake in their reputations and the hotels also are responsible for their own water supplies.

The five finest hotels in any major city will each have several restaurants of excellent quality, serving food that is authentic, well presented, and regional. They'll also usually have restaurants that serve food from other parts of India. Usually I recommend against buffets, but if you see an Indian buffet in a good Indian hotel it is likely tasty and extremely fresh. (Indian food, which often simmers, is especially well-suited to the buffet format.) Good Indian hotels also have "stands," usually within the restaurants, where talented cooks are asked to re-create quality regional street food for the guests, as if they were cooking at an actual food stand. In other words, you can sample local street delicacies, cooked in front of your eyes, without much fear of getting sick.

These hotel restaurants will cost much more than most of the food available in India, but by American or European standards they remain affordable. If you know the Indian street, you can eat very well on the absolute cheap, but for India in particular I don't trust a lot of the food, perhaps because I have read too much about water policy in Indian cities. Home-cooked food in India is generally good, because so many people have quality servants, including servant cooks. I recommend trying to get some; and if you know anyone in India this shouldn't be hard, in part because servants are so common. Most Indian food, by the way, isn't very spicy, contrary to its reputation in the United States and home-cooked food in India is very often not spicy at all.

India is also probably the world's best country for eating vegetarian. Even if you're not vegetarian, I find that many of the best dishes in the Indian hotel restaurants are the vegetables. (You're also less likely to get sick eating vegetarian there, because there is no question of what the animals have been eating.) The best two or three Chinese restaurants in a major Indian city are likely world class, but otherwise avoid cuisines that are not from India or the immediate region, such as Nepal. India has opened itself up to the world only recently and for the most part there is not enough cooking experience with cuisines outside of the subcontinent, apart from Chinese. I also recommend the sweets shops, most of all in Calcutta. Don't be put off if you don't like Indian sweets in the United States, because they are not made from scratch. The labor-intensive product is done properly only in a low-wage country, namely India.

Adventures in Europe

Cheap food in Europe isn't easy to do, because Europe itself isn't very cheap, least of all in recent times when the euro has hit some highs against the dollar. That currency alignment may or may not last, but

European dining has some fundamental structures that can be dissected and understood. In this section I can't quite promise good cheap food by Asian price standards, but I can promise good food that is cheap compared to a lot of what else goes on in Europe.

Let's start with France, the most classic food destination, and it has some of the most economically sophisticated food supply networks in the world. You're still looking for fresh supplies and informed demanders. But unlike in Tokyo, you can't track down the cheap noodle shop; and unlike in Nicaragua, you're not spying the neighbor's small chicken farm across the road or finding tamales in the street. You're dealing with high wages, wealthy customers, and a lot of government regulation of work hours and benefits.

By the way, I save up most of my fine dining experiences for travel in Europe and Japan, not for my typical time in the United States. There are some splendid expensive restaurants in the United States, but Western Europe still has a comparative advantage in this sector of the market, based on centuries of history and the refinement of sophisticated recipes and raw ingredients. If you have the chance to travel abroad, consider holding off on some of that expensive food-spending at home. A fine meal in Europe also gives us a better chance to share a special memory with another person and to make a journey and narrative out of the meal.

There's another reason for saving up the expensive places for Europe, and that has to do with memory and also sociality. It's the same reason why you might go to an especially fancy place on a birthday or an anniversary. You want your trip abroad to be special, so you can remember it for your entire life. Toward that end, reserve some categories of restaurants for your trips (and maybe birthdays too). Your anticipations and your memories will be all that more potent.

France

You'll hear, from equally serious people, both that France has the best food in the world and that the French culinary empire is tumbling. On one hand it has marvelous, talented chefs, reinventing old ideas for a sophisticated global audience, while serving foie gras and wheeling out cheese carts. On the other hand it is a stale, corrupt, overregulated, under-innovating, hierarchical system, losing its lead to Spain and England while inducing its leading chefs to commit suicide in their futile quest for overrated Michelin stars. There's even a whole book on the decline of French cuisine: Michael Sternberger's well-argued *Au Revoir to All That: Food, Wine, and the Decline of France.*

How could intelligent people so disagree on such an easy to sample set of dishes and restaurants? Is it really just a matter of taste?

Both sides are right, as they are touching different sides of the proverbial elephant. French food is blossoming and collapsing at the same time. I think of French food in terms of this apparent paradox: Paris has more fine restaurants than ever before, but cheap food in Paris continues to decline in quality.

To oversimplify a bit, consider two differing ways of supporting quality cuisine. The first relies on a tightly knit local network of quality food suppliers, and counts on those suppliers to throw off enough good ideas and good raw ingredients to make for a vibrant culinary tradition. Restaurants, for instance, might have close links to slaughterhouses, fishing boats, and wise grandmas, from which they draw basic foodstuffs and inspired recipes. There is a part of Paris—La Villette—where the slaughterhouses and cattle market used to be located, and formerly that was an area for good restaurants serving meat and offal. These days it's just another part of town and not an especially interesting one at that, except perhaps for its science museum.

The second way to support quality cuisine relies on artisanal production—usually at higher cost. It's like hiring Picasso to do your portrait. It's good, but you have to pay an outlandish price. In the context of food, these fancier outputs tend to occupy expensive real estate—near the major museums and expensive hotels—and often they are funded by tourist demand. In any case most of the old neighborhoods are gone. The ingredients are sometimes local but often hurried in by expensive methods of transport and care. Culinary knowledge is bought and sold to a greater degree, and is less "in the air." Chefs fly around the globe and oversee multiple restaurants. The global replaces the local, and the inspiration comes from apprenticeships with famous chefs, not from local grandmothers or the family's Sunday cooking.

Many cities have a bit of both food networks (a good thing), but in Paris the balance of power has been shifting away from the neighborhood model. That means good food is still in abundance, but it's becoming more and more expensive.

As Parisian land prices rise, every square commercial inch is used to exacting standards and that means that most of the food supply network is pushed out of the city center. A Starbucks, Internet café, or clothing shop needs to be near lots of tourists but a food supply market does not. For some time now, it's been cheaper to put the market further away and truck in the supplies to the city center.

One turning point came in 1968, when the classic Parisian food market of Les Halles closed, signifying a shift from one mode of quality food production to another. Whereas Les Halles was a short walk from the main sights of the Right Bank, the current central food market site of Rungis is near Orly airport and outside the peripheral highway of Paris. Les Halles had been operating, with few breaks, almost continuously for eight centuries in its previous locale; Zola referred to it as the stomach of Paris. But Les Halles was too crowded and the surrounding neighborhoods offered little scope for expansion. Les Halles took up one small neighborhood in the center of Paris and even that was not big enough, as the opening of the sprawling Rungis included forty large warehouses, 25,000 parking spaces, modern cold storage facilities, and a large number of accompanying office buildings and restaurants. Rungis claims to be the world's largest fresh food market and arguably it is also the best.

At Les Halles the market was small-scale and person-to-person. Refrigeration was minimal and mechanized transport within the market was difficult or impossible. The dominant method of sale was to bring a relatively small quantity of fresh things and offer them to the market immediately. The surrounding neighborhood was known for its bistros, cafes, and restaurants. Nowadays Les Halles is dominated by a tacky shopping mall and it is one of the least appealing parts of the center city. It's a dump.

How much was the shuttering of Les Halles a cause of these changes and how much was it a mere symptom of broader changes? I incline toward the latter view, that it was a symptom, but for my purposes that is a moot point. In any case Paris has been moving away from the neighborhood model of food production. The best food in Paris is now directed toward Japanese tourists, Chinese businessmen, and American software entrepreneurs. At the same time that the local food markets get crowded out to more distant locales, wealthy tourists arrive in greater numbers and their purchasing power has made Paris the world's focal city for itinerant gourmets. The upscale restaurant market becomes higher cost, more commercial, more based on global publicity, and more dependent on bringing together ingredients and ideas from many geographic locales.

Yet there is a subtler point: using economic language, the *marginal cost of quality rises*. That means the best food is more expensive than before, compared to so-so food, which keeps on getting cheaper. On average, it is the wealthier buyers who stick with quality food purchases and a lot of the poorer buyers give up on good taste and simply eat cheaply. Think of it as a gentrification effect, but for food rather than real estate. Good, cheap food has become harder to find in Paris, just as a good, cheap apartment is difficult or impossible to come across in Manhattan or London. That's a sign of overall success for those cities but still it makes life harder for some people, clearly those without lots of money.

Here's another way of putting the point. More people enjoy Parisian Michelin-starred restaurants than ever before. But mediocre food is now remarkably cheap, and Parisians are going to pay more for the better stuff only if they're really interested in it. And that brings us to the result: In Paris the food is more splendid, but you have to pay a higher premium than before for the fanciest meals. What this means is that if you stop on the boulevard of the Champs-Élysées for a random meal, it's probably not going to be special. I'd rather eat in the suburbs of San Diego.

On top of those developments, the French labor market is stifled and overregulated. It's hard to hire workers cheaply. Hours are regulated, costly benefits are mandated, and it can be very hard to fire the bad workers. It's not just about food; most of the French labor market works (or rather doesn't work) this way. That makes good cheap food much, much harder to produce. Since workers will be fairly highly paid, and "here to stay," restaurants and other businesses are more likely to invest in tried-and-true workers. That's good for reliability but bad for innovation and bad for price. Labor costs are stuck at a high level and that means most of the food is pretty expensive.

It's also about real estate. It's very hard to build in the city center of Paris, or to modify the existing buildings, basically because so many of them are historic landmarks. That's good for the beauty of the city, but it's bad for the food. They're not about to open a strip mall of low-rent ethnic eateries next to the Musée d'Orsay and Parisian food will suffer for that. I'm not suggesting those rules must be changed (they do have aesthetic benefits), but it is another way to understand why the Parisian food market is in some regards so stagnant.

On the bright side, for the ordinary eater, Paris has more kinds of ethnic food than before, although this is usually away from the main city center. These ethnic restaurants are found, as you might expect, in the less beautiful neighborhoods. These places range from Algerian to Tex-Mex to Indian to the cuisine of the Reunion Islands (where else can you find that?). The efficient supply apparatus of the modern world, as represented by the Rungis food market, enables this plentitude. Cheaper food processing means more variety, even though this variety includes both good and bad, including more junk and also more cheap, mediocre food.

This variety also includes a fairly efficient supply network to local supermarkets and small food shops. If I'm in France, especially Paris, the supermarket, or better yet a few small cheese, bread, and fruit shops remain some of the best options. Usually the tourists are absent and the level of quality is high.

When it comes to affordable restaurants in France, I recommend the provinces, where land remains much cheaper than in Paris. A forty-dollar meal in Nice or Strasbourg, even in the center of the city, is much better than a comparably priced meal along the Right Bank or next to Notre Dame.

So here's a simple principle: *Unless you are spending a lot of money, Paris is the worst place to eat in all of France.*

For traveling around France more generally, I have another piece of advice. *Buy and use a Michelin guide, but use the guide for the very cheapest restaurants it recommends.* Look for restaurants that are certified with one or two forks and no stars. That's right, no stars, even though stars are supposed to represent the highest reach of culinary achievement. The forks, in contrast, signify that the restaurants offer something of interest and the guide defines a two-fork restaurant ("two-forkers," I call them) in the following terms: "Comfortable." That's vague but also pretty accurate.

It's not just that the non-starred restaurants are cheaper, or easier to get into, but they are also more likely to serve the classic French dishes. Often the stars are awarded for culinary innovation and for the overall profile of the chef. That's fine, but as a tourist so much of the food in France is new to me or at least the quality execution of the dishes is new to me. I don't need the extra innovation and probably I am trying to *avoid* the innovation. I seek that perfect pot-au-feu. I'm usually going to enjoy the classic dishes—done well—at least as much as I will like the innovations for culinary specialists.

So, despite its much-rumored problems, I am a believer in the red Michelin guide, and I think it overall does a good job in communicating the food glories of France and other locales. But I use the guide in a different way than do many of its partisans. I've been to France many times (twenty?), but some of those were short trips and so I don't think I have spent six months of my life in France. That's more than most visitors but, still, much in French food remains new to me and I don't need to seek out the very latest. And by going for the lower-rated-but-still-excellent places, it is possible to avoid whatever corruption and hype the Guide and its star system might fall prey to.

Keep in mind the economics of the Michelin guide itself: The guide loses money (about $21 million a year by one estimate)—but the name and profile provide publicity for the tire company, which owns the guide. The tire company does make money, or at least it can make money in good times. That means the guide is arranged to maximize its publicity value and not to maximize its usefulness to the ordinary reader. I adjust my use of the guide accordingly, to compensate for this economics-driven bias.

There is one final problem with dining in Paris, at least for tourists and especially for lunch. If you're just walking around and looking for a good place to eat, it's hard to get the timing right. I've found that most good places fill up immediately at 12:30, upon opening, if they aren't fully booked already. (This is a common problem in cities where space is tight.) You have a window of maybe five to ten minutes to get a seat and then your chances are gone; and if you get a seat, it often means you are at a lemon. The first lesson is to make a point to book in advance. The second lesson is that if you can't book or haven't booked, and you see a decent-looking place at 12:34, grab it. The idea of walking around another fifteen minutes to find somewhere better, or to enjoy the window-shopping, probably isn't going to pay off. That is again a result of the relatively high rents in the city and the only way to cope with that problem is to be well prepared in the first place. If you can't do advance research and booking when it comes to Paris—again, for your meal, I direct you to cheese, bread, and fruit shops.

London

London has fantastic food of many varieties, but it's almost always expensive, even after the depreciation of the British pound during and after the financial crisis. Pay up, suffer, or get out. If you love fish and chips, New Zealand is the place, not the United Kingdom. Even British pub food is being reified into an expensive form of fine cuisine. London is a wonderful place to be eating on an expense account, but otherwise it's tough to do well there for the amount you have to spend.

That's short coverage of a major city and leading tourist destination, but pretty much you're stuck, unless you visit the somewhat distant East End and feast on Pakistani, Bangladeshi, and Indian delights. That said, you don't have to enter the triple digits range—$100 and up—for an excellent meal. If you visit the better Indian, Portuguese, Chinese, or otherwise ethnically unusual places, you can get a very good meal for less than $50.

London is also the best European city for Michelin-starred Thai, Indian, and Chinese restaurants. They're not cheap, but they're much cheaper than their French counterparts, and they are perhaps the best way to spend $100 on food in the city, less if you go for lunch.

For England, more generally, I am enamored of the Pakistani, Bangladeshi and Indian restaurants in the north. It is often the case that the more run-down and decrepit the city, the better the food from the subcontinent. The run-down Bradford was a manufacturing and textiles center in the nineteenth century, but today it sometimes resembles a war zone. It's the best Pakistani food I've had; and for restaurants, the main streets are perfectly safe to visit.

Germany

German food is underrated. Maybe you think of a plate of fatty meat, with potatoes, served by a stout Bavarian waitress. Or maybe you just think of Oktoberfest and beer.

Yet a deeper look reveals some riches. Germany is right next to France and it has a free-trade zone with most of Europe, giving it access to some of the best raw culinary materials. Germany is a prosperous nation and it supports a wide variety of service industries. Germans have a long cultural history of being good at precision manufacturing, so why should they all be terrible cooks? They're not. Furthermore, the free migration clause of the European Union treaties makes it easy for Germany to import cooks from other nations. Finally, Germany has moved away from the "eurosclerosis" cliché into a vibrant and dynamic economy, which attracts immigrants from all over the world. While Western Europe is rarely cheap by global standards, by regional standards you can find many bargains in Germany.

Germany competes with France on fresh ingredients and often wins, but doesn't have informed or interested customers to the same degree. That means a dedicated foodie can find the good product but has to search more along the way. It also means less crowding and lower prices, when you do find the good stuff.

Germany has excellent Michelin-starred restaurants. They are not as good as the very best ones in France, but they are as good as the typical Michelin-starred restaurants in France. By a 2011 count, Germany had over two hundred restaurants with some kind of Michelin star and the nine three-starred restaurants placed them second in Europe after France. These restaurants have access to a lot of the same ingredients as their French peers and very often the chef comes from France anyway. Yet these restaurants can be half the price of a French equivalent or less, and they are also much easier to get into without an advance reservation. Very often a top German restaurant can be called up a mere day or even an hour in advance for a table.

Why are the German restaurants both cheaper and easier to visit? Sadly, German consumers don't have the same commitment to food culture as French consumers do and thus the average standard is lower. A lot of Germans really are happy with meat and carbohydrates in stereotypical form. Happily the visitor is not stuck with the average. There are numerous nooks and crannies, and many of those will be excellent. A top German restaurant is operating less in the limelight, and that can mean less pressure, and more creativity.

The German Michelin restaurants have excellent levels of service and only rarely are they snooty, a quality that would alienate some of their German patrons. The other customers often aren't dressed as well as they might be in a French Michelin-starred restaurant, so as an American often I feel more comfortable in the German version. For all of these reasons, visiting Germany is one good way to fulfill your desires for Michelin-star dining.

German restaurants and bistros just below the Michelin-star level often have outstanding vegetables, mushrooms, and fish.

Many of the best German meals I have had have been at cheaper restaurants in the southwest of the country, especially in country restaurants in the Black Forest. It makes for a nice foodie vacation simply to spend a week going around from one village to another. The food has a French feel, and Colmar and Strasbourg are, from most parts of southwest Germany, no more than an hour away. The game, the berry sauces, and the salads based on wild greens plucked by hand from the neighboring fields are usually excellent.

The bottom line is that Germany is still an underappreciated food country. Furthermore, buying bread, cheese, and especially sausage in the supermarket will almost certainly not be disappointing.

The best ethnic food in Germany is often from groups that don't make their way in very large numbers to the United States. I spent a chunk of a recent summer living and teaching in Berlin and the best ethnic meals I had were from Georgia (the country, not the state) and Sri Lanka. The former restaurant attracted a large number of Georgians, but the latter had more German customers. The Sri Lankan place was good, in part, because it had no hope of "crossover" potential and thus it marketed itself to well-educated German customers with its relatively authentic and spicy offerings. I also found about half a dozen Mexican places that were run by Mexicans cooking real Mexican cuisine. They were better than anything I can get in northern Virginia and better than most places in Los Angeles. These Mexican sites were typically in the lower-rent areas of East Berlin. The other German cities cannot compare with the ethnic offerings of Berlin, but still if you look around there are gems, including good Greek food. Beware: Most of the Chinese restaurants in Germany are too influenced by the blandness and starchiness of a lot of German food.

Turkish food in Germany is overrated, and it is a partial exception to the principle that you should look for lots of competition in an ethnic cuisine. There are a lot of Turkish restaurants in Germany, in part because the Turks are Germany's largest ethnic minority, due to decades of guest-worker programs. Some of the Turkish restaurants are quite good, but I don't recommend random selection. You need to know where you are going.

The underlying problem has to do with dysfunctional German fast food. McDonald's never achieved the foothold in Germany that it has in the United States, in part because Germans are skeptical about the quality of the cuisine, in part because many Germans view it as a symbol of

Americanization, and also, in part, because compared to the United States, German family eating is less centered around the child.

The result is that Germans have had to evolve their own fast food. Many Germans will order wurst in the street, but still there remains a gap and in large part this gap is filled by Turkish food and in particular the doner kebab. Very often in Germany Turkish food is fast food, and often the standards for it have fallen. There is far too much Turkish food in Germany that consists of not great meat, served in bread with a gloppy bland yogurt-based sauce.

Doner kebab, by the way, is often thought of as a Turkish dish, but it was invented by a Turk living in Berlin and it was geared toward the German market from early on. "Meat and carbohydrates with a creamy sauce"—does that sound familiar? Again, that doesn't have to be bad, it just means caution is in order. When you're eating Turkish food in Germany, make sure you are not eating what is actually German fast food.

Finally, Berlin deserves some special remarks. For its size and political importance, Berlin has arguably the least developed fine dining scene in Europe, except perhaps for Moscow. The city doesn't have much of a business class, first because of the Nazis and then because of the East German communists. Berlin was, in the early part of the twentieth century, a center for German business, but that was a long time ago. Very often it is businessmen and financiers who sustain expensive restaurants. Today the financial capital of Germany is Frankfurt, not Berlin. Berlin also does not have wealthy multilateral institutions to sustain its fine dining scene, as do Geneva and Brussels and Washington, D.C.

What Berlin does have is remarkably cheap rents. Because of the weak business climate in the city, there are not so many jobs. A disproportionate share of the population either works for the government or receives subsidy income from the government; or young people live there while they try their hand at art, design, music, and so on. That supports cultural riches, but the city itself is not economically vital. Yet it is a city that was originally built up to be a major commercial center, and as a result it is considerably overbuilt. Rents are very cheap and even today it is not difficult to find a reasonable apartment for three hundred dollars a month, which is unthinkable in New York City or London. That makes for a vibrant cultural scene, unparalleled in the Western world. It also makes for a lot of very good and very diverse ethnic restaurants. When it comes to food, Berlin is more or less the opposite of central Paris.

Switzerland

For food discussions, it's common practice to divide Switzerland into its linguistic regions, but I find that practice more misleading than illuminating. Food aside, I start with two very basic lessons about Switzerland:

1. Everything in Switzerland is good.

2. Everything in Switzerland is expensive.

Food is not an exception to either rule, no matter what language they are speaking. I have visited every canton in Switzerland—in many cases more than once—and they are all impressive. Price and quality are well aligned in the country, as in London, and thus it is hard to find bargains. Note that Switzerland almost always has an overvalued currency, precisely because it is so stable and so many investors find it to be a "safe haven" country. Many people want to keep some money there, and that pushes the exchange rate in an unfavorable direction for the tourist. Being a financial haven isn't good for cheap food.

Still, I have a few tips:

- The larger Swiss cities have some vegetarian, alternative, and Indian-related, often religious and Buddhism-related, alternative restaurants. In general they are excellent and they are also bargains. Don't worry if they smell like incense, that's part of what helps keep the prices low.

- Swiss shops are excellent sources for cheese, bread, and cold cuts. These items aren't cheap either, but a do-it-yourself picnic in Switzerland can be very good and the country has the scenery to match.

- The country cooks too frequently with cream sauce. They have some of the best cream sauces in the world, but I am happier when I don't order it more than once on a trip. If I have ended up with a slightly boring dish, very often Swiss cream sauce is the culprit. Caveat emptor.

- Switzerland has taken in many Sri Lankan immigrants and its Sri Lankan restaurants are quite good, quite spicy, and also much cheaper than most of the other restaurants. Look for them on the outskirts of the larger cities.

Italy

The problem is this: Most American tourists are likely to visit the cities of Rome, Florence, and Venice—and, unfortunately, those are exactly the cities with the worst food in Italy, precisely because they attract so much tourist attention. Those cities do not have a historically poor food record; the problem really is the tourists, the package tours, and the large groups. Even the informed visitors, whether they like or dislike a restaurant, probably will never go back there in any case. Tourism and high rents work together to lower the quality of food in these locales. If you're just walking into an average-looking Italian restaurant, in the centers of any of those three cities, the odds are it will be mediocre and also fairly expensive.

In this case, the standard tips about location will serve you well: Get as far out of the city center as you can, to avoid both the tourists and the high rents and to capture some excellent food. The Tuscan food in the non-touristy neighborhoods of Florence is very, very good. It's simply becoming increasingly hard to find. If you're determined to eat well, take a short train or taxi ride out of town. It will pay off.

Venice has an excellent set of local eateries, which you can find listed in a *Time Out* guide, or may be Michelin-rated as a "two-forker." Venice eateries serve local and regional dishes, attract a largely local clientele (along with some perspicacious Frenchmen, which is not a bad sign), and while they are not cheap they are inexpensive compared to most of the other dining options. What these places share in common is that they are hard to get to, in terms of the walking and navigational directions, at least. And I *mean,* they are *very* hard to get to. Use GPS. Nothing in Venice is extremely far, by the nature of the city, but finding these places is like threading your way through a maze. It's worth it, as they can serve tastier food than some of the dishes at the Michelin-starred restaurants there, and at lower prices. The rule of thumb for Venice is— if you found it easy to get there, it won't be very good. You also must reserve in advance to have much chance of getting in, or show up right at opening.

Rome is large enough, and densely populated, so that there are still plenty of outlying neighborhoods that are not so far away. Again, it's worth the trip. I've also had first-rate Ethiopian food in Rome, probably the best I've ever sampled. However, for all of its cooking prowess, Italy has some of the worst ethnic food in the world—and, all of a sudden it seems, they cannot do anything good with a noodle.

For superb food in Italy, I've done best in less heralded places such as Torino, Genoa, Bologna, Bergamo, Trento, Naples, Parma, and Padua (I'll get to Sicily below.) If you can't name a famous landmark in an Italian city, it is likely to have superb food at affordable prices. Overall, once you get past the three "ruined cities," mentioned above, Italy is one of the most consistent locations for food in the world. You don't need too many tips to do well; just make sure you are fishing in untouristed waters. The rest will take care of itself.

As in France, you can stop at a gas station, or rest stop, and find some pretty good food. It may be in the bottom tier of food in Italy, but it's still better than the Italian food in many an American-Italian restaurant. The last time I visited Italy, my first meal coming off the plane was in a highway rest stop, on the way to a conference in the Alps. There were, at the same stop, men dressed as gangsters and glamorous women in impossibly tall high heels. It was cheap. At about 10:30 P.M., I chose some pasta that was sitting under a lamp. It was the worst meal of my trip to Italy, but still comparable to the best Italian food in northern Virginia.

No matter how run-down or low-class a venue in Italy may seem, there remains an excellent chance it will serve some very good food.

Sicily

Sicily is my favorite place to eat in Europe. Standards are remarkably high, quality raw ingredients are plentiful, prices are cheap by European standards, and a lot of the key dishes you can't get elsewhere. Imagine a cross of European, Arabic, and medieval influences, where mint, orange, and pistachio remain important flavors in the food and quality seafood and pasta are everywhere. The flavors are bold and direct, and it is hard to believe how good the ricotta cheese is. The sweets rival those of Istanbul or Calcutta. Each region of Sicily has its own dishes.

I once spent six days in Palermo, in August, and most of the leading restaurants were closed for vacation, as is common in many parts of Europe in August. Every advance recommendation I received from friends and blog readers turned out to be shuttered, save for one exception. My Michelin guide was producing dead ends. It was still one of the best eating weeks of my life, even though I picked restaurants simply by walking around and showing up. By the way, Sicily has a low density of Michelin-starred restaurants, typically no more than a handful. Good for them. The problem is, if you were to give stars to three or four more Sicilian restaurants, you'd have to give stars to three or four hundred more. The French aren't going to do that.

I deviated from Sicilian food for one meal (or did I?) and tried Indian food, mostly out of curiosity, when I was walking around some of the alleys in an immigrant neighborhood. I was served a kind of "fusion" cuisine, namely a dosa stuffed with Sicilian sardines. It blew me away. I can't say enough good things about the food in Sicily. You don't need much further advice, other than to go to Sicily and stay as long as you can. And eat.

Spain

Food in Spain already gets plenty of coverage, especially at the high end and for tapas joints. I have another angle, most useful in the cities: Spain has much better ethnic food than is commonly realized. In Madrid and Barcelona, there are large numbers of migrants from South and Latin America and they inhabit entire portions of those cities, although you will not find this mentioned in Fodor's or Frommer's guidebooks. You can find excellent servings of Ecuadorian, Bolivian, Peruvian, and other Latino cuisines, better than what you get in most parts of the United States. The dishes are also quite cheap and although some Spaniards will refer to those parts of town as sketchy, to this visitor they seem relatively safe by American standards. They are a good way to get off the beaten track when eating in Spain. You get all the benefits of good Spanish ingredients, but without having another round of oversalted tapas, ham, and bacalao (dried salt cod). I'm not saying you will get sick of the food in Spain, but sometimes I do—much as I like it—and that is where I go for a change of pace. I haven't found that any research is needed about quality: Just walk into a Latino restaurant and it is very likely to be good.

Istanbul

You can eat the traditional dishes, in simpler settings, or you can pay extra to eat them—slightly modified—in more gussied-up surroundings. The key to eating well here is to go simple and to look for the best and purest versions of straightforward dishes. World-class raw ingredients are at the visitor's disposal, and the main task is simply to avoid their ruination. That isn't hard to accomplish.

Thousands of street restaurants offer seafood (the fried small smelts are my favorite, then the sea bream or *levrek*, "sea bass"), eggplant, fava beans, kebabs of various kinds, including spicy kebab with sumac, fried mussels, fried oysters, salads with cheese and tomatoes, lamb brains, fried and baked potatoes, Turkish ravioli (good but harder to find), and other delicacies. It is common for the small restaurants to specialize, an indication of quality. A meal in these places, with one small portion, will cost six to ten dollars, so for the sake of variety order more. Forget about your waistline on vacation and dig in to the Turkish sweets for dessert. I prefer something with pistachio.

Avoid all restaurants near the main sights or near clusters of tourist hotels, especially in Sultanahmet. Avoid most of the places—even Turkish ones—on the main thoroughfares. Avoid fish restaurants with a water view. Look for the neighborhood side streets with clusters of these small restaurants just off the larger roads, and preferably in neighborhoods off the beaten path. If you order small dishes, you can visit two or three restaurants in one meal, no problem.

My favorite small Istanbul restaurants have been the tripe soup houses, even though I don't usually like tripe. You ladle in some liquid garlic sauce, paprika, a bit of chili pepper, and a green herb of some kind. Some of these places are open for breakfast.

Unless you've sampled all the major dishes (which would take a good while), the return to going upscale, or seeking innovation, is not overwhelming. The basic market model here is segregation of restaurant type and price discrimination on the basis of social status of the visitor, rather than on the basis of food quality. If it's food you're after, don't pay more for the culinary twists. At the more expensive places, the food will remain recognizably Mediterranean but it just won't be the classic treatment.

Go simple and stay cheap. The good here is very good, and the best isn't that much better.

I've had just as good fortune searching for food in the more obscure parts of Turkey. My wife and I recently visited Konya, which is regarded as one of the most religious places in Turkey. The population is about three-quarters of a million people, it is located in the Turkish agricultural heartland, and except for the tomb of the famous Sufi poet Rumi, it has few tourist attractions. Those are all recipes for good cheap food, and indeed the city delivered. I enjoyed wonderful yogurt soup and also one of the local specialties, etli ekmek, which resembles a thin pizza with beef on top, and into which the diner rolls a long green pepper and some spicy ground red pepper for flavor. All for a few dollars. Again, it's about finding the pure local ingredients combined with experienced craftsmanship and the desire to serve regular, informed customers. Turkey is not only a wonderful vacation spot, it's one of the world's best locales for cheap, first-rate food.

Of course there are many places I haven't covered but no matter where you go, you should return to the same general principles when selecting a place to eat on the road and, if you will indulge me, I will state those principles once again. *Food is a product of economic supply and demand, so try to figure out where the supplies are fresh, the suppliers are creative, and the demanders are informed.*

11

The Stuff and Values of Cooking at Home

One of the most rewarding experiences is to take the food knowledge you have acquired, and bring people into your home for sharing. It wasn't long ago that we had about sixty people over our house for an evening, including a visit from my sister and her partner, who drove all the way from New Jersey to Virginia. We wanted to do something to make it memorable, to add to the perfect weather of the spring season, the flowers in bloom, and the very special crowd we had assembled.

I am a fan of Costco for party uses, and we did go there to buy paper plates, a large chunk of cheese, and soft drinks, including Mexican Coca-Cola. Still, we did a lot more to make the experience stand out for our guests.

I drove to my favorite gas station—the Shell branch that contains R&R Tacquería—off Route 95 in Maryland, on an especially dumpy part of Highway 1. The proprietor is a former airplane pilot from Mexico City who decided to start cooking authentic Mexican food, including huaraches, tacos del pastor, and chile relleno. His stuff is the best around, by a long mile, and it's very cheap. It's cheap enough to buy in large quantities. I drove back with two big, hot plastic containers in the backseat of the car—lamb soup and a soup with pureed chili peppers. I knew both would reheat very well the next day.

Usually I am the family cook, but on this occasion my wife and daughter were in charge of food preparation. We were having many Russian guests (my wife was born in Moscow), so she prepared a variety of Russian salads. These work great for a party, at least for the Russians. If you recall, there is a tension between fresh food and food that can be produced and served at a scalable level. But a lot of Russian food evolved to remain workable under the days of communism, bread lines, and lots of canned goods. The Russian salads, though I do not care for them, succeeded because they don't have to be served very fresh. The older Russians in the group cleaned off those plates rather quickly and felt right at home.

One quick lesson is that home cooking and outside food are complements and not always substitutes. Bring some core dishes in for a larger group, and then supplement it with some of your favorite cooking or home-prepared items. If you don't have to plan to cook a whole meal for sixty people, you'll feel less overwhelmed and perhaps you'll attempt a personal contribution, when instead you might never have held the party in the first place. Let the division of labor—namely, reliance on outside commercial supplements—be the friend of your cooking and food preparation, not its enemy.

Finally, and most important, we hired our favorite Bolivian food truck—Las Delicias—to camp out in the driveway for five hours. It's not just Bolivian food; it's a special variety of that food from the Cochabamba region. We paid them in advance to prepare a few key Bolivian dishes: peanut soup, wheat soup, silpancho (thin breaded meat with potatoes, rice, tomato, egg, and spicy green sauce), pique (a big pile of meats and starches), and charque. The charque, the most popular and best, is a dry, stringy, salty beef jerky, mixed with a lusciously moist white Bolivian cheese. Most of our visitors had never tried such a dish before and many of them fell in love with it. They went away talking about it.

Again, the dish is easy to prepare and store in advance, in relatively large quantities. When serving a lot of people, a key question is to figure out what is scalable, while remaining tasty. Simply picking your favorites, and hoping they will survive the process of being translated into a major party event, won't do.

Hiring the food truck had a lot of big advantages. They took away a lot of the extra food and dirty plates. That made it easier for us to prepare and serve the Russian salads, and to use the kitchen for putting out a lot of fruit and drinks. The woman who ran the truck was charming and gave the whole thing a homey feel. The party felt exotic and unique, just like its food.

In general, if you are going to select a caterer, use your common sense. Don't opt for the expensive, mediocre services that supply rubber chicken for banquets and weddings. Rather, follow the principles of cheap labor and low wages. Ask around at ethnic supermarkets and restaurants and see who does local ethnic catering. Is there a small Mexican, Haitian, Afghani, Korean, or Indian business that will cook and transport a cheap meal for you and your guests? How about inviting your favorite food truck to cater while parked in your driveway? We knew about Las Delicias, our Bolivian food truck, because we had eaten there on many a Sunday afternoon. We knew all of the best dishes. There are plenty of local cooks who are keen to get the cash, and they will work hard to make you happy. Think of it as customized takeout, but from a home kitchen rather than a restaurant.

That's for a large home event. If it's just me doing the cooking, maybe for a smaller group of four to eight, I'll put to work my knowledge of Mexican food, again based on some simple economics. Based on what's in chapter nine, and given our understanding of dining out, and the food supply chain, here are some rules on how home cooks can make better Mexican food in the United States.

1. Mexican recipes based on chili-based sauces, or for that matter pumpkin seeds, travel pretty well. Cook those dishes.

2. Typical Mexican salsa can be replicated. You need white onions, chilies, garlic, and tomatoes, heated on a pan and pureed to a blend or perhaps the tomatoes are left chunky.

3. The beef dishes won't work well without a good source of dry-aged beef. Seek one out and splurge on it every now and then.

4. Use fresh lard, which you can buy at Latino markets or you can try making it yourself. Don't neglect this one.

5. Mexican chicken dishes will be least affected by relatively bland U.S. ingredients.

6. Consider looking for handmade tortillas in your local Latino community or try making them from scratch yourself.

7. Find thick and gooey cheeses, and if you can get them, risk the nonpasteurized Mexican cheeses. (Don't shudder—you eat seafood and maybe sushi, don't you?)

8. Buy fresh, small, and ugly tomatoes and don't refrigerate them.

In the final analysis, you still won't have the pure Mexican product, but it will be good everyday food and a lot more authentic than what you get at most American Mexican restaurants. The overall idea is thinking in terms of supply and demand. Find the markets you can get to from home (real or online) that serve the customers who demand the flavors you want.

There is another supply everyday foodies experience at home. It is very cheap, but it can really clutter up your refrigerator. Leftovers. To figure out how to make your leftovers taste better, again use some logic. What sits best are complex sauces and dishes that are cooked slowly, rather than flash fried. Curries are an obvious choice here, as are Mexican molé sauces, or also any dish involving beef jerky. Most of those taste better the next day, not worse. The sauces have more of a chance to blend and become richer. Ground beef and lamb also hold up better than does a rib-eye steak, again because blending is more important for the final taste than freshness.

Food waste is a big problem in the United States, in large part because the decay of the food on compost heaps emits methane and creates environmental problems. One approach to the problem is to feel guilty and lecture ourselves about the evils of food waste. That's fine, but let's also think about incentives. You'll do best if you don't *want* to throw your food out, and that sometimes means cooking with the next day in mind. Make the refrigerator and Tupperware your friend, rather than the enemy, of good food. That will likely do more for the environment than eating local food.

This book will I hope inspire readers to go beyond memorizing particular answers, and pursue an understanding of processes and their codes. Cooking at home helps us appreciate good restaurants and figure out where bad restaurants go wrong. But what's the sweet spot where cooking, dining out, and food reading all work together to put you on a path of continuous improvement as a chef and gourmand? Arguably the most influential artifacts in the home food economy are books. Cookbooks, that is.

Influential Cookbooks

When I was an undergraduate, I frequented library used-book sales with my friend Daniel Klein in the quest to find reasonably priced great economics classics. The door would open in the morning and the vultures would swoop into the room, hoping to grab early editions of great economists like Hayek or Hawtrey for a bargain price. But we were hardly ever first in line, because a woman named Mrs. McGillup was there before us. She bought cookbooks and sought out rare, old cookbooks, just as Dan and I sought out rare, old economics books. Mrs. McGillup didn't seem very interested in cooking the recipes from those cookbooks, rather she wanted the books themselves. She was a collector and she loved learning about how people used to cook, even if she didn't want to copy them. A big part of the cookbook market works that way. It isn't always about cooking.

People buy many more cookbooks than they use for their cooking. That's because people don't usually buy cookbooks for actual cooking advice. Often people buy cookbooks out of wishful thinking and the books sit on the shelf. Other times we buy a cookbook for emotional reasons. We wish to affiliate with a celebrity chef or restaurant, to remember a vacation, to express an alliance with an ethnic food or ethnicity, or to look at pretty pictures. Freud famously noted that sometimes a cigar is just a cigar, but this is hardly ever the case with a cookbook. When they marketed Bourland and Vogt's *The Astronaut's Cookbook: Tales, Recipes, and More* they were well advised to put the word tales before the word recipes.

Especially in these days of the Internet, information about cooking isn't scarce, so the key is to have a good plan for building and arranging your knowledge so you can innovate in exciting and tasty ways. A few cookbooks can be used repeatedly to get a sense of differing approaches. Cookbook A says build a curry paste this way, cookbook B has a radically different process—or not. What goes well with a tomatillo-based Mexican sauce? My cooking has improved by focusing on information-rich books that are designed for actual use—not narrative storytelling.

The cookbooks by Fuchsia Dunlop on Hunan and Sichuan, by Diana Kennedy, Patricia Quintana, Mark Miller, and Rick Bayless on Mexican, and by Julie Sahni on Indian food have long informed my thinking. For simpler, standard dishes I look to Mark Bittman, and for general knowledge on the chemistry of cooking I have learned a lot from Harold McGee. I am *not* suggesting these should be your picks, as that depends on what you wish to cook, but these books reflect my vision of good food, few of the recipes involve great expense, and the books are informationally dense in a useful manner.

Most of these books have few if any glossy photos, which indicates the strengths of each one stems from its practical information on food preparation. There are exceptions, but I'm suspicious of cookbooks associated with a particular restaurant run by a celebrity chef. Usually a celebrity chef- and restaurant-branded cookbook is a souvenir product and the dishes are too complicated to make. They almost seem designed to make you feel humiliated by your lack of cooking skill. Say it's a magnum opus by Jean-Georges or Ferran Adrià. Do you think the message of the book will be: "You too can do this with only a small amount of extra work and a single trip to your local Safeway"? No. The goal of the book is to make the chef look impressive, not to bring you up to the chef's level. Famous chefs make money not just from their cookbooks but also from their TV appearances, endorsements, and consulting for food companies. That means their recipes are often too demanding and the cookbooks are a form of self-promotion, not instruction. Few people will visit the fancy, expensive restaurant of a man who shows us how to find and use cheaper russet potatoes, even if that information is of practical value.

I opened up *Susur: A Culinary Life* by the brilliant Susur Lee, of Toronto and Singapore fame, and I found his writing compelling and the photos full of striking colors. I am glad I bought the book—it was fun and told his moving life story. Still, I don't think it will influence my cooking much. At random, I turned a page to a recipe for: "Roast Duck Breast and Burdock Root and Duck Leg Confit Crepe with Spiced Caramelized Chestnuts and Goat Cheese." A lot of my actual *recipes* are shorter than that title. Within this recipe, I count 55 different ingredients or applications of ingredients and six referrals to different pages of the cookbook, each of which involves further multiple ingredients. It's not just that it's hard, but I also feel that if I did something wrong along the way (which is likely), it would be especially hard for me to learn from my mistake. How could I trace back what went wrong? A book like this, whatever its merits, won't get an everyday foodie like me on a path of sustainable learning.

There are some good cookbooks written by famous chefs, for instance *Authentic Mexican* by Rick Bayless. But these books are geared toward teaching actual cooking skills, and an understanding of Mexican cuisine, rather than promoting a particular restaurant. The titles of his best books don't mention any restaurant. Once the famous chef gets away from restaurant promotion, the book is less likely to be a travel or visit memento and more likely to be a useful distillation of what the chef has learned through many years of practice.

Seek out a very deliberate variety of cookbooks, with regard to their level of detail and their presuppositions. I often compare *Classic Indian Cooking* by Julie Sahni, with its American perspective, to the small, cheap "everyman" cookbooks that I've picked up while visiting India. The latter cookbooks cost me about two dollars apiece, each one covering a different culinary region. They are easy to hold folded open and read while stirring a pot or turning on the sink faucet. I like to compare what they take for granted and what Sahni explains in detail. The Sahni book has ninety-five pages of preliminary materials, full of information with relatively little chaff. Those pages cover questions such as what poppy seeds are, what "curry" means, how to squeeze water from Indian cheese, how Indians braise, and what can and can't be done in your food processor. The Indian books have none of this material, not a page of it. They are taking it for granted.

I started with the Sahni, over twenty years ago, but now I cook mostly with the shorter Indian guides. They are a constant challenge as to whether I have mastered various codes of Indian cooking and their lack of detail gives me room to improvise, learn, and make mistakes. Every now and then I go back to the more thorough cookbooks (another is *1,000 Indian Recipes* by Neelam Batra) to learn new recipes and techniques, and then I do a batch more Indian cooking from the shorter guides. It's an iterative process where I step back and forth between a food world where I am told what to do and a food world where I am immersed in the implicit codes of meaning and contributing to innovation within established structures.

Some of your cookbooks, or more broadly your recipe sources, should have very short recipes for use in this manner. Maureen Evans posts recipes at @cookbook on Twitter and has a book called *Eat Tweet*. Here's a nice one, as I'm a fan of German food, at least as it is served in Germany:

"Knödels: Germany. Peel, boil 6tater. Finely grate; mix+2egg/½c flr/ 1½t salt. Form1" balls; boil10m. Rmv w slotted spoon; srv w soup or gravy."

That's it. A lot of old recipes were this simple, as you'll see in old cookbooks. It's not that all the food was unsophisticated, but rather the cooks were operating with a lot of background knowledge, including an understanding of the proper raw materials, or what it meant when you read "srv w soup or gravy." In economics this is sometimes called "tacit knowledge" and it is an important part of how business firms succeed.

Here's a Thai recipe from her site:

"Yam Khao Pot: Thailand. Blend t rdcurrypaste/2T cocontmilk& peanut&lime&cilantro/T fishsauce&dryshrimp(opt). Toss+2c sweetcorn/¼c tstdcoconut."

I've cooked a lot of Thai food so I have a good sense of the proper portions on the items where it is not indicated. This isn't a place to *start* (How much fish sauce was that? Doesn't the stuff stink? Why should I add it at all?); it's a way to proceed. Bouncing back and forth between detailed, information-intensive cookbooks and quite abbreviated recipes works. The switches force you to refine your knowledge of an area and they are a continual test of which ingredients and processes you have understood and which not.

One of my favorite cookbook sets is a series of fifty-plus volumes (they are still producing them) titled *Cuisine Indigenous and Popular* [*Cocina Indígena y Popular*]. Volume 26, on cuisines of San Luis Potosí and Querétaro, has a typical recipe on page 124. It asks for one large squash, five normal-size mushrooms, water, and cinnamon bark according to your taste. You clean the squash, cut it into large pieces and boil it in water with the other ingredients until the water diminishes, pull it out and then let it cool. That's all. The only details given are that two liters of water are required (no specifics on the other portions or on how long the whole thing should take) and that the resulting pieces will be "sweet." There is no indication which kind of mushrooms to use, except that in the native language they are called "Nchyawl," a word that does not match any single document in Google, as of summer 2011.

I tried this recipe and I was surprised how fragrant and delicate the taste turned out. I recommend Mexican rather than Asian cinnamon (a whole stick, but of the sort which breaks apart easily) and a kind of mushroom softer than the Golden Trumpets I selected at my local

Wegmans. There's no reason why you can't use more than five of them. An hour and a half of boiling seemed fine, and now I am on a path toward converting this recipe to an American setting and refining it for my uses. I also preferred the squash pieces while they were cooling but still somewhat warm and before they reached room temperature.

In the same series there is a 509-page volume on "The Food of the Tarahumaras," the Tarahumaras being an indigenous group of 50,000 to 70,000 people, living in the north of Mexico and renowned for their long-distance running ability. I have never visited their towns and to the best of my knowledge I have never sampled their cuisine.

On page 292, there is a recipe for Palo Amarillo, given first in the language of the Tarahumaras and then translated into Spanish. If Google is to be believed, Palo Amarillo is a kind of rubber tree. The recipe starts by noting that the tree is an old one, and that its brush can be combined with wool for sewing and knitting. Then we are told that the fruit can be eaten when ripe, that the fruit is sweet, and that it comes in black and white colors. Next, the recipe relates that the tree no longer grows in the canyon and that the fruit ripens in May. We are then told what the wood of the tree is good for and that the flower of the tree has an attractive yellow color. Then the "recipe" ends.

Most of us have an excessively restricted sense of what a recipe does or what a recipe can mean. Indigenous fruits in Mexico usually are delicious, but they require knowledge of location and also conservation. Reading strange or unusual cookbooks gets us out of the loop of thinking that we know all we need to know about the world's food ways.

Reading indigenous Mexican cookbooks also will teach you how much cooking knowledge is in people's heads and not on paper. Classes, or other forms of access to experts, are wonderful, but maybe you can't afford them or you don't have the time. So I have one final pointer. Probably somebody else is eating your food, at least some of the time. Ask them what they think. But you have to ask the right way. Asking "What did you think?" will be heard as a request for compliments. Instead, ask something like "what was the worst thing about this meal?" or "I know you really liked everything, but what was the least satisfying thing about this meal?" Then push a bit. This can provide the kind of useful instruction a cookbook can never really offer.

Non-Food Stuff Clutter

I've noticed two things about people's kitchens.

First, just as with cookbooks, most people don't use most of the cooking equipment they own or they use it only rarely. I am a relatively active cook, experimenting with a wide diversity of dishes and cuisines, and still well over half of my cooking equipment sits dormant. I don't use the plastic bowl or that whisk or that CorningWare tray. I would throw them away, except that my wife does not like it when I throw things away.

Second, most people have a few favorite items which they use again and again and again, until they wear them out and have to buy new ones. Most kitchens function as a "winner-take-all" market, where a few items receive all the use and most are neglected and left alone.

For me, the winning items are a very-good-at-conducting-heat frying pan, a wok, a large blue casserole, a small pot for cooking rice, an all-purpose Cuisinart/spice grinder, a large boiling pot for pasta, and a baking tray. Add a few sharp knives to that list and two long wooden spoons for tossing in the wok. If I had only those items—and nothing more—I still could do most of my cooking. My kitchen also would be less cluttered. Again, this list is a description of my cooking life, not purchase advice for you.

Thinking through the realities of what you will cook should come before receiving lots of advice on particular pieces of cooking equipment. You will learn the most about cooking if you get to know some particular pieces of cooking equipment—those that match your cooking interests—relatively well. That's the way to understand what is going on in a recipe, and eventually modifying or improving it, rather than simply memorizing it.

Let's think through the general patterns of how you use cooking equipment. Either you already have your favorite cooking items or you're a neophyte and you don't yet have clear favorites. Let's start with the neophyte case first, because it is pretty easy to handle.

If you are a neophyte, buy a cheap set of cooking equipment, knowing that you will use some parts of it much more than others. Once you've figured out what is useful to you, go back and consider buying more expensive versions of the important items. Don't start off by spending lots of money because much of your expenditure will be wasted. In the language of economics, think of yourself as engaged in "optimal search." If you start by buying expensive cooking items, it's like bringing a diamond ring to every first date. Search first and learn your preferences.

Alternatively, let's say you already have some favorites. What can you do to improve your cooking experience?

Buy better and more expensive versions of what works for you, but only once you know it works for you. There is a high return to having very good and very durable versions of what you use all the time. So take your five kitchen item "winners" and spend more money on them. That's usually a better bet than trying new kitchen equipment, which will likely lie fallow and over time make you feel bad about having wasted your money. The cognitive bias here is a common one: new, shiny toys hold great appeal for us, because in some ways we are still kids. But we're being tricked by the marketing and by the fun of the buying experience itself, so spend your money on what will turn out to be more reliable pleasures. We actually learn cooking by mastering how to use well-understood equipment, to make some specialized dishes of great interest to us, rather than by making new purchases or by having one of each item.

Consider buying multiple versions of what works for you. For instance at home we have three woks and four(!) machines capable of serving as spice grinders.

Why might three woks be needed? Sometimes I use one wok for cooking the main dish and the other wok for steaming the vegetables. Sometimes one wok is full with cooked curry, sitting in the basement refrigerator, waiting to be eaten the next day. If we're having company over for dinner, it's likely that I'll end up using all three woks.

Actually, I have a fourth wok, an electric wok with heated sides, which I have never used. Maybe it's great, I don't know. When I find out I'll tweet.

How about four spice grinders? Isn't that absurd? Posh.

My wife, Natasha, uses one of those grinders for her coffee. It smells like coffee most of the time and I'm not going to use it for chilies or nutmeg. Then I have a small spice grinder, which I use when I am grinding up small amounts, which is about half the time I need a grinder. Grinding up two chilies and one clove doesn't work well in a large Cuisinart because the items get lost in the toss. The large Cuisinart is used for pureeing tomatoes, onions, making Mexican molé sauces, and other larger-scale endeavors.

What about the fourth Cuisinart, the midsize one? Well, it's never used. But I feel better having it around. I know that if either the small or large spice grinder "went down," the midsize model could step in and perform either set of duties. I can cook for others without feeling nervous that the entire venture will fail at the last minute.

I'm not thinking of buying a fifth spice grinder, but I am considering another wok. That's likely a better investment than a torch for making crème brûlée.

How might you identify "winning" kitchen items that you don't already know? For instance last year my colleague Veronique de Rugy (a good cook, I might add) came to me and swore I should buy a Thermomix, which is manufactured by a rather intimidating German company called Vorwerk. Vorwerk is best known for its especially powerful vacuum cleaners. Their all-purpose cooking machine is a food processor that also allows you to weigh, blend, grind, knead, steam, and emulsify, all in one contraption, and I doubt if that is the end of its functions. Vero insists it is worth the $1,400 or so, as do many other users (you may need to order it from outside the United States and prices will vary). It is reputed to be especially good at kneading dough and making warm, volatile sauces. Chef Ferran Adrià, formerly of the renowned modernist cuisine restaurant El Bulli in Spain, uses one.

Still, I haven't bought one. Maybe I am too old. I was intimidated by the notion that the machine will overturn my entire cooking routine. Let's say I could swap in seven of my current cooking devices for this one. I'm not sure I would be better off. Every time I would cook something I would have to learn a new function for the machine. It could be that I'd save time within a year of working with the machine, but when it comes to cooking, I need an initial "nudge" that the whole venture will be easy in the first place. There was a Vorwerk company spokesman who, not having me in mind as his model customer, once said: "We discourage them [customers] from buying one if they don't already know how to use it." Buying the machine is like deciding to make it one of my specialties and I'm not ready to do that.

Furthermore, when I cook I usually leave "half-baked cakes" scattered around the kitchen, as I work on several dishes at once. I need a bunch of devices, if only to accommodate my jerky, back-and-forth methods of cooking (the Thermomix can accommodate more than one function at a time, but I am talking about five to seven functions here). I might have changed those methods at age 23, or even 27, but probably I won't change them at 49.

I think of cooking equipment as falling into a few discrete categories:

1. New contraptions that perform familiar uses.

2. New contraptions that enable you to perform entirely new operations.

3. Improved versions of contraptions you already have.

If you are going to improve your foodie life through cooking, you need to ask yourself which of these categories you are ready for.

I am busy enough, for instance, that I'm not looking to learn entirely new cooking techniques. I already have a "research program" of learning more and better uses of cilantro in Indian curry blends, different variants of French roast chicken, and making Thai curry pastes from scratch. I'd also like to learn some new stocks and to master Bengali mustard curries. Maybe by the time you are reading this book, I will have done all of those and be moving on, but probably not. If you tell me that a new device will enable me to make cheesecake, which I have never done before, I'm simply not interested. It doesn't matter how good the device is. I'd like more and better knives, a new casserole (the old one works fine, but it's twenty-three years old and starting to crust), and maybe that extra wok. The rest of my cooking energy I'll spend on perfecting recipes and procuring better raw ingredients.

Again, the key here is to understand your own cooking temperament, at your current stage in life, and to look past the self-deception and the lure of the shiny and new. The big questions aren't about selecting the best cooking contraptions; you can find answers online to those any time. For answers to the most important questions, you must look inward.

Bringing Americans Back to the Kitchen

So far we've covered some economic factors of production in the kitchen: capital (equipment) and ideas (cookbooks), so now we must turn to labor—namely, your own proclivity for cooking. Capital and ideas don't much matter if you never step into the kitchen. So, if you don't wish to eat out much, what can you do to force, trick, or otherwise induce yourself to eat at home more often?

For me this is still largely an unsolved problem. Nonetheless, my fellow everyday foodies, here is what I propose.

First, frozen food doesn't have to be bad. I've said that refrigeration is bad for flavor, but not all refrigeration is created equal. Freezing can retain flavor far more effectively than mere chilling, so the quality of the food frozen matters. In France they have a whole chain—Picard— devoted only to frozen food and it is common for sophisticated French eaters to patronize the store. It's not cheap like a lot of our frozen food, but the quality is higher. Refrigeration technologies today support higher-quality foodstuffs than in the 1950s, the nadir of the frozen food era. Flash-freezing allows quality foodstuffs to be preserved without

AN ECONOMIST GETS LUNCH

causing them to dry out so badly. Even a lot of foodies don't know that most of the sushi they eat—and I mean the good stuff—relies on the flash-freezing of fish on the open sea.

The truth in America today is that the frozen fruits and vegetables— flash-frozen near the site of production—are often "fresher" than the ones that have been trucked, kept cold for days, and chosen for maximum size and ease of packing. Mark Bittman in his often brilliant, long-running cooking column "The Minimalist," often made this point. Frozen cherries are often better than what are called "fresh" cherries, which are in fact not so fresh, due to transportation and storage. Canned tomatoes are often better than non-canned tomatoes (I can't bring myself to call them "fresh"), including for tomato sauce. Good canned sardines are of higher quality than most of the fish in the seafood department, even at a gourmet grocery store. Your cooking will be easier and cheaper if you can use economics to figure out when an extra trip to the supermarket is unnecessary.

Experiment with precommitment. Thaw some frozen foods before leaving for work in the morning. Get guilt to kick in on your side. If you don't eat the thawed corn that evening, it will either go bad and you'll lose some money or you'll feel silly freezing it again. On the way home, you'll be that much less likely to pull in to Thai Hut and order a green chicken curry.

There are plenty of ways you can take technology and make it the friend of good home cooking rather than the enemy. I began the second chapter of this book explaining how American food—including food at home—became pretty bad throughout most of the twentieth century. Fortunately for Americans, many of these negative trends have been reversed over the last thirty or so years and many modern technologies now favor quality household production.

For instance, microwave ovens are used more and more for good food rather than for junk; it is now commonly known that a microwave can cook many fish dishes without loss of quality. Entire cookbooks are devoted to how to use the microwave for quick but tasty recipes, a far cry from the early Swanson frozen dinners. Julie Sahni's *Moghul Microwave* is entirely devoted to recipes for microwaves. And then there is the tremendous value in dealing with leftovers discussed above. The microwave is a good example of a technology that at first was an enemy of good cuisine but has been turned toward better and more sophisticated culinary purposes.

As to getting good or better ingredients for your home meals, use mail order, through the Internet. A lot of good restaurants and food suppliers will ship you their product direct. For the last six years or so, we've ordered frozen barbecue from Lockhart, Texas, as part of our main Thanksgiving meal. As you will recall from the chapter on barbecue, Lockhart is arguably America's best town for Texas sausage, ribs, and brisket. One of the major Lockhart restaurants, Kreuz Market, ships to anywhere in the continental United States.

The barbecue itself is relatively cheap and it costs no more than eating out in a mid-priced restaurant near home. The brisket and spicy sausages, when thawed out, taste 90 percent as good as the fresh product on-site. (The ribs I find lose more value.) So now we get the brisket and sausage, and they ship it packed in ice, FedEx. Not only is the food impressive but it's a good story, and the holiday guests feel they are getting something special, which, believe me, they are.

It may sound like cheating, but using services like this inevitably gives me more time to prepare, say, vegetables and side dishes. Thanksgiving dinner is a pretty big undertaking, even for relatively small groups of people. If it wasn't for delivery from Kreuz Market, we probably would have eaten out a lot of those meals or simply taken some not-so-tasty shortcuts. On net I am saving money or breaking even, as Kreuz Market food, ordered in moderate quantity, is cheaper than a lot of what you get at gourmet supermarkets.

I'm also an advocate of ordering high-quality bacon (I like the product from Benton's Smoky Mountain Country Hams, a source favored and used by David Chang of Momufuku fame), freezing it, and then cooking it over many months, often in Sichuan style. The bacon is cured and preserved in any case and the freezing doesn't seem to involve much loss in taste. These meats do cost more than Whole Foods bacon, but they cost less trying to find comparable quality meat in a restaurant. If I use the bacon to cook Chairman Mao's Pork Belly, it probably runs me about twelve dollars or so for two, for the whole meal. That's hardly an outrageous expenditure and in the meantime I am dining on world-class ingredients. Most important, it's always ready to go.

The cheap transport of goods often favors eating out, but if you are creative you can mobilize this feature of modernity to improve dining at home. Home cooking doesn't mean you have to produce all the food yourself. That point reflects my economic themes of cooperation and division of labor and, of course, the expertise of the United States at long-distance food transport.

There are many ways to trying to eat more at home; it's the oppressive paths that are likely to fail and the fun, innovative approaches that are going to succeed. Cooking at home, no matter how modest the attempt, should have some special element each and every time. Your cooking life should not necessarily involve the work of a party for dozens of people but it should have the feel of a joyous collective event, offering some bit of meaning for everyone involved. That's the best way to fight the lure of all those excellent restaurants out there. Most of all, a food revolution succeeds when it wins a permanent place in individual hearts and minds.

The next step is up to you.

Notes

1. On the Eve of the Revolution

On Fourier, see Priscilla Parkhurst Ferguson, *Accounting for Taste: The Triumph of French Cuisine* (Chicago: University of Chicago Press, 2004) p. 100.

2. How American Food Got Bad

On Holiday Inn and Tad's, see Harvey Levenstein, *Paradox of Plenty: A Social History of Eating in Modern America* (New York: Oxford University Press, 1993), p. 128.

See Charles Merz, *The Dry Decade* (Seattle: University of Washington Press, 1969), pp. 19–23 for descriptions of various state laws on alcohol. Not all were so strict on the home consumption of alcohol, although they did rule out serving alcohol in public restaurants. On town laws, see Norman H. Clark, *Deliver Us From Evil: An Interpretation of American Prohibition* (New York: W.W. Norton & Company, 1976), pp. 101–2.

The quotations about how Prohibition affected dining are from Harvey Levenstein, *Revolution at the Table: The Transformation of the American Diet* (Berkeley: University of California Press, 2003), p. 183. On the British visitor and the Post, see Andrew Barr, *Drink: A Social History of America* (New York: Carroll & Graf Publishers, 1999), pp. 104–5. For the views of Herbert Asbury, see his *The Great Illusion: An Informal History of Prohibition* (Westport, Connecticut: Greenwood Press, 1968 [1950]), p.193. Asbury (pp. 194–96) discusses the restaurant closures and related matters. See also Michael Karl Witzel, *The American Drive-In* (Osceola, Wisconsin: Motorbooks International, 1994), p. 19 on general changes in the dining scene.

On French chefs, Harvey Levenstein wrote: "Within two years of Prohibition, most of the French chefs who had flocked to New York, Chicago, San Francisco, and the other major cities in the prewar days were on the streets, looking for non-existent jobs, or at the steamship offices, booking their passage home." That is from Harvey Levenstein, *Revolution at the Table: The Transformation of the American Diet* (Berkeley: University of California Press, 2003), p. 184.

On the effects of the New York City alcohol raids, see Andrew Sinclair, *Era of Excess: A Social History of the Prohibition Movement* (New York: Harper & Row, 1964), p. 232; on bribery and other costs of speakeasies, see pp. 222, 230–34, which discusses the bad food in speakeasies more generally.

On how much Prohibition hurt drinking, and how long it took to recover, see Andrew Barr, *Drink: A Social History of America* (New York: Carroll & Graf Publishers, 1999), pp. 111-12, 239. On 1973, see Daniel Okrent, *Last Call: The Rise and Fall of Prohibition* (New York: Scribner, 2010), p. 373. For the estimates on when culinary recovery began in New York, see Herbert Asbury, *The Great Illusion: An Informal History of Prohibition* (Westport, Connecticut: Greenwood Press, 1968 [1950]) p. 196, and Andrew Barr, *Drink: A Social History of America* (New York: Carroll & Graf Publishers, 1999), p. 111.

On how the wartime experience shaped America and its food networks, see Amy Bentley, *Eating for Victory: Food Rationing and the Politics of Domesticity* (Chicago: University of Chicago Press, 1998), p. 9, and Susan M. Hartmann, *The Home Front and Beyond: American Women in the 1940s* (Boston: Twayne Publishers, 1982), pp. 77–78. On wartime rationing, see Bentley, p. 91, passim. On chicken consumption, see Steve Striffler, *Chicken: The Dangerous Transformation of America's Favorite Food* (New Haven: Yale University Press, 2005), pp. 43–45. On canned spam, and U.S. meat consumption during the war, see Bentley, pp. 71, 131–32. On beef consumption during the war, see Bentley, pp. 91–92. On the rise of processed food and vegetables, see John L. Hess and Karen Hess, *The Taste of America* (Urbana: University of Illinois Press, 2000), p. 269. On sugar, see John Mariani, *America Eats Out: An Illustrated History of Restaurants, Taverns, Coffee Shops, Speakeasies, and Other Establishments That Have Fed Us for 350 Years* (New York: William Morrow and Company, 1991), pp. 156–57.

For some basic references on dry counties, see David J. Hanson, "Dry Counties," http://www2.potsdam.edu/hansondj/controversies/1140551076.html and the Wikipedia page http://en.wikipedia.org/wiki/List_of_dry_communities_by_U.S._state. For a more extensive look at dry localities, there are the various editions of the *Statistical Abstract of the United States*. On wine and the 1970s, see the restaurant figures for allowed drinking in different states and counties drawn from various editions of the *Statistical Abstract of the United States*. See http://www2.pots dam.edu/hansondj/Controversies/1140551076.html for information on dry counties. On wine and the 1970s, see Andrew Barr, *Drink: A Social History of America* (New York: Carroll & Graf Publishers, 1999), p. 254, and p. 112 for the quotation.

On the North Korean restaurant, see "Hermit Kitchen: How Did a North Korean Restaurant Wind Up in Northern Virginia?" http://www.washingtoncitypaper.com /articles/40495/hermit-kitchen/full.

Notes

For some more details on the process of culinary acculturation among ethnic groups, see Harvey Levenstein, *Revolution at the Table: The Transformation of the American Diet*, (Berkeley: University of California Press, 2003), p. 176. On spicy and garlicky foods, see Jeffrey M. Pilcher, *Que Vivan los Tamales: Food and the Making of Mexican Identity* (Albuquerque: University of New Mexico Press, 1998), p. 93. For some general observations, see Hasia R. Diner, *Hungering for America: Italian, Irish, and Jewish Foodways in the Age of Migration* (Cambridge: Harvard University Press, 2001).

On Duncan Hines, see Harvey A. Levenstein, "The Perils of Abundance: Food, Health, and Morality in American History," in *Food: A Culinary History from Antiquity to the Present*, English edition edited by Albert Sonnenfeld (New York: Columbia University Press, 1999), pp. 516–29; especially pp. 524-25.

For the figures on Chinese immigration, see J.A.G. Roberts, *China to Chinatown: Chinese Food in the West* (London: Reaktion Books, 2002), p. 165.

On the varieties of Mexican-derived foods, Tex-Mex tends to use venison and beef, fajitas, puffy tacos, and cabrito (goat). New Mexico foods are more likely to use fresh green chilies and green tomatillo sauces. Pork is the preferred meat, not beef. Mexican food from California uses more produce, as befits the diversified agriculture of the state. Avocados, sour cream, and Spanish olives are especially common.

See Tyler Cowen, *Creative Destruction: How Globalization is Changing the World's Cultures* (Princeton: Princeton University Press), 2002, chapter four, for information on the differential spread of television across the United States and Europe.

For the figures on working women, see Martha Hahn Sugar, *When Mothers Work, Who Pays?* (Westport: Bergin and Garvey, 1994), p. 27. The quotation from the Jell-O pamphlet is from Carolyn Wyman, *Jell-O: A Biography* (New York: Harcourt, Inc., 2001), p. 23.

For the figures on housework, Stanley Lebergott, *Pursuing Happiness: American Consumers in the Twentieth Century* (Princeton: Princeton University Press, 1993), p. 59.

On the origins of the microwave, see Nell du Vall, *Domestic Technology: A Chronology of Developments* (Boston, Massachusetts: G.K. Hall & Co., 1988), p. 117. On microwave prices, see Gerry Schremp, *Kitchen Culture: Fifty Years of Food Fads* (New York: Pharos Books, 1991), pp. 89–90.

On the early Swanson meals, see Martin J. Smith and Patrick J. Kiger, *Poplorica: A Popular History of the Fads, Mavericks, Inventions, and Lore that Shaped Modern America* (New York: Harper Resource, 2004), pp. 121–26, and Richard Pillsbury, *No Foreign Food: The American Diet in Time and Place* (Boulder, Colorado: Westview Press, 1998), pp. 65–66.

On the history of pizza in the United States, see John A. Jakle and Keith A. Sculle, *Fast Food: Roadside Restaurants in the Automobile Age* (Baltimore: The Johns Hopkins University Press, 1999), pp. 242–46.

On various American food critics, see Leslie Brenner, *American Appetite: The Coming of Age of a Cuisine* (New York: Avon Books, 1999), pp. 46–47, 62–64. On Betty Crocker, see Karal Ann Marling, *As Seen on TV: The Visual Culture of Everyday Life in the 1950s* (Cambridge: Harvard University Press, 1994), p. 206.

On doughnuts, see John A. Jakle and Keith A. Sculle, *Fast Food: Roadside Restaurants in the Automobile Age* (Baltimore: The Johns Hopkins University Press, 1999), pp. 197–98.

On the clustering of fast foods near high schools, see S. Bryn Austin, Steven J. Melly, Brisa N. Sanchez, Aarti Patel, Stephen Buka, and Steven Gortmaker, "Clustering of Fast-Food Restaurants Around Schools: A Novel Application of Spatial Statistics to the Study of Food Environments," *American Journal of Public Health*, September 2005, vol. 95, no. 9, pp. 1575-81.

3. Revolutionizing the Supermarket Experience

No published references, based on fieldwork.

4. The Rules for Finding a Good Place to Eat

On Masa restaurant, see G. Bruce Knecht, "The Raw Truth," *The Wall Street Journal*, Saturday/Sunday, March 25–26, 2006, pp. P1, P6.

On Nobel Prizes for Americans, one source is here: http://www.jinfo.org/US_Nobel _Prizes.html.

On the Coca-Cola markup, Eric Schlosser, *Fast Food Nation: The Dark Side of the All-American Meal* (New York: Perennial, 2002), p. 54, offers some typical figures: "The fast food chains purchase Coca-Cola syrup for about $4.25 a gallon. A medium Coke that sells for $1.29 contains roughly 9 cents' worth of syrup. Buying a large Coke for $1.49 instead, as the cute girl behind the counter always suggests, will add another 3 cents' worth of syrup—and another 17 cents in pure profit for McDonald's."

For some recent estimates on wine markups, see Juliet Chung, "Cracking the Code of Restaurant Wine Pricing," *The Wall Street Journal*, Friday, August 15, 2008, and Gretchen Roberts, "The Lowdown on Restaurant Markups," *Wine Enthusiast Magazine*, May 7, 2010, http://www.winemag.com/Wine-Enthusiast-Magazine/May-2010/ The-Lowdown-on-Restaurant-Markups. It has been estimated that New York's Daniel restaurant stores up to about $800,000 worth of wine; see Brenner, *American Appetite*.

On the notion of "shrouding" the prices of secondary importance, such as drinks in a restaurant, see Xavier Gabaix and David Laibson, "Shrouded Attributes, Consumer Myopia, and Information Suppression in Competitive Markets," *Quarterly Journal of Economics*, May 2006, pp. 505–40.

On the history of the free lunch, see Madelon Powers, *Faces Along the Bar: Lore and Order in the Workingman's Saloon, 1870–1920* (Chicago: University of Chicago Press), 1998.

On drink pricing and the use of table space, see John R. Lott Jr. and Russell D. Roberts, "A Guide to the Pitfalls of Identifying Price Discrimination," *Economic Inquiry,* January 1991, vol. 29, no. 1, pp. 14–23.

On the history of popcorn, see Andrew F. Smith, *Popped Culture: A Social History of Popcorn in America* (Columbia: University of South Carolina Press, 1999), pp. 102, 119–120, 159. For a study of the empirics of popcorn pricing, see Ricard Gil and Wesley Hartmann, "Empirical Analysis of Metering Price Discrimination: Evidence from Concession Sales at Movie Theaters," working paper, 2008.

For one look at the economics of movie distribution, see Peter Caranicas, "Studios at the Brink," *Variety Magazine,* May 3–9, 2010, pp. 1, 70.

On popcorn pricing, the movie studios are no dummies. They fear that excessively priced popcorn will drive down movie demand and drive down their profits. So when a movie is rented to theaters, the accompanying contract typically specifies a maximum price for the popcorn. Ideally, the movie studios would prefer a high price for the movies and a very low price for the popcorn. A tug-of-war ensues, with the following result. The movie studio can regulate the easily monitored price of the popcorn, but cannot so well regulate its quality. The movie studio fixes the popcorn price. The theater pushes back by lowering popcorn quality. Lower quality, per unit, is another (sneaky) way of charging consumers a higher per unit price. And that is why the quality of popcorn—and other foodstuffs—is typically so poor in movie theaters.

On rates of restaurant failure, see the work of H.G. Parsa, including his "Why Restaurants Fail," coauthored with John T. Self, David Njite, and Tiffany King, *Cornell Hotel and Restaurant Administration Quarterly,* August 2005, vol. 46, no. 3, pp. 304–22.

On McDonald's see Philip Langdon, *Orange Roofs and Golden Arches: The Architecture of American Chain Restaurants* (New York: Alfred A. Knopf, 1986), p. 107. On panini, see Janet Adamy, "Dunkin' Donuts Tries to Go Upscale, But Not Too Far," *The Wall Street Journal,* Saturday/Sunday, April 8–9, 2008, pp. A1, A7.

5. Barbecue: The Greatest Slow Food of All

On Mike Whitely, see http://thelittledixieweekender.com/archive/page/4/.

On failed attempts to construct barbecue chains, see John A. Jakle and Keith A. Sculle, *Fast Food: Roadside Restaurants in the Automobile Age* (Baltimore: The Johns Hopkins University Press, 1999), pp. 171–72. On the Reverend Deuteronomy Skaggs, see Greg Johnson and Vince Staten, *Real Barbecue* (New York: Harper & Row, 1988), p. 145, and on the Times Square barbecue outlet, see p. 107. A very good general history of barbecue is Robert F. Moss, *Barbecue: The History of an American Institution,* (Tuscaloosa: University of Alabama Press, 2010).

For the estimate on how often Americans barbecue, see Rick Browne and Jack Bettridge, *Barbecue America: A Pilgrimage in Search of America's Best Barbecue* (Alexandria, Virginia: Time-Life Books, 1999), p. 11.

For the time to cook pork shoulder, see Steven Raichlen, *BBQ USA* (New York: Workman Publishing, 2003), pp. 160, 230.

See for instance Eric Lolis Elie, *Smokestack Lightning: Adventures in the Heart of Barbecue Country* (Berkeley: Ten Speed Press, 2005), p. 26 on the etymology of barbecue.

On early barbecue see Dotty Griffith, *Celebrating Barbecue: The Ultimate Guide to America's 4 Regional Styles of 'Cue* (New York: Simon & Schuster, 2002), pp. 20, 32. On the Caribbean origins of barbecue, see Eric Lolis Elie, "Barbecue," in *Encyclopedia of Food and Culture,* edited by Solomon Katz and William Woys Weaver (New York: Charles Scribner's Sons, 2003), pp. 164–66.

On Texas history, and also barbecue and political rallies, see Robb Walsh, *Legends of Texas Barbecue Cookbook: Recipes and Recollections from the Pit Bosses* (San Francisco: Chronicle Books, 2002), pp. 28–30, and Sharon Hudgins, "A Feast for All: Texas Barbecue as a Meal and Social Gathering," *Culture* 6, 1992.

On barbecue as roadside eateries, see John A. Jakle and Keith A. Sculle, *Fast Food: Roadside Restaurants in the Automobile Age* (Baltimore: The Johns Hopkins University Press, 1999), p. 171. On barbecue and bread, see John Egerton and Ann Bleidt Egerton, *Southern Food: At Home, On the Road, in History* (Chapel Hill: The University of North Carolina Press, 1993), p. 150.

On coleslaw in North Carolina, see Bob Garner, *North Carolina Barbecue* (Winston-Salem, North Carolina: John F. Blair, 1996), pp. 20–25.

For rough estimates on participation in barbecue contests, see Rick Browne and Jack Bettridge, *Barbecue America: A Pilgrimage in Search of America's Best Barbecue* (Alexandria, Virginia: Time-Life Books, 1999), p. 102, and Steven Raichlen, *BBQ USA* (New York: Workman Publishing, 2003), p. 12.

On idiosyncratic barbecue names, see Greg Johnson and Vince Staten, *Real Barbecue* (New York: Harper & Row, 1988), pp. 187–89.

On pit masters, see the remarks of Bob Garner, *North Carolina Barbecue* (Winston-Salem, North Carolina: John F. Blair, 1996), pp. 29–30, and also Eric Lolis Elie, *Smokestack Lightning: Adventures in the Heart of Barbecue Country* (Berkeley: Ten Speed Press, 2005), p. 11.

On Blue Smoke and its obstacles, see "Where the Smoke Rises (and Rises)," *The New York Times,* Wednesday, March 27, 2002.

For a tale of grandfather clauses, from San Antonio, see Robb Walsh, *Legends of Texas Barbecue Cookbook: Recipes and Recollections from the Pit Bosses* (San Francisco: Chronicle Books, 2002), pp. 172–74.

On goat's head barbecue, see Daniel D. Arreola, *Tejano South Texas: A Mexican American Cultural Province* (Austin: University of Texas Press, 2002), pp. 167–69,

Robb Walsh, *Legends of Texas Barbecue Cookbook: Recipes and Recollections from the Pit Bosses* (San Francisco: Chronicle Books, 2002), pp. 190–91, and Mario Montaño, *The History of Mexican Folk Foodways of South Texas: Street Vendors, Offal Foods, and Barbacoa de Cabeza* (Ann Arbor: University of Microfilms, University of Pennsylvania doctoral dissertation, 1992), pp. 257–63.

On the difficulties of open pit barbecue in Hawaii, see Rachel Laudan, *The Food of Paradise: Exploring Hawaii's Culinary Heritage* (Honolulu: University of Hawaii Press, 1996), pp. 238–40.

On Mexican techniques for making cochinita pibil, see Peter Kaminsky, *Pig Perfect: Encounters with Remarkable Swine and Some Great Ways to Cook Them* (New York: Hyperion, 2005), chapter seventeen. On the meaning of *pib,* see Diana Kennedy, *The Essential Cuisines of Mexico* (New York: Clarkson Potter, 2000), pp. 277, 320.

For a discussion of rural Mexican barbecue, and its seasonings, see James W. Peyton, *El Norte: The Cuisine of Northern Mexico* (Santa Fe: Red Crane Books, 1995), pp. 112–14.

On how gyro came to Mexico, see Jeffrey M. Pilcher, *Que Vivan los Tamales: Food and the Making of Mexican Identity* (Albuquerque: University of New Mexico Press, 1998), p. 136.

On the costs of barbecuing with wood, see, for instance, the comments in Greg Johnson and Vince Staten, *Real Barbecue* (New York: Harper & Row, 1988), p. 70.

For Wilber Shirley's view on the positioning of the meat and why it matters, see Bob Garner, *North Carolina Barbecue* (Winston-Salem, North Carolina: John F. Blair), 1996, pp. 31–32.

On Korean barbecue, see for instance Hi Soo Shin Hepinstall, *Growing Up in a Korean Kitchen* (Berkeley: Ten Speed Press, 2002), p. 177.

On the barbecue sauce in Guam, see Steven Raichlen, *BBQ USA* (New York: Workman Publishing, 2003), pp. 244, 657.

The list of ingredients in barbecue sauces draws upon Mike Mills and Amy Mills Tunnicliffe, *Peace, Love, & Barbecue: Recipes, Secrets, Tall Tales, and Outright Lies from the Legends of Barbecue* (Emmaus, Pennsylvania: Rodale Books, 2005), pp. 53, 61, 65. On p. 53 they discuss Miracle Whip vs. mayonnaise.

On the production and marketing of barbecue sauce, see Nell du Vall, *Domestic Technology: A Chronology of Developments* (Boston, Massachusetts: G.K. Hall & Co., 1988), p. 79.

Sous vide techniques were introduced to France about thirty years ago. They failed to catch on for fear of botulin poisoning and listeria, but since then both the equipment and methods have improved.

On the cooking of Lockhart sausage, see Rick Browne and Jack Bettridge, *Barbecue America: A Pilgrimage in Search of America's Best Barbecue* (Alexandria, Virginia: Time-Life Books, 1999), pp. 11–12, and Eric Lolis Elie, *Smokestack Lightning: Adventures in the Heart of Barbecue Country* (Berkeley: Ten Speed Press, 2005), p. 49.

6. The Asian Elephant in the Room

On the number of Filipinos and Filipino restaurants, and also on the number of Chinese restaurants, see Steven A. Shaw, *Asian Dining Rules: Essential Strategies for Eating Out at Japanese, Chinese, Southeast Asian, Korean, and Indian Restaurants* (New York: William Morrow, 2008), pp. 130–31.

7. Another Agricultural Revolution, Now

On the history of corn breeding, see "Rio Balsas most likely region for maize domestication," Christine A. Hastorf, *Proceedings of the National Academy of Sciences,* March 31, 2009, vol. 106, no. 13, pp. 4957–58.

The book is W.P. Hedden, *How Great Cities are Fed* (Boston: D.C. Heath and Company, 1929), see pp. 74–81, p. 88 on speeds of trains, p. 299 on distribution costs.

On the boom in American agricultural productivity, see Bruce L. Gardner, *American Agriculture in the Twentieth Century: How It Flourished and What It Cost* (Cambridge: Harvard University Press, 2002), pp. 20–22, 44.

On the decline in foodstuffs prices since 1950, see Indur M. Goklany, *The Improving State of the World: Why We're Living Longer, Healthier, More Comfortable Lives on a Cleaner Planet* (Washington, D.C.: Cato Institute, 2007), p. 21.

On Borlaug and the spread of Borlaug's Green Revolution, see Leon Hesser, *The Man Who Fed the World: Nobel Peace Prize Laureate Norman Borlaug and His Battle to End World Hunger* (Dallas: Durban House Publishing Company, 2006), and chapter seven on the spread.

On famine in Mao's China, see Frank Dikötter, *Mao's Great Famine: The History of China's Most Devastating Catastrophe, 1958–1962* (New York: Walker & Company, 2010).

For the figures on pressure on the land, see Goklany, *The Improving State*, pp. 120–22, p. 190.

For the study of the tax on food, see Jonah B. Gelbach, Jonathan Klick, and Thomas Stratmann, "Cheap Donuts and Expensive Broccoli: The Effects of Relative Prices on Obesity," March 13, 2007, http://www.law.yale.edu/documents/pdf/Intellectual_Life/JKlick_Cheap_Donuts.pdf.

For another look at the difficulty of designing workable obesity taxes, see Jason M. Fletcher, David Frisvold, and Nathan Teff, "Can Soft Drink Taxes Reduce Population Weight?" *Contemporary Economic Policy,* January 2010, vol. 1, no. 28, pp. 23–35.

For some hunger estimates, see http://en.wikipedia.org/wiki/Hunger. For a more skeptical view, see Abhijit Banerjee and Esther Duflo, "More Than 1 Billion People Are Hungry in the World, But What if the Experts Are Wrong?" *Foreign Policy,* May/June 2011.

For the information on declining U.S. agricultural productivity, see Julian M. Alston, Matthew A. Andersen, Jennifer S. James, and Philip G. Pardey, *Persistence Pays: U.S. Agricultural Productivity Growth and the Benefits from Public R&D Spending* (New York, Springer, 2010), pp. 147–57. For the Jonathan A. Foley quotation, see "A Warming Planet Struggles to Feed Itself," *The New York Times,* June 4, 2011.

On wheat price spikes, see Robert J. Samuelson, "The Great Food Crunch," *The Washington Post,* Monday, March 14, 2011, p. A19.

On how much agriculture is taken up by biofuels, see Elisabeth Rosenthal, "Rush to Use Crops as Fuel Raises Food Prices and Hunger Fears," *The New York Times,* April 6, 2001.

On Yemen, see Hugh Macleod and John Vidal, "Yemen Threatens to Chew Itself to Death over Thirst for Narcotic Qat Plant," *The Guardian,* February 26, 2010.

On Saudi Arabia, see "Wheat and Water Subsidy Datapoints of the Day," June 23, 2008, http://www.portfolio.com/views/blogs/market-movers/2008/06/23/wheat-and-water -subsidy-datapoints-of-the-day/#ixzz1KGRWIOzS, drawing upon work by Elie Elhadj, see for instance his "Saudi Arabia's Agricultural Project: From Dust to Dust," http:// www.globalpolitician.com/print.asp?id=5059.

On malnutrition rates in India, see Vikas Bajaj, "Galloping Growth, and Hunger in India," *The New York Times,* March 8, 2011, which also cites the especially rapid rise of food prices in India. On the restrictions on food production in India, one very good source is Maurice Landes, *The Environment for Agricultural and Agribusiness Investment in India,* USDA, *Economic Information Bulletin,* Number 37, July 2008, p. 19, for instance, covers land law and p. 27 covers restrictions on foreign direct investment. On spoilage rates, see estimates (which should be taken as very rough, but they are high nonetheless) in "Fling Wide the Gates," *The Economist,* April 14, 2011, and for spoilage rates on wheat see *"WSJ* Interview with Kaushik Basu," *The Wall Street Journal,* March 22, 2011. On the relaxation on FDI in 2011, see "100% FDI allowed in some areas of farm sector," *The Hindu,* March 31, 2011.

For background on GMOs, in addition to the National Research Council study (The Impact of Genetically Engineered Crops on Farm Sustainability in the United States,

Washington, D.C.: National Academies Press, 2010), see Pamela C. Ronald and Raoul W. Adamchak, *Tomorrow's Table: Organic Farming, Genetics, and the Future of Food* (New York: Oxford University Press, 2008), and "Global Status of Commercialized Biotech/ GM Crops: 2010," ISAAA Brief 42-2010, http://isaaa.org/resources/publications/briefs/ 42/executivesummary/default.asp.

Also useful are Indur M. Goklany, *The Improving State of the World: Why We're Living Longer, Healthier, More Comfortable Lives on a Cleaner Planet* (Washington, D.C.: Cato Institute, 2007), and Henry I. Miller and Gregory Conko, *The Frankenfood Myth: How Protest and Politics Threaten the Biotech Revolution* (Westport, Connecticut: Praeger, 2004). For a brief popular overview, see Gregory Conko, "The Benefits of Biotech," *Regulation,* Spring 2003, and also James E. McWilliams, "The Green Monster: Could Frankenfoods be good for the environment?" *Slate,* Wednesday, January 28, 2009, http://www.slate.com/id/2209168/pagenum/all/#p2.

On how GMOs can make crops more nutritious, see Pamela C. Ronald and James E. McWilliams, "Genetically Engineered Distortions," *The New York Times*, May 14, 2010, and also the National Research Council report.

On cotton and pesticides, see Gregory Conko, "The Benefits of Biotech," *Regulation,* Spring 2003, p. 22.

The excerpt from Laura Ticciati and Robin Ticciati is in their *Genetically Engineered Foods: Are They Safe? You Decide* (Los Angeles: Keats Publishing, 1998), p. 45.

On ecoterrorism in Spain, see http://foodfreedom.wordpress.com/2010/07/14/uprooting -ecoterrorism-syngenta-gm-crops-sabotaged-in-spain/.

On the Amish and GMOs, see for instance http://news.bbc.co.uk/2/hi/science/nature/ 7745726.stm. On GMOs in Africa, and also on European regulations, see Robert Paarlberg, *Starved for Science: How Biotechnology Is Being Kept Out of Africa* (Cambridge: Harvard University Press, 2009).

8. Eating Your Way to a Greener Planet

On Ed Begley, see for instance http://www.johnnyjet.com/folder/archive/I-Flew-with -Ed-Begley-Jr-Possibly-the-Greenest-Person-Alive.html, http://www.edbegley.com/ environment/tipsandfaq.html.

On Mathias Gelber, see http://greenmanplanet.blogspot.com/.

For one article on Mike Duke and Wal-Mart, see Tom Rooney, "The greenest man alive is . . . Mike Duke of Wal-Mart!" *Pittsburgh Post-Gazette,* July 18, 2010, http:// www.post-gazette.com/pg/10199/1073252-109.stm#ixzz1KGYRMjsm.

On Pygmy life expectancy, see Roger Highfield, "Pygmies Life Expectancy Is Between 16 and 24," *The Telegraph,* December 10, 2007.

On the studies, see for instance, Ro'i Zultan and Maya Bar-Hillel, "When Being Wasteful Appears Better than Feeling Wasteful," *Judgment and Decision Making*, vol. 5, no. 7, December 2010, pp. 489–96. On green products, see Nina Mazar and Chen-Bo Zhong, "Do Green Products Make Us Better People?" *Psychological Science*, March 5, 2010, XX(X), pp. 1–5.

On green eating, two standard sources are Peter Singer and Jim Mason, *The Way We Eat, Why Our Food Choices Matter* (Emmaus, Pennsylvania: Rodale Publishers, 2006), and Mark Bittman, *Food Matters: A Guide to Conscious Eating* (New York: Simon & Schuster, 2009).

On Annina Rüst, see Jascha Hoffman, "Carbon Penance," *The New York Times*, December 12, 2008.

On plastic, see for instance "Paper or Plastic?" *The Washington Post*, October 3, 2007. On cotton, see Martin Hickman, "Plastic Fantastic! Carrier Bags 'Not Eco-villains After All'" *The Independent*, February 20, 2011.

On the energy cost of transporting food, see Stephen Budiansky, "Math Lessons for Locavores," *The New York Times*, Friday, August 19, 2010, p. A19. The original source is "Energy Use in the U.S. Food System," by Patrick Canning, Ainsley Charles, Sonya Huang, Karen R. Polenske, and Arnold Waters, United States Department of Agriculture, March 2010; the 29 percent figure is taken from p. 17; see also p. 20. On Pirog, see James E. McWilliams, *Just Food: Where Locavores Get it Wrong and How We Can Truly Eat Responsibly* (New York, Back Bay Books, 2009), pp. 25–26.

On the refrigerated apple example, see Mike Berners-Lee, *How Bad Are Bananas?: The Carbon Footprint of Everything* (London, England: Profile Books, 2010), p. 27.

For information on April, see her blog and twitter feed, http://web.me.com/aprildavila/MWM/Check_My_Work.html.

http://web.me.com/aprildavila/MWM/Blog/Blog.html.

http://web.me.com/aprildavila/MWM/Blog/Entries/2010/2/20_Food_For_Thought.html.

https://twitter.com/WithoutMonsanto.

There is also this article, http://blogs.riverfronttimes.com/dailyrft/2010/04/la_woman_boycotts_monsanto_for_a_month.php?page=1 and the piece on rats can be found here http://www.biolsci.org/v05p0706.htm.

On boycotts, see Brayden G. King, "A Political Mediation Model of Corporate Response to Social Movement Activism," *Administrative Science Quarterly*, 2008, vol. 53, no. 3, pp. 395–421, and also a summary at http://insight.kellogg.northwestern.edu/index.php/Kellogg/article/why_boycotts_succeed_and_fail.

On the new cutlery for the House of Representatives, see "Stick a Fork in Hill's 'Green' Cutlery," by David A. Fahrenthold and Felicia Sonmez, *The Washington Post*, Saturday, March 5, 2011, pp. A1, A4.

For a sustained environmental defense of aquaculture, see the excellent book by James E. McWilliams, *Just Food: Where Locavores Get It Wrong and How We Can Truly Eat Responsibly* (New York: Back Bay Books, 2009), chapter five.

On the energy costs of home preparation and storage of food, see "Energy Use in the U.S. Food System," by Patrick Canning, Ainsley Charles, Sonya Huang, Karen R. Polenske, and Arnold Waters, United States Department of Agriculture, March 2010. British estimates run at about twenty percent, for the contribution of food to total energy use; see Mike Berners-Lee, *How Bad Are Bananas?*, p. 177.

On the energy costs of sugar refining and processing, and also gasoline versus food, see "Energy Use in the U.S. Food System," by Patrick Canning, Ainsley Charles, Sonya Huang, Karen R. Polenske, and Arnold Waters, United States Department of Agriculture, March 2010.

9. Why *Does* Mexican Food Taste Different in Mexico?

On the strong Latin influence in El Paso, see Kathleen Staudt, *Free Trade? Informal Economies at the U.S.-Mexico Border* (Philadelphia: Temple University Press, 1998), pp. 35, 46, and see p. 33 on the history of border relations between the two cities.

Juárez is one of the wealthiest parts of Mexico. El Paso has been slipping in wealth compared to the rest of the United States. El Paso per capita income was slightly above the national average in 1950, but by 1991 had declined to 59 percent of the national average; see Staudt, *Free Trade?*, pp. 35–36. Its former manufacturing jobs have been transformed into low-wage labor, most of all in the apparel industry.

For general background on the economics of factory farms, as it relates to the difference between the two countries, see Ann Cooper, with Lisa M. Holmes, *Bitter Harvest: A Chef's Perspective on the Hidden Dangers in the Foods We Eat and What You Can Do about It* (New York: Routledge, 2000), pp. 108–109, and Peter Kaminsky, *Pig Perfect: Encounters with Remarkable Swine and Some Great Ways to Cook Them* (New York: Hyperion, 2005), p. 243.

On dry vs. wet aging of beef, see, for instance *Steaks, Chops, Roasts, and Ribs: A Best Recipe Classic*, by the Editors of *Cook's Illustrated* (Brookline, Massachusetts: America's Test Kitchen, 2004), p. 234. On the price premium for dry-aged beef, see, for instance, Katy McLaughlin, "Steakhouse Confidential," *The Wall Street Journal*, Saturday/Sunday, October 8–9, 2005, pp. P1, P4.

On skirt steak vs. flank steak, see, for instance, *Steaks, Chops, Roasts, and Ribs: A Best Recipe Classic*, by the Editors of *Cook's Illustrated* (Brookline, Massachusetts: America's Test Kitchen, 2004), p.40, and Mario Montaño, *The History of Mexican Folk Foodways of South Texas: Street Vendors, Offal Foods, and Barbacoa de Cabeza* (Ann Arbor:

Notes

University of Microfilms, University of Pennsylvania doctoral dissertation, 1992), p. 227. *Fajita* means "little girdle" in Mexican Spanish (*faja* is "girdle"). The skirt steak is taken from exactly the part of the cow that would wear a girdle, thus the name; see Jeanne Voltz, *Barbecued Ribs, Smoked Butts, and Other Great Foods* (New York: Alfred A. Knopf, 1990), pp. 63–64.

For the Peter Kaminsky quotation on pigs, see Peter Kaminsky, *Pig Perfect: Encounters with Remarkable Swine and Some Great Ways to Cook Them* (New York: Hyperion, 2005), p. 159.

On when beef consumption became more important than pork consumption in the United States, Richard Pillsbury, *No Foreign Food: The American Diet in Time and Place* (Boulder, Colorado: Westview Press, 1998), pp. 71–73.

On the decline in fat in American pork, see Kaminsky, *Pig Perfect,* p. 190.

The origins of the U.S. restrictions on nonpasteurized cheeses are obscure. The law dates from 1947, when refrigerated trucks were not in wide use for cheese transportation. The Mexican government recently has been encouraging moves toward cheese and dairy pasteurization, although this has not involved an outright ban. Mexican milks tend to be runnier and less thick, which also influences the taste of the cheese. On Mexican milks, see Arturo Lomelí, *La Sabiduría de la Comida Popular* (Miguel Hidalgo, Mexico: Random House Mondadori), 2004, pp. 303–4.

On Mennonite cheeses, see Cheryl Alters Jamison and Bill Jamison, *The Border Cookbook: Authentic Home Cooking of the American Southwest and Northern Mexico* (Boston: The Harvard Common Press, 1995), p. 141. For a broader history of the Mennonites in Mexico, see Harry Leonard Sawatzky, *They Sought a Country: Mennonite Colonization in Mexico* (Berkeley: University of California Press), 1971.

On the use of lard and beef suet in Mexico, see James W. Peyton, *El Norte: The Cuisine of Northern Mexico* (Santa Fe: Red Crane Books, 1995), p. 16. On the history of lard consumption in Mexico, see John C. Super, *Food, Conquest, and Colonization in Sixteenth Century Spanish America* (Albuquerque: University of New Mexico Press), 1988, p. 85, and Jeffrey M. Pilcher, *Que Vivan los Tamales: Food and the Making of Mexican Identity* (Albuquerque: University of New Mexico Press, 1998), p. 36.

See *The El Paso Cookbook.* El Paso: Ladies' Auxiliary, YMCA, 1898, republished (no date) by Applewood Books, Bedford, Massachusetts, introduction by Andrew F. Smith.

On the history of vegetable oil and its advertising, see Susan Strasser, *Satisfaction Guaranteed: The Making of the American Mass Market* (Washington: Smithsonian Books, 2004), chapter one. For the 1929 English-language Mexican cookbook, see Pauline Wiley-Kleeman, *Ramona's Spanish-Mexican Cookery: The First Complete and Authentic Spanish-Mexican Cook Book in English.* 1929, no publisher listed.

Tortilla means "omelet" in Spanish; when the Spanish first came to Mexico the flat corn tortillas reminded them of their flat omelets back home. On the percentage of

273

flour tortillas in the United States, see Daniel D. Arreola, *Tejano South Texas: A Mexican American Cultural Province* (Austin: University of Texas Press, 2002), p. 175.

On corn syrup, see Betty Fussell, *The Story of Corn: The Myths and History, the Culture and Agriculture, the Art and Science of America's Quintessential Crop* (New York: North Point Press, 1992), pp. 7–8, and Margaret Visser, *Much Depends on Dinner* (New York: Grove Press, 1986), p. 23.

On wheat and flour tortillas in Mexico, see Jeffrey M. Pilcher, *Que Vivan los Tamales: Food and the Making of Mexican Identity* (Albuquerque: University of New Mexico Press, 1998), pp. 31–36, 86–87, 493, and also Arreola, *Tejano South Texas*, p. 173, who discusses Texas.

On the story of Fritos, see Betty Fussell, *The Story of Corn: The Myths and History, the Culture and Agriculture, the Art and Science of America's Quintessential Crop* (New York: North Point Press, 1992), p. 209.

On U.S. corn breeding in the 1920s, see Visser, *Much Depends on Dinner,* p. 48. Mexican corn, of course, was bred by human beings as well but at a much earlier point in time. A far greater number of varieties have survived.

Tortilla-making machines in Mexico date from the 1920s and 1930s. During transitional times, women would bring the kernels to a central machine in the village. And until electricity came to a village, the machine often would be run by gas, giving the tortillas an inferior taste. For a general history of the growth of tortilla machines in Mexico, see Jamie A. Aboites, *Breva Historia de un Invento Olvidado, Las Maquinas Tortilladoras en Mexico* (Mexico City: Universidad Autonoma Metropolitana, 1989). On tortilla production in Mexico, see, for instance, Pilcher, *Que Vivan,* pp. 100–102, and Jeffrey M. Pilcher, "Industrial Tortillas and Folkloric Pepsi: The Nutritional Consequences of Hybrid Cuisines in Mexico," in *Food Nations: Selling Taste in Consumer Societies,* edited by Warren Belasco and Philip Scranton (New York: Routledge, 2002), pp. 222–39. On *masa harina,* and tortilla history more generally, see Janet Long-Solís and Luis Alberto Vargas, *Food Culture in Mexico* (Westport, Connecticut: Food Culture Around the World, 2005), p. 27. On moisture content, see Robert L. Wolke, *What Einstein Told His Cook 2: The Sequel* (New York: W.W. Norton & Company, 2005), p. 231. On tortilla factories, see Donna R. Gabaccia, *We Are What We Eat: Ethnic Food and the Making of Americans* (Cambridge: Harvard University Press, 1998), p. 221, Jeffrey M. Pilcher, *Que Vivan los Tamales: Food and the Making of Mexican Identity* (Albuquerque: University of New Mexico Press, 1998), pp. 103–105, and Arturo Lomelí, *La Sabiduría de la Comida Popular* (Miguel Hidalgo, Mexico: Random House Mondadori), 2004, p. 136. On the history of Mexican tortilla subsidies, see Enrique C. Ochoa, *Feeding Mexico: The Political Uses of Food since 1910* (Wilmington, Delaware: Scholarly Resources Books, 2000), and Lomelí, *La Sabiduria,* p. 53. On larger tortilla factories in the U.S., and also on the boom in handmade tortillas in the United States, see Himilce Novas and Rosemary Silva, *Latin American Cooking Across the U.S.A.* (New York: Alfred A. Knopf, 1997), p. 8.

Pápalos, Pipizca, verdolaga, and *quelite* are some indigenous Mexican greens not generally available in the U.S.

For a good discussion of tomato and tomato transport, see Deborah Barndt, *Tangled Routes: Women, Work, and Globalization on the Tomato Trail* (Lanham, Maryland: Rowman & Littlefield, 2002), pp. 12–13, 16–17, 21–22, and 48.

10. The Finding Great Food Anywhere Encyclopedia

On the histories of various Singapore foods, see Lee Geok Boi, "Part One: Food in Singapore," in *The Food of Singapore: Authentic Recipes from the Manhattan of the East* (Singapore: Periplus Editions, 2001), pp. 5–24, especially pp. 14–15, and Chua Beng Huat and Ananda Rajah, "Food Ethnicity and Nation," in *Life is Not Complete Without Shopping: Consumption Culture in Singapore*, edited by Chua Beng Huat (Singapore: Singapore University Press, 2003), pp. 93–117. On the history of Singapore hawker stalls, see, for instance, Selina Ching Chan, "Consuming Food: Structuring Social Life and Creating Social Relationships," in *Past Times: A Social History of Singapore*, edited by Chan Kook Bun and Tong Chee Kiong (Singapore: Times Editions, 2000), pp. 123–35, see, in particular, pp. 124–26.

On the history of Les Halles, see, for instance, John Hess, *Vanishing France* (New York: Quadrangle/The New York Times Book Co., 1975), pp. 4–5 and also Susanne Freidberg, *French Beans and Food Scares: Culture and Commerce in an Anxious Age* (Oxford: Oxford University Press, 2004), pp. 130, 142, 144, and 149.

On the financial losses involved with publishing the Michelin guide, see Paul Betts, "Flavour of austerity taints Michelin guide," *The Financial Times*, March 5, 2011, p. 2.

11. The Stuff and Values of Cooking at Home

For the advice on how to get honest feedback from your guests, see the remarks of Hang at http://blog.figuringshitout.com/my-hn-dinner-party-3/.

On Vorwerk, see Amanda Hesser, "The Way We Eat: Dream Machine," *The New York Times Magazine*, November 11, 2005, at http://www.nytimes.com/2005/11/20/magazine/20food_.html?_r=1.

Acknowledgments

For useful comments and discussions the author would like to thank Stephen Morrow, Teresa Hartnett, Kara Abramson, Marc Abramson, John Nye, Kevin Grier, Natasha Cowen, Yana Chernyak, Randall Kroszner, Robin Hanson, Alex Tabarrok, Carrie Conko, Ezra Klein, Thomas Head, Mike Whitely, Megan McArdle, Veronique DeRugy, Mark Bittman, Karen Black, Michael Rosenwald, Alex Cohen, Nelson Head, Seth Roberts, Chug Roberts, Moltani, Bryan Caplan, Saria Sheikh, Siyu Wang, Rong Rong, Charlie Liu, Michelle Lim, Daryl, Jodi Ettenberg, two anonymous readers, and numerous others, most of all those who have served me wonderful food and taken the time to talk about it.

Index

The El Paso Cookbook (1898), 201
El Salvadoran food, 5, 50, 76,
    77, 203
Emergency Quota Act, 29
entertaining, 243–47
environmental issues, 167–86
    and barbecue smoke, 105, 109–11
    and consumer choices, 167–68,
        169–75, 176–86
    and cost effectiveness, 175
    and Genetically Modified
        Organisms, 162
    and methane emissions, 162, 178, 182,
        185, 247
    and seafood, 183, 185
Erie Railroad, 144
ethanol, 155
Ethiopian food, 238
ethnic foods. *See also* immigrants;
    specific ethnicities and countries
    and barbecue, 95, 110
    in Germany, 234
    and influential cookbooks, 248
    in Italy, 238
    in London, 231–32
    and low-rent areas, 75–76
    in Spain, 240
    and the suburbs, 28
    supermarkets, 40–55, 245
    in Tokyo, 217, 218
    variety within, 188
Ettenberg, Jodi, 211, 218
Europe, 161, 162–63, 224–42. *See also*
    specific countries
European Union, 163, 232
Evans, Maureen, 250

fajitas, 190, 192
family restaurants, 121–22
famines, 147
Farber, Billy, 91
fast foods, 24, 32–35, 188, 234–35
fermented foods, 126–27
fertilizers, 155
Filipino food, 110, 128–29
financial crises, 74–75, 231
Financial Times, 176
fine dining, 1, 11, 217–18, 225, 228
firemen, 78

fish. *See also* seafood
    and Bangladeshi food, 126
    and ethnic supermarkets, 46–51
    fish and chips, 12, 231
    fish head curry, 220
    and German food, 233
    and microwave ovens, 258–59
    and transportation infrastructure, 7
flash-freezing, 257–58
Florence, 237
flour, 201–2, 202–3
flowers, 171
Flushing, Queens, 74, 75, 130–31
Fogo de Chao, 111
fois gras, 184
Foley, Jonathan, 153
Food, Inc. (2008), 168, 172
food crises, 154
Food Network, 18, 120
"The Food of the Tarahumaras," 251
Food Rules (Pollan), 8
food safety
    and barbecue, 105, 108
    and beef aging, 191–92
    and Chinese restaurants, 137
    and Genetically Modified
        Organisms, 163
    and Indian food, 223–24
    and lard, 200, 201
    and liability laws, 192
    and meats, 192
    and Mexican food, 187, 195–96, 222
    before modern food system, 9
    and nonpasteurized cheeses, 197
    safety standards, 59
    and street food, 222–23
    and water safety, 6
food stands and stalls, 220, 223–24
food trucks, 2, 76–77, 243–45
fossil fuels, 178, 179–81, 186
Fourier, Charles, 13
France and French food, 22, 32–33,
        87–88, 116, 218–19, 225–31
free-range poultry, 194
fresh foods, 49, 125
Fritos, 203
frozen foods, 49, 196, 257–58, 259
fruits, 24, 46, 207–8, 251
frying, 194

labor costs (*cont.*)
  and rules for finding good food, 59
  and women in the workforce, 34–35
lamb, 110, 136, 173–74, 246
language barriers, 41–42, 216, 251
Laos and Laotian food, 212–13
La Paz, Nicaragua, 4
lard, 199–201, 221, 246
Laredo, Texas, 106
Las Delicias, 76–77, 244, 245
Latin America. *See also specific countries*
  and Chinese food, 130
  and ethnic supermarkets, 50
  and food markets, 194
  and food trucks, 76
  immigrants from, 41–42
  Latin-Asian fusion cuisine, 80
  restaurants of, 73
La Villette, 226
laws and legal issues, 36. *See also*
    government policies and
    regulations
  and agribusiness, 158
  and animal welfare, 182
  and barbecue, 105–7
  and intellectual property, 164
  and lard, 200
  and Mexican food, 187, 190
  and nonpasteurized cheeses, 197
  and Prohibition, 18, 20–26, 29, 36
  and shipping of produce, 209
Lebanon and Lebanese food, 76,
    99–100, 157
Le Bernardin, 73
Lee, Susur, 249
leeks, 171
León, Nicaragua, 4–5
Le Pavillon, 24
Les Halles market, 227–28
Lexington, North Carolina, 96, 103–4
Lexington Barbecue #1, 96
liability laws, 192
Lion Head in Hot Pot, 133
liquors, 23, 25–26
listeria, 197
Living with Ed (television), 167
local foods and locavores, 1, 8, 158,
    171–72, 177, 186
Lockhart, Texas, 95, 111, 259

London, England, 231–32
Lonnie Ray's BBQ, 86
Los Angeles, California, 75, 122, 128,
    133, 135
Los Angeles Kogi (food truck), 76
loss leaders, 44–45
Lotte Plaza, 127
lumpia, 128
Luther's, 91

mackerel, 46
mad cow disease, 162–63
Madrid, Spain, 240
mail-order foods, 259–60
maize, 202. *See also* corn
mala sauce, 132
Malawi, 163
Malaysia and Malaysian food, 129, 146,
    220, 221
malnutrition, 150–59
Manhattan, New York, 73, 101, 105–6
Manila, Philippines, 128
mani soup, 60
Maori culture, 88
Mao Tse Tung, 147
Ma Po Tofu, 138–39
marketing of foods
  and barbecue, 101
  and ethnic supermarkets, 42
  impact on quality of American food,
    18–19
  and kitchen equipment, 254
  and loss leaders, 44–45
  and politics, 13–14
  and prospective clientele, 82–83
  and restaurants, 73
masa, 58, 204
Maseca, 206
mass food production, 25. *See also*
    agriculture and agribusiness
Matthews, Scott, 171, 172
Ma Young-Ae, 26–27
Mazar, Nina, 169
McDonald's, 33–34, 82, 234–35
McGee, Harold, 248
meats. *See also* beef; chicken; fish; pork
  and animal welfare issues, 181–82
  and barbecue, 89
  consumption rates, 154